One Currency, Two Markets

This book is for anyone who is interested in the economic analysis of the future of the international monetary system and the USD, and the rising importance of the RMB. It points out the unsustainability of the dollar standard in the long run, that China has unique incentives to internationalize its currency, and how Hong Kong plays an important role. It explains the real reasons for China to internationalize its currency, including using external commitments to force financial sector reforms ("daobi" in Chinese). It applies economic theories accessible to laymen to establish that financial development and openness are crucial for RMB internationalization to succeed, and that greater exchange rate volatility is inevitable due to the "open-economy trilemma". Employing the "gravity model," the book predicts quantitatively that, by 2030, the RMB can be a distant third payment currency after the USD and the euro but surpassing the British pound sterling.

EDWIN L.-C. LAI is Professor of Economics at HKUST. He has been Senior Research Economist and Adviser at the Federal Reserve Bank of Dallas, a consultant with the World Bank, and a visiting fellow at Princeton University. He is an associate editor of *Review of International Economics* and has published numerous papers in leading economics journals.

One Currency, Two Markets

China's Attempt to Internationalize the Renminbi

EDWIN L.-C. LAI

Hong Kong University of Science and Technology

CAMBRIDGE
UNIVERSITY PRESS

University Printing House, Cambridge CB2 8BS, United Kingdom

One Liberty Plaza, 20th Floor, New York, NY 10006, USA

477 Williamstown Road, Port Melbourne, VIC 3207, Australia

314–321, 3rd Floor, Plot 3, Splendor Forum, Jasola District Centre, New Delhi – 110025, India

103 Penang Road, #05–06/07, Visoncrest Commercial, Singapore 238467

Cambridge University Press is part of the University of Cambridge.

It furthers the University's mission by disseminating knowledge in the pursuit of education, learning, and research at the highest international levels of excellence.

www.cambridge.org
Information on this title: www.cambridge.org/9781108491686
DOI: 10.1017/9781108647236

© Edwin Lun-Cheung Lai 2021

First published 2021

Printed in the United Kingdom by TJ Books Limited, Padstow Cornwall

A catalogue record for this publication is available from the British Library.

Library of Congress Cataloging-in-Publication Data
Names: Lai, Edwin L.-C., author.
Title: One currency, two markets: China's attempt to internationalize the renminbi / Edwin L.-C. Lai, Hong Kong University of Science and Technology.
Description: Cambridge, United Kingdom ; New York, NY : Cambridge University Press, 2021. | Includes bibliographical references and index.
Identifiers: LCCN 2021000172 (print) | LCCN 2021000173 (ebook) | ISBN 9781108491686 (hardback) | ISBN 9781108740586 (paperback) | ISBN 9781108647236 (epub)
Subjects: LCSH: Renminbi. | Money–China. | Foreign exchange–China. | Capital market–China. | Finance–China.
Classification: LCC HG1285 .L35 2021 (print) | LCC HG1285 (ebook) | DDC 332.4/50951–dc23
LC record available at https://lccn.loc.gov/2021000172
LC ebook record available at https://lccn.loc.gov/2021000173

ISBN 978-1-108-49168-6 Hardback

To the memory of my parents, Shuxin and Yi

Contents

Figures

Tables

Boxes

Preface

The Chinese government is trying to internationalize the renminbi (RMB). But what are the real reasons for doing it? Will it succeed? What are the factors working in its favor? What are the impediments? What are the implications for the rest of the world?

In this book, I explain how the problem with the international monetary system since the demise of the Bretton Woods system and the recent global financial crisis prompted China to seek independence from the dollar standard. One way is to make the RMB a widely accepted currency internationally. China, however, is in an awkward position. On the one hand, it is the second largest economy and the largest trading nation in the world, and it will likely become the largest economy before long. This works in favor of the internationalization of the RMB. On the other hand, China is still an emerging economy, meaning that its financial and legal institutions are still immature compared with the more advanced system in the West. Yet, China does not want to fully integrate its financial system with the West any time soon. As currency internationalization requires the currency to be largely convertible in the capital account, this factor works against the internationalization of the RMB. Thus, China tries to internationalize its currency in its own unique way, i.e., by adopting the "one currency, two markets" approach, which entails establishing a global offshore RMB market. Through this strategy, China sets up a firewall between the onshore and offshore markets, allowing full convertibility of RMB in the offshore market but partial convertibility in the onshore market. Behind this approach are a number of policy measures. Among all the policy measures, I shall highlight financial market liberalization, capital account opening and the offshore RMB centers, especially Hong Kong. In telling my story, I shall invoke economic theories to support my arguments and empirical facts to support my theory. Based on my theory, I conclude that China's economic size, its commitment to sufficiently free capital mobility, the development of a deep, broad, and liquid financial market, and people's confidence on the RMB are the four key factors for the success of RMB internationalization. China has economic size, but it needs to work on the other three factors. It is not at all clear whether and when China would achieve the degree of capital mobility and financial market development sufficient to make the RMB a significant international currency on a par with, say, the euro, not to mention the USD. Moreover, it seems unlikely that a country without a contestable democracy, independent judiciary, and a truly free press to constrain the government can secure the confidence of the world in its currency. Thus, my conjecture is that, in the intermediate term, the RMB can only be a distant third payment currency (behind the USD and the euro). In the longer run, because of China's large GDP and continuing reforms and opening, and the world's central banks' demand for safe assets for foreign exchange reserves, the world may become a multi-reserve-currency system, with the USD, euro, and RMB being the three main reserve currencies. However, the road for the RMB to get there may be quite long and uncertain.

LITERATURE REVIEW

Many outstanding books directly or indirectly related to RMB internationalization have been written. For example, Eichengreen (2011) gives a historical account and interpretation of the rise and fall of the USD and conjectures concerning the future of the international monetary system (IMS). He thinks that it is more likely for the RMB to become a regional currency than a global currency as it is hard for China to give up exchange rate stability and capital controls entirely. He argues that to give up those things China has to let go of its development model, the pillars of which are financial repression and a stable exchange rate. He argues that the dominance of the USD will continue in the foreseeable future unless the United States causes self-inflicted injuries to its own financial system, such as a dollar crash caused by the budget deficit running out of control. However, even if there is no dollar crash, the dominance of the USD will weaken with the rise of the Chinese RMB and currencies of other developing countries such as the Indian rupee. He conjectures that the future will be one with multiple international currencies, and that the USD will have to compete for business in order to maintain its dominant position.

Eichengreen and Kawai (2015) is a valuable and informative edited volume about RMB internationalization consisting of multiple articles discussing a wide range of topics concerning the internationalization of the RMB. Its strength is its broad coverage and the expertise of the authors. However, because it is written by many authors dwelling on many topics, it does not have a consistent theme.

Overholt, Ma, and Law (2016) is a well-researched, comprehensive, and informative book about RMB internationalization with a consistent theme. They project an optimistic view about the future of RMB internationalization. One distinguishing feature of the book is the emphasis of the importance of the development of the onshore bond market in China, which I think is interesting. It is worth reading for anyone who cares about RMB internationalization.

Cheung, Chow, and Qin (2017) is an insightful book about the RMB. It focuses more on the RMB exchange rate than its internationalization, though it devotes two chapters on RMB internationalization, encompassing topics as wide as the offshore market, the measures taken by the Chinese government to promote the use of RMB overseas, and the latest developments. It is quite an informative source.

Prasad (2017b) is a well-written and comprehensive book on RMB internationalization that focuses exclusively on RMB internationalization, with a lot of details about the history, the policies, and the latest developments. Prasad points out the rapid rise of the use of the RMB internationally, but he also cautions that the currency started from a very low base, and that China is still a developing country with a relatively immature financial system and a rather closed capital account. He emphasizes that the RMB will fail to be a safe-haven currency as long as China lacks a set of credible checks and balances to discipline its government so as to give foreigners confidence about the currency. He thus concludes that the degree of RMB internationalization will only be moderate in the foreseeable future, with the RMB comprising no more than 10 percent of total foreign reserves of the world (as of the end of June 2019, the shares for the USD and euro are 61.6 percent and 20.3 percent respectively).

Subacchi (2017) is an informative book about RMB internationalization. The author points out that although China is the second largest economy and the largest trading economy, its currency is a "dwarf currency," and this is one of the motivations for the Chinese to internationalize the RMB. However, China is still under financial repression, and its currency is still not convertible in the capital account. So, China has to adopt an unconventional approach. Subacchi points out that the main "RMB strategy" of China is to build offshore RMB centers, especially the one in Hong Kong, in order to facilitate capital account opening and to encourage RMB trade settlement so as to allow the RMB to flow outside China and create the market thickness of the RMB outside China.

Eichengreen, Mehl, and Chiṭu (2018) explores the more general topic of how global currencies work instead of focusing on RMB internationalization. The authors propose a "new view" to replace the "traditional view" about the extent to which the leading reserve currency dominated the market. The traditional view argues that the leading currency all but monopolized the market as network externalities and first-mover advantage led to a "winner takes all" situation. This is due to the high liquidity and low transaction cost of keeping, buying, and selling the assets denominated in the leading currency. The new view, however, argues that the force of network externalities is not strong enough to lead to a "lock-in effect" and "winner takes all" effect for the leading currency. Instead, several reserve currencies can coexist so as to realize the benefits of diversification. The theoretical basis of the new view is built on a literature on technology standards that focuses on open systems, in which users of a particular technology or system can interact with those using other technologies or systems. The technical barriers between different systems can be circumvented by "gateway technologies" that enable users to overcome incompatibilities between systems and integrate competing systems into an extended network. The implication of the new view is that "The twenty-first-century Triffin Dilemma [of the USD] can be resolved through the development of other national sources of international liquidity." The euro and the RMB are two obvious candidates. Consequently, the book seems to support a somewhat optimistic view about the prospects of RMB internationalization.

However, none of the books above has devoted enough space to rigorously explaining economic theories to the general reader and applying them to analyze the issues related to RMB internationalization. By contrast, in this book, I base my arguments on economic theory that is accessible to readers who only have some basic knowledge of economics but no deep knowledge of international macroeconomics and finance. For example, I explain in simple economic language the theories of the "open-economy trilemma," coalescing effect, thick market externalities, uncovered interest parity, and the sequence of liberalization, and apply them to the real world. A second distinguishing feature of this book from the previous literature is that, instead of just qualitatively assessing the prospects of RMB internationalization, I carry out rigorous quantitative assessments. Making use of a proprietary data set from SWIFT, I carry out an econometric study to estimate the determinants of a currency's share in total international payments and use it to predict the future payment share of the RMB, an indicator of the degree of internationalization of the currency. I find that financial development and capital account openness are much more important than the GDP of China in determining the payment share of its currency. My model predicts that it is possible that, by 2030, RMB can rank a distant third (behind the USD and the euro) in the global ranking of payment currencies, but this is possible only if China greatly speeds up its financial development and capital account opening in the next decade. I believe my quantitative assessment is more convincing than any qualitative one in making the point that China's economic size alone cannot make the RMB an international currency. The third distinguishing feature of this book is that I argue that there is a positive feedback effect (or synergy) between capital account liberalization and domestic financial sector reform. This argument provides the rationale for using the internationalization of RMB to force domestic financial sector reform. This is the idea of *daobi* (倒逼), which I believe is (silently) advocated by some quarters in the Chinese government. I argue that *daobi* is one important motivation of internationalizing the RMB. For this reason, the sequence of liberalization in China should not strictly follow that of conventional wisdom, namely financial market liberalization should take place before capital account liberalization. Instead, the two liberalization initiatives should proceed interactively in tandem. Finally, my book differs from the previous literature by providing a detailed coverage of the offshore RMB market in Hong Kong and the new international payment system of China (Cross-Border Interbank Payment System, CIPS), complete with a mathematical model that explains the relationship between economic variables in the onshore and offshore markets, such as the interest rates and exchange rates.

I have inserted a few "boxes" in the book to carry more technical/theoretical materials or case studies. They are intended for readers who are interested in the details. For general readers, the boxes can be skipped without missing the main storyline of the book.

Acknowledgments

This book is the culmination of nine years of my research on RMB internationalization and many years of teaching international macroeconomics and finance. In 2012, Leonard K. CHENG, then the Dean of the Business School at HKUST, encouraged me to study RMB internationalization and appointed me as the Associate Director of the Center for Economic Development to spearhead the research. In retrospect, I am so happy that I accepted that task. Since then, I have read many papers and articles, talked to many people, hired many research assistants to work for me, given many talks, taught an MBA course in RMB internationalization, served as a Research Fellow for the Hong Kong Institute of Monetary Research, twice, to work on the topic, and written a few papers along the way. This journey paved the way for me to write this book, which summarizes and crystallizes my findings on the topic. I would like to thank all those whom I met in this journey. Without them, the book would not be as good as I hope it is.

I would like to thank especially Paul Sau-Him LAU and Paul LUK for tirelessly reading the entire manuscript and giving me very detailed and useful comments. They are true friends. They pointed out some literature that I had overlooked, offered valuable suggestions, and helped me to improve the book. I am truly grateful to Kim-Man NGAN, who kindly spent time to discuss with me the real world of the Hong Kong RMB market, and later wrote very detailed comments on my manuscript. Yatang LIN kindly read the manuscript and offered some interesting suggestions. I would also like to offer my gratitude to Kang SHI for offering his insights on the topic by engaging in two enlightening discussions.

I would like to express my gratitude to the Hong Kong Institute of Monetary Research of the Hong Kong Monetary Authority for offering me the position of Research Fellow twice, in 2013 and 2018, to work on the topic of RMB internationalization. During those periods, I had the valuable opportunity to interact with many experts in the HKMA and came to understand better the RMB offshore market of Hong Kong and RMB internationalization in general. They include, but are not limited to, Giorgio VALENTE, Edmund LEE, Jacqueline ZHANG, Alfred WONG, Cho-Hoi HUI, Dong HE, and Hongyi CHEN. I sincerely thank all of them for the interactions.

During the years, I have benefited from my discussions with many outstanding economists, scholars, and practitioners who enlightened me a lot. They include, but are not limited to, Yin-Wong CHEUNG, Shu LI, SUN Lijian (Fudan University), Ben CHAN, Carmen LING, Ilhyock SHIM, Francis LUI, BA Qing, WU Jun, Shang-Jin WEI, Chao HE (IMF), and Paola SUBACCHI.

Many research assistants have helped me in writing this book or papers related to the topic of RMB internationalization. They have been indispensable for the completion of this book. In this regard, I offer my greatest gratitude to Weili CHEN, who has tirelessly collected data and carried out analyses with outstanding performance. Without him, the book would be of a much lower quality. I am also grateful to Barron Yiu-Hing TSAI, Xiaoyan ZHUANG, and Vincent Pok-Ho LO for offering a lot of very high quality research assistance. JIANG Yang (February) and BIAN Ce (Eileen) provided assistance with the figures, referencing, and indexing of the book. ZHOU Jing, BAI Xue, CUI Yiye, Erica Wai-Chu CHUNG, Victor Cheuk-Hin YAU, YANG Rui, and YE Muyang all made important contributions.

HKUST provides an excellent environment for writing this book. I would like to thank the School of Business of HKUST for giving me the opportunity to teach an MBA course in RMB internationalization so that I could look at the issue from the point of view of the students. I also want to thank the Institute of Emerging Market Studies and Center for Economic Development of HKUST for their support.

I am grateful to the Society for Worldwide Interbank Financial Telecommunications (SWIFT) for giving me permission to use their proprietary historical data on bilateral inter-country payments flows to analyze the potential of the RMB as a significant payment currency. The analysis is an important part of this book.

The work in this book has been supported by the Strategic Public Policy Research (SPPR) Scheme of the Central Policy Unit of the Hong Kong Government Project No. SPPR17RG01 and General Research Funds of the Research Grants Council of Hong Kong (Project No. 16506820). Data relating to SWIFT messaging flows are published with permission of S.W.I.F.T. SCRL. SWIFT © 2019. All rights reserved. Because financial institutions have multiple means to exchange information about their financial transactions, SWIFT statistics on financial flows do not represent complete market or industry statistics. SWIFT disclaims all liability for any decisions based, in full or in part, on SWIFT statistics, and for their consequences.

Last but not least, I would like to express my wholehearted gratitude to my publisher, Joe Ng of Cambridge University Press, for his enormous patience and offer of assistance whenever needed, making the writing of the book much less burdensome.

A Short Summary of This Book

Below I summarize each chapter and provide a diagram that summarizes the theoretical framework of the book.

Chapter 1 is the introduction. I discuss the current state of the international monetary system (IMS), the "exorbitant privilege" of the United States and the history of the IMS. I explain how the United States seized the opportunity in the Bretton Woods conference to establish the USD as the reserve currency, and how the Bretton Woods system collapsed in 1973. Today, under the post-Bretton Woods system, a developing country like China adopts the "dollar standard" and pegs its currency to the USD. In doing so, China accumulates huge amount of USD foreign reserves. It falls into the "dollar trap." However, the global financial crisis sounded an alarm for China that the dollar-based IMS could be quite unreliable – for example, there might be a shortage of the USD for trade finance. Thus, China began to accelerate the pace of RMB internationalization, aiming to make the RMB an international unit of account, medium of exchange, and store of value. However, this implies that its capital account has to be open, the financial market must be liberalized, and its exchange rate has to be more volatile. Is China ready to meet this challenge? This book investigates the necessary conditions for RMB internationalization to succeed and its prospects.

In Chapter 2, I explain why China desires a stable exchange rate. International trade has been very important to China's economic development ever since the "reform and opening" that started in 1978. In the early years of its reform and opening, China had plenty of cheap labor but very little capital. Thus, it opened its door to inward foreign direct investment (FDI), which brought in capital and technological know-how. China had a huge rural labor surplus (an under-employed rural labor force) that had to be absorbed by the economy.

Thus, it needed to keep its labor employed by expanding external demand through exporting. In order to sustain export-promotion during the period 1996–2005, China had been maintaining a stable and undervalued exchange rate versus the USD. In other words, China adapted to the dollar standard and made good use of it during its development process. As a result of this exchange rate policy, China rapidly became an important player in international trade. For example, its processing trade and its engagement in the global value chain would not have been so successful had China not pegged the RMB to the USD. A stable and undervalued exchange rate with the USD has therefore become the cornerstone of China's initial development strategy. This policy, however, becomes an obstacle in RMB internationalization, which requires that China allows much freer capital mobility. A very stable exchange rate and a high degree of capital mobility cannot be achieved at the same time if autonomy in monetary policy is to be maintained, according to the open-economy trilemma. So, in order to internationalize the RMB, China must give up a certain degree of exchange rate stability.

In Chapter 3, I discuss why China wants to internationalize the RMB. I define internationalizing a currency as making it widely used as a unit of account, medium of exchange, and store of value outside of the issuing country. In the private sector, it is used to invoice and settle international trade in goods and services and to denominate bank deposits and financial assets in foreign countries. In the public sector, it is used as a reserve currency in foreign central banks. There are multiple reasons that motivate China to try to internationalize the RMB. Here I list just a few. First, the IMS, which is dominated by the USD as the major reserve currency, has many problems. It is asymmetric in the sense that as developing countries like China try to peg to the USD, they lose their autonomy in monetary policy. Yet the United States has all the autonomy in monetary policy as it does not need to adjust its exchange rate of its currency against those of other countries. Second, as China wanted to safeguard the dollar peg, it accumulated a huge amount of USD foreign exchange reserve, which earned a very low rate of interest and was subject to losses due to USD depreciation. It triggered complaints from the Chinese people. At the same time, the United States has kept running large current account deficits year after year for four decades. Essentially, the United States is using its special status to borrow overseas at very low interest rates from countries like China. Third, the global financial crisis in 2007 – 2009 caused a shortage of dollars all over the world. This gave further impetus to China to grab the window of opportunity to promote the use of RMB internationally so as to eventually escape from the "dollar trap." China has two additional reasons to internationalize its currency, which countries like Japan did not have: a strong desire to become independent of the United States and an IMS dominated by the USD, and the desire to use external commitment to force internal reforms. I also discuss the pros and cons of RMB internationalization to China and to the world, and why Japan did not internationalize the yen.

In Chapter 4, I discuss China's strategy of internationalizing the RMB. China is probably the first country in history not considered among the most advanced trying to internationalize its currency. Historically, the financial market of a country that issues an international currency needs to be large, reliable, efficient, and liquid. These features are usually associated with a more developed country. China is special because it is a developing country that is expected soon to become the largest economy in the world. But its financial system is still immature compared with those of the most advanced countries, and still needs to improve regarding reliability, efficiency, breadth, depth, and liquidity. Moreover, its currency is still not fully convertible in the capital account. Thus, market forces alone would not be able to make the RMB a significant international currency, and government policy is required. Borrowing the "one country, two systems" idea, the Chinese government decided to create an offshore RMB market that is not completely integrated with the onshore one. They facilitated the formation of offshore RMB centers in Hong Kong, Singapore, Taipei, and London. The CNH (offshore RMB) is a fully convertible currency in the offshore market. In the offshore centers, the markets for CNH-denominated bonds, loans, bank deposits, and other financial products gradually developed. Trade settlement in RMB is allowed and even encouraged. China also entered into bilateral currency swap agreements with 36 countries as of March 2018. The capital account is gradually being liberalized through schemes such as Qualified Foreign Institutional Investor (QFII), Qualified Domestic Institutional Investor (QDII), RMB-Qualified Foreign Institutional Investor (RQFII), Shanghai–Hong Kong Stock Connect, Shenzhen–Hong Kong Stock Connect, Bond Connect, Mutual Fund Connect, Shanghai Free Trade Zone (FTZ), Shenzhen Qianhai FTZ, and so on. At the same time, China is increasingly building up its international interbank payment system, called the Cross-Border Interbank Payment System (CIPS), which clears and settles RMB-denominated payments. In this chapter, I explain how China gradually experiments with capital account liberalization and currency convertibility. I also discuss an "RMB Internationalization Index."

In Chapter 5, the importance of capital account liberalization is discussed. I explain how the "coalescing effect" and "thick market externalities effect" determine the use of a currency for trade invoicing and denominating financial assets and use the theory to explain why capital account opening, in addition to financial development and the size of the economy, is essential to RMB internationalization. Capital account opening is not non-controversial even among well-regarded economists. For example, well-known economists such as Dani Rodrik and Joseph Stiglitz are against it. It carries non-trivial risks, especially for emerging economies with immature banking and financial sectors. We ask two questions: Given that capital account opening carries risk, should China open its capital account just because it wants to internationalize the RMB? Do the benefits of capital account opening outweigh the costs regardless of whether or not China pursues RMB internationalization? To answer these questions, we discuss the benefits and costs of capital account liberalization, including the loss of exchange rate stability due to the open-economy trilemma. We explain the theoretical basis of the tri-lemma and the empirical evidence for it. We then point out that there is a positive feedback effect between capital account opening and financial market reform. Thus, the initiative to internationalize the RMB, which calls for capital account opening, can set forth a chain reaction that facilitates capital account opening and financial market liberalization in tandem in a gradual and interactive manner. This provides the rationale for using RMB internationalization as an external commitment device to force the reform of the domestic financial market.

In Chapter 6, I concentrate on the importance of financial sector reform, focusing on the banking sector, the bond market, and the stock market. The banking system, which is tightly controlled by the state, is an important institution in the development model of China. Under this system, deposit rates are kept artificially low so as to channel cheap credits to the state-owned enterprises for investment. In a country that was short of capital in its early stage of development, this might have been a justifiable policy. This is in fact a classic example of financial repression. However, it is also economically inefficient in the later stage of development. The largest banks are all state-owned, the interest rates are not market-determined, and state-owned enterprises (SOEs) still enjoy preferential access to credits compared with the private sector, which consists of many small and medium-sized enterprises (SMEs). Thus, it leads to misallocation of capital. There are no significant private financial institutions or banks to challenge their large state-owned counterparts. Because of the lack of external competition, the financial sector is quite inefficient. A deep, broad, and liquid financial market cannot be developed. This is unfavorable to RMB internationalization. At the same time, because subsidized credits are available, many state-owned enterprises lack the incentives to attain the best international standards. Thus, the financial sector cannot be reformed without reforming the state-owned enterprises. The vested interests in the financial sector are serious obstacles to reform as well. The bond market developed only recently. Most important developments in the

Chinese bond market have happened only since about 2015. China's bond market is characterized by its relatively small size relative to its GDP, low turnover ratio, and low foreign ownership. The Chinese government bond market, which is most important for the internationalization of the RMB, needs to be much further developed in order to pave the way for the RMB to serve as a significant reserve currency. The market capitalization of the stock market is small relative to the GDP of China. It is characterized by low fund-raising capacity, excessive government intervention, lack of transparency, capital controls, and other issues. Despite the obstacles, however, financial sector reform continues to be carried out. For example, the interest rate reform continues as an ongoing task; an onshore bond market is developing; and foreign financial institutions are gradually being allowed to operate onshore with majority ownership. Another positive signal for the financial sector is that market opening and integration with the rest of the world has not slowed down in recent years.

Chapter 7 explains the importance of the offshore RMB market. Historically, an international currency had to be largely convertible in the capital account, meaning that there had to be a high degree of capital mobility. Examples are the post-war United States, Britain, and Japan. But China wants to open its capital account only in a controlled manner as its institutions are still immature. Besides, China wants to retain the option of adjusting the extent of its capital controls when the needs arise. Thus, making use of offshore RMB centers located in international financial centers, such as Hong Kong, Singapore, and London, is a crucial step in launching RMB internationalization. Through this strategy, China sets up a firewall between the onshore and offshore markets, allowing full convertibility of RMB in the offshore market but partial convertibility in the onshore market. In this chapter, I study the operation of the offshore RMB centers, in particular that of Hong Kong, which is by far the largest offshore center. I describe in detail the difference between the onshore and offshore foreign exchange (FX) markets. I discuss the settlement and clearing of offshore RMB payments, the operation of RMB liquidity provision, and the RMB financial products being offered by banks and financial institutions such as the Hong Kong Exchange. Importantly, I describe in detail the Cross-Border Interbank Payment System (CIPS) of China, explain how it speeds up international payments of RMB, and compare it with the Clearing House Interbank Payments System (CHIPS) of the United States. I explain the economics behind the operation of the Hong Kong offshore market; in particular, I explain the relationship between the onshore and offshore interest rates and exchange rates using an economic model based on the "uncovered interest parity" condition. I compare the offshore USD market with the offshore RMB market so as to understand what improvements are necessary in the offshore RMB market.

A qualitative analysis is not enough for us to understand the quantitative importance of the various factors in determining the success of RMB internationalization. In Chapter 8, I carry out a quantitative study of the determinants of RMB internationalization, focusing on assessing the potential of the RMB as an international payment currency. I present an econometric study to demonstrate that financial development and capital account openness are distinctly more important than the GDP of China in determining the share of the RMB in international payments. Using the inter-country payments flows data provided by SWIFT and the "gravity model" as the theoretical framework, I carry out a regression analysis to identify the determinants of bilateral inter-country payments flows by currency. Then, I use the model to predict the future share of the RMB in global payments. I find that, in the best-case scenario, the RMB can possibly become the (distant) third payment currency (behind the USD and euro) by 2030. However, despite China's large expected economic size, it would be hard for the RMB to come even close to the status of the euro as a payment currency because it would be hard for China to attain the required levels of financial development and capital account openness, given the underdevelopment of China's institutions. I also carry out a very simple exercise to estimate the impacts of the Belt and Road Initiative on the payment share of the RMB and its share in denominating international debt securities. I find that the impacts are not very large.

In Chapter 9, the concluding chapter, I discuss the prospects of RMB internationalization. There are plenty of reasons to be pessimistic. First, the population is ageing, and the labor force had already begun to shrink in 2012. The shrinking labor force can have a nontrivial impact on economic growth. Without sufficiently large economic size, it is hard for China's currency to attain the market thickness necessary for internationalization. Second, China is too wary of the risks of a high degree of capital mobility to relinquish capital controls in the onshore market any time soon. Third, the development of a deep, broad, and liquid financial market in the onshore market will probably take a long time. Fourth, in order to be a "safe-haven currency," China must gain foreigners' trust in China's institutions, such as having an independent judiciary, an independent central bank, democracy, and freedom, which China still lacks. There are, however, reasons for cautious optimism as well. First, despite a possible slowdown in the growth rate, China's economy is probably going to become the largest economy before long, giving it size advantage. Second, China has more incentives than other countries, such as Japan, in internationalizing its currency. It has a strong desire to be more independent from the United States and the USD-based IMS; and the external commitment associated with RMB internationalization can be used as a tool to force domestic financial sector reform. Third, as the United States' GDP share of the world is set to fall continuously because of the fast growth of developing countries, the United States eventually will not be able to supply the assets for reserves and payments needed by the world. Some other currency(ies) is (are) needed to fill the gap, and the RMB is a strong candidate. It may not be too far-fetched to imagine that, eventually, the world will become a multipolar system, with the USD, euro, and RMB being the three main reserve currencies. The road for the RMB to get there, however, may be quite long.

The theoretical framework of this book can be summarized by Figure 0.1.

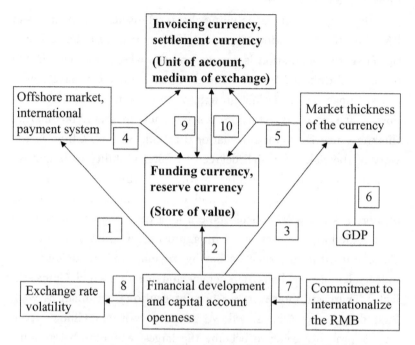

FIGURE 0.1 A summary of the theoretical framework of this book. Text in bold represents the goals of RMB internationalization. Numbers in the figure correspond to the notes below.

1: Scale and scope of offshore market activities increase with onshore financial development and capital account openness (Chapter 7).

2: (a) Freer capital mobility increases inward and outward investment flows (Chapter 5);(b) deeper, broader, and more liquid financial markets (e.g., bond market, stock market, and banking sector) increase inward foreign investment flows (Chapter 6).

3: Financial development and capital account openness increase the extent to which the currency is used internationally (Chapters 5 and 8).

4: (a) Creation of an offshore market where RMB is fully convertible while maintaining a partially convertible RMB market onshore, with a firewall in between, is a key strategy in launching the internationalization of RMB (Chapter 7);(b) Offshore currency centers and an international payment system facilitate efficient flows of funds between the onshore and offshore markets and enhance the impacts of financial development and capital account opening on RMB internationalization (Chapter 7);(c) Offshore currency centers and an international payment system facilitate efficient operation of the offshore financial markets and offshore use of the RMB (Chapter 7).

FIGURE O.I *(cont.)*

5: Thicker market for the currency lowers transaction costs of currency conversion and increases convenience of using the currency, increasing FX turnover and liquidity of the currency (Chapters 5 and 8).

6: GDP increases the global usage of the currency as the country's international economic activities expand (Chapters 5 and 8).

7: Commitment to internationalize the RMB creates pressure for capital account liberalization and financial sector liberalization (*daobi* [倒逼]). With RMB internationalization as a catalyst, the two liberalization initiatives can proceed gradually and interactively in tandem, defying conventional wisdom concerning the "sequence of liberalization" (Chapter 5).

8: According to the open-economy trilemma, opening the capital account will lead to higher exchange rate volatility if autonomy in carrying out monetary policy is to be retained (Chapter 5).

9 and 10: The functions of unit of account, medium of exchange, and store of value reinforce each other (Chapter 3).

Abbreviations

ABC	Agricultural Bank of China
ADBC	Agricultural Development Bank of China
AIIB	Asian Infrastructure Investment Bank
AREAER	Annual Report on Exchange Arrangements and Exchange Restrictions
ASEAN	Association of Southeast Asian Nations
AUD	Australian dollar
B&R	Belt and Road
BIS	Bank for International Settlements
BOC	Bank of China
BOCHK	Bank of China (Hong Kong)
BRI	Belt and Road Initiative
CAD	Canadian dollar
CBIRC	China Banking and Insurance Regulatory Commission
CBRC	China Banking Regulatory Commission (later combined with CIRC to form CBIRC)
CCB	China Construction Bank
CCWAEC	China-Central Asia-West Asia Economic Corridor
CDB	China Development Bank
CDC	China Government Securities Depository Trust & Clearing Co., Limited
CFETS	China Foreign Exchange Trade System
CGB	Chinese Government Bond
CHATS	Clearing House Automated Transfer System
CHIPS	Clearing House Interbank Payment System
Chexim	Export–Import Bank of China
CHF	Swiss franc
CIBM	Chinese Interbank Bond Market

CICPEC	China–Indochina Peninsula Economic Corridor
CIP	covered interest parity
CIPS	Cross-Border Interbank Payment System
CIRC	China Insurance Regulatory Commission (later combined with CBRC to form CBIRC)
CMREC	China–Mongolia–Russia Economic Corridor
CNAPS	China National Advanced Payment System
CNH	offshore RMB
CNY	onshore RMB
COFER	Composition of Official Foreign Exchange Reserves
CPC	Communist Party of China
CSRC	China Securities Regulatory Commission
DF	deliverable forward
DKK	Danish kroner
DNS	deferred net settlement
ECB	European Central Bank
EUR	euro
FDI	foreign direct investment
FTZ	Free Trade Zone
FX	foreign exchange
GBP	British pound sterling
HKD	Hong Kong dollar
HKICL	Hong Kong Interbank Clearing Limited
HKMA	Hong Kong Monetary Authority
HVPS	High Value Payment System
ICBC	Industrial and Commercial Bank of China
IMF	International Monetary Fund
IMS	international monetary system
IPO	initial public offering
JPY	Japanese yen
LCP	local currency pricing
LPR	loan prime rate
LVPS	large-value payment system

MLF	medium-term lending facility
MNCs	multinational corporations
MOF	Ministry of Finance
MRF	Mutual Recognition of Funds
MSCI	Morgan Stanley Capital International
MSR	21st-Century Maritime Silk Road
NDF	non-deliverable forward
NOK	Norwegian kroner
NPL	non-performing loans
NSA	National Security Agency
ODI	outward direct investment
OMO	open market operations
OTC	over-the-counter
P2P	peer-to-peer
PAP	People's Action Party
PBC	People's Bank of China
PCP	producer currency pricing
QDIE	Qualified Domestic Investment Enterprise
QDII	Qualified Domestic Institutional Investor
QDLP	Qualified Domestic Limited Partner
QFII	Qualified Foreign Institutional Investor
QFLP	Qualified Foreign Limited Partner
RFDI	RMB-settled inward foreign direct investment
RGI	RMB Globalization Index
RMB	Renminbi (It stands for the name of the currency as well as the unit. When used as a unit, it also stands for Chinese yuan.)
RODI	RMB outward direct investment
RQDII	RMB Qualified Domestic Institutional Investor
RQFII	RMB Qualified Foreign Institutional Investor
RQFLP	RMB-Qualified Foreign Limited Partner
RTGS	real-time gross settlement
SAFE	State Administration of Foreign Exchange

SAR	(Hong Kong) Special Administrative Region
SDR	special drawing right
SEHK	Stock Exchange of Hong Kong
SEK	Swedish kroner
SGD	Singapore dollar
SME	small and medium-sized enterprise
SOB	state-owned bank
SOE	state-owned enterprise
SREB	Silk Road Economic Belt
STP	straight-through processing
SWIFT	Society for Worldwide Interbank Financial Telecommunications
TFP	total factor productivity
TMA	Hong Kong Treasury Markets Association
USD	US dollar (It stands for the name of the currency as well as the unit.)
WTO	World Trade Organization

I   Introduction

On 11 August 2015, the onshore RMB, China's currency, depreciated by 1.9 percent against the USD, the largest one-day drop since the adoption of the managed float of the currency in 2005. China's yuan had been on an upward track for a decade, during which the country had been growing rapidly, and the market had been expecting the RMB to appreciate. So, what happened on that day?

Before 11 August 2015, the central bank, the People's Bank of China (PBC), set a midpoint for the value of the yuan against the US dollar (USD) (called the "central parity rate") at 9:15 a.m. on each trading day. In daily trading, the yuan was allowed to move 2 percent above or below the central parity rate. Under this mechanism, the central parity rate might not follow the trend of movement of the exchange rate the day before: The PBC sometimes set the central parity rate so that the yuan was stronger against the dollar a day after the market had indicated it should be weaker. In other words, the central bank intervened in the foreign exchange market to reverse the market trend from time to time under this mechanism. As the government intervened in the foreign exchange market, the RMB did not depreciate much against the USD even though capital began to move out of China starting from around October 2014, apparently due to the weakening growth momentum of the economy. The RMB would have depreciated more had the government not intervened to support its value.

On 11 August 2015, China implemented a new mechanism for setting the central parity rate. The central parity rate would now be largely based on how the yuan closed in the previous trading session. In other words, the central parity rate would follow the market trend the day before, which means that it became more market-driven.[1] As a result of the reform on 11 August 2015, the yuan's central parity value was weakened by 1.9 percent on that day from the previous day, leaving it at 6.2298 to the USD, compared with 6.1162 the day before. As a consequence, the CNH/USD (the offshore RMB exchange rate against the USD) and CNY/USD (the onshore RMB exchange rate against the USD) exchange rates fell by 2.83 percent and 1.86 percent respectively on 11 August 2015, and they further depreciated by 2.08 percent and 0.96 percent respectively in the following trading day (see Figure 1.1). The market expected further, and possibly large, depreciation of the RMB. Before 11 August 2015, the market was still expecting the currency to appreciate relative to the USD in the short and medium term. It now was quite confident that it would depreciate in the short and medium term. This definitive reversal of the expected future exchange rate of the RMB was quite remarkable. As a result, it triggered capital outflows. To stem these outflows, the government soon reimposed certain measures of

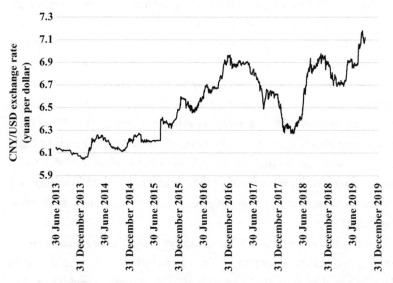

FIGURE I.I Historical CNY/USD exchange rate (yuan per dollar), 2013–2019.
Source: Bloomberg

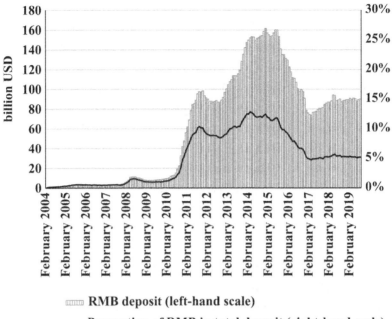

RMB deposit (left-hand scale)

—— Proportion of RMB in total deposit (right-hand scale)

FIGURE 1.2 Monthly RMB deposits in Hong Kong in billion USD, 2004–2019 (excluding certificates of deposit).
Sources: CEIC and "HKMA – Size of Renminbi Deposit in Hong Kong": www.hkma .gov.hk/media/eng/doc/market-data-and-statistics/monthly-statistical-bulletin/ T030302.xls

capital controls. CNH deposits in Hong Kong fell; so did cross-border capital flows into Mainland China.[2] Figure 1.2 shows that the RMB deposits in Hong Kong underwent a sharp decline from its peak (about the equivalent of USD 160 billion) after 11 August 2015. It never attained that level again even up till the time of writing (May 2020). In the third quarter of 2019, the amount of RMB deposits in Hong Kong was only slightly higher than 50 percent of the peak in the summer of 2015.

The change caused turmoil in the global financial market both immediately and long after the event took place. It not only marked the beginning of fundamental changes in Chinese exchange rate policy but had further repercussions, as indicated by the other events that took place after 11 August 2015. For example, some months later, there were crashes in the Chinese stock market, which prompted measures to halt trading when stock prices became too volatile.

In the months after 11 August 2015, the state-owned banks in Hong Kong intervened in the Hong Kong offshore market to keep the CNH and CNY exchange rate aligned. That meant reducing the supply of CNH so as to raise the interest rate so that it became expensive to short the yuan. That kind of intervention greatly hurt the offshore market. The Hong Kong RMB offshore market suddenly lost steam. This was a serious setback to the internationalization of the RMB after many years of progress on that front. The Chinese government clearly underestimated the response of the market to its policy change.

In the aftermath of 11 August 2015, the momentum of RMB internationalization weakened substantially. The main reason is capital controls. Capital outflows were restricted so as to sustain a stable exchange rate of the RMB against the USD. This is due to a principle called the open-economy trilemma (see, for example, Obstfeld, Shambaugh, and Taylor 2005). The trilemma states that out of the three "desirable" goals of monetary policy autonomy, a stable exchange rate, and free capital mobility, it is impossible to achieve all three at the same time. Another interpretation of the trilemma is that when one goal (e.g., autonomy in monetary policy) is to be maintained, there is a tradeoff between the other two goals (i.e., free capital mobility and exchange rate stability)—if you have more of one, you will have less of the other. It dictates that if China wants to retain monetary policy autonomy and a very stable exchange rate, it cannot have a high degree of capital mobility.[3] The highest level of the government seemed to think that maintaining exchange rate stability took priority over allowing capital mobility. But capital mobility was essential for the internationalization of RMB, in particular the offshore RMB market. Thus, RMB internationalization was effectively put to the back burner.[4]

The fact that the above events caused a serious setback to RMB internationalization was quite ironic. One of the reasons for the change in the mechanism of setting the central parity of the RMB exchange rate was supposed to make the RMB exchange rate more market-determined and more flexible so as to satisfy the requirements of the International Monetary Fund (IMF) for the RMB to be included in the basket of currencies that made up the special drawing right (SDR).[5] The SDR is a fictitious currency established by the IMF for lending to countries for short-term needs to fill the payment gap in their balance of payments account. Being included in the SDR basket was considered an important milestone of RMB internationalization by the Chinese government.

Indeed, subsequent to the central parity reform, the IMF announced on 30 November 2015 that the RMB would be included in the basket of currencies that made up the SDR on 1 October 2016. China's dream of making the RMB an internationally respected currency finally materialized on that date. The irony was that in the course of making the exchange rate more flexible so as to increase the chance of the RMB becoming an internationally recognized member of the club of elite currencies, China inadvertently put a brake on the pace of internationalization of RMB, one of whose aims was to increase the international status of the RMB.

Why then does China want to internationalize its currency in the first place? To answer this question, we first have to understand the IMS and its history.

I.I   THE DOLLAR STANDARD

Under the current IMS, many well-established currencies choose to adopt a floating exchange rate regime. However, many other countries, especially less-developed ones, choose to adopt a pegged exchange rate regime, meaning that they peg their exchange rate to a hard currency or a basket of hard currencies, such as the USD, euro, pounds sterling, and Japanese yen because they want to maintain stable exchange rates with these currencies. There can be multiple reasons for a country to adopt a pegged exchange rate regime. For example, it may want to maintain an undervalued exchange rate so

as to facilitate an export-oriented growth strategy, to minimize the
risk of destabilizing the weak domestic banking system due to excessive volatility in the exchange rate, to anchor the domestic inflation
rate, and to minimize the exchange rate risks faced by domestic firms
that incur debts denominated in foreign currencies. In order to peg to a
hard currency, these countries have to accumulate sufficient amounts
of foreign reserves denominated in the hard currency in case they have
to intervene in the foreign exchange market so as to sustain the
exchange value of their currency. Suppose, for example, a country
wants to peg its currency to the USD. If the market exerts depreciating pressure on the currency, the central bank has to sell USD and
buy the domestic currency in the foreign exchange market so as to
defend its peg to the USD. To safeguard the currency peg against
market shocks and speculative attacks, the country has to keep a
sufficient amount of USD reserves. Thus, the USD has to be a major
reserve currency kept by the central bank of the country. A currency's
share in the total foreign reserves of all countries is positively related
to the extent to which they want to maintain a stable exchange rate
with that currency. As of the end of the second quarter of 2019, the
shares of USD, euro, Japanese yen, and pounds sterling in the total
amount of allocated central banks' reserves in the world were 61.6
percent, 20.3 percent, 5.4 percent, and 4.4 percent respectively[6] (see
Figure 1.3). Thus, the USD is by far the most important reserve
currency. Moreover, the reason that many countries want to maintain
a stable exchange rate with the USD is that it is also the dominant
trade invoicing currency, trade settlement currency, and funding
currency (the currency in which financial assets are denominated).
Thus, the functions of reserve currency, invoicing currency, settlement currency, and funding currency are mutually reinforcing,
making the USD the dominant currency in the world. As most countries want to maintain a stable exchange rate against the USD, they
accumulate large amounts of USD reserves. However, the USD does
not have to be pegged to any currency or to any asset such as gold.
Thus, the United States does not have to keep any substantial amount

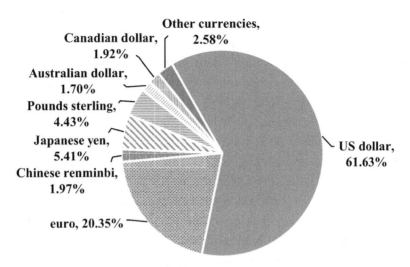

FIGURE I.3 Shares of currencies in the total amount of allocated foreign exchange reserves across the globe by 2019 Q2.
Sources: IMF Currency Composition of Official Foreign Exchange Reserves (COFER), International Financial Statistics (IFS), International Monetary Fund. http://data.imf.org/?sk=E6A5F467-C14B-4AA8-9F6D-5A09EC4E62A4

of foreign exchange reserves. More importantly, being the major reserve-currency country, the United States has the autonomy to use monetary policy to influence its own national income, unemployment rate, and inflation rate, while other countries that peg their currency to the USD do not have the autonomy to use monetary policy to influence their national income, unemployment rate, and inflation rate unless they limit capital mobility. (This is because of the open-economy trilemma.) This asymmetry is remarkable.

I.2   THE "EXORBITANT PRIVILEGE" OF THE UNITED STATES

Because of the reserve currency status of the USD, American citizens are able to borrow in their own currency at very low interest rates. This is because a major reserve currency is also a major invoicing currency and funding currency. Thus, there is a large supply of USD funds in the international capital market, lowering the borrowing rate. The assets held by foreigners in the United States as of the end of 2017 was composed of 17.3 percent in US Treasury bonds, 11.5 percent in US corporate bonds, 2.8 percent in US agency debt, 22.4 percent in US stocks, 25 percent in inward foreign direct investment, 4.5 percent in financial derivatives, and 15.5 percent in other investments.[7] The overseas assets held by Americans as of the end of 2017 was composed of 12.4 percent in foreign debt securities, 32.7 percent in foreign stocks, 32.1 percent in US outward direct investment, 5.9 percent in financial derivatives, 15.4 percent in other investment, and 1.6 percent in reserve assets.[8] So, foreigners held a lot more US bonds than Americans held foreign bonds (in percentage terms). Since foreigners held more US assets than Americans held foreign assets, this difference is even larger in absolute terms. This reflects the fact that foreign central banks held a lot of US Treasury bonds as foreign exchange reserves.

On average, during the period 2005–2017, the overseas assets held by Americans earned around 3 percentage points higher interest rate per year than the assets held by foreigners in the United States.[9] This means that Americans can spend more than they produce year after year (i.e., running a current account deficit year after year) without incurring more net international debt. We shall discuss this issue further in Chapter 3.

Approximately 70 percent of US foreign assets are denominated in foreign currencies, while close to 100 percent of US liabilities to foreigners are denominated in USD.[10] Thus, when the USD depreciates, the international investment position of the United States improves, as the dollar value of American liabilities is unchanged but the dollar value of American assets rises. Consequently, when the United States is in a recession, say caused by a fall in foreign demand for its goods and services, its currency depreciates but this negative shock is mitigated by a wealth transfer from foreigners to the United States in the form of the increased net international investment position of the United States. Such an international transfer serves as an insurance payment and partly offsets the damage caused by a negative demand shock to the country's economy. Admittedly, this "privilege" or advantage is not confined only to the United States but also accrues to any country that can borrow in its own currency, such as the eurozone countries, the UK, or Japan. However, the absolute values of the total foreign assets and total foreign liabilities of the United States are much higher than those of the UK or Japan, which means that the United States, as a country, benefits most through this privilege among all the countries that can borrow in their own currencies.

1.3   SEIGNIORAGE

Seigniorage is the real resources a government earns when it prints or creates money that it spends on goods and services. The dollar amount of US currency held outside of the United States is an indicator of the value of the seigniorage the US government earns from foreigners. There is no official data on the amount of US currency circulating outside the United States. Some researchers have provided estimates: Ruth Judson (2012) of the Federal Reserve Board of Governors of the United States estimated that "about half of all U.S. currency, and about 65 percent of the hundred-dollar notes, were held abroad as of the end of 2011." Edgar L. Feige (2012) estimated that "the percentage of U.S. currency currently held overseas is between 30–37 percent." An older report provided by the US Treasury Department in 2000 cited the following figure: "Estimates by the Federal Reserve suggest that at the end of 1998, 50 percent to 70 percent of the $500 billion in U.S. currency outstanding, or $250 billion to $350 billion, was held outside the United States."[11] The average of the above three estimated percentages is 47.8 percent. The total amount of USD in circulation as of 6 June 2018 was USD 1,661 billion, according to the Federal Reserve Bank of St. Louis.[12] So, assuming the above estimated percentages remain constant over the years, the total amount of US currency circulating outside the United States as of June 2018 was approximately USD 800 billion, which was about 4 percent of US GDP, a non-trivial amount.

Thus, the United States benefits a lot from the advantage that it enjoys as a major reserve currency. Valéry Giscard d'Estaing, French President Charles de Gaulle's finance minister, called it the "exorbitant privilege" of the United States. However, the IMS was not always like that of today. As Zhou Xiaochuan, the former governor of the People's Bank of China, once said, "The acceptance of credit-based national currencies as major international reserve currencies, as is the case in the current system, is a rare special case in history."

I.4 SOME HISTORY OF THE INTERNATIONAL MONETARY SYSTEM

During 1870–1914, most of the world was under the Gold Standard, in which all countries fixed the prices of their currencies in terms of gold. This avoided the asymmetry that exists in a reserve currency standard and put constraints on the supplies of money in all countries.

During 1944–1971, most of the world was under the Bretton Woods system, in which all countries fixed their exchange rates to the USD, while the USD fixed its value to the price of gold at USD 35 per ounce. Thus, the USD became the reserve currency of all countries that joined the Bretton Woods system. The monetary policy of the member countries other than the United States was disciplined as their currencies were fixed to the USD. As the USD was pegged to the price of gold, it provided discipline to the monetary policy of the United States. Thus, there existed no asymmetry as is seen in the reserve currency system. Because the exchange rates of countries were ultimately fixed to gold via the USD, it was called a gold exchange standard.

From 1973 to the present time, a large part of the world economy has been under a floating exchange rates system as mentioned above. Nonetheless, many countries continue to maintain a stable exchange rate with the USD, while the value of the USD is no longer fixed to the price of gold. There is no external commitment by the United States to discipline its monetary policy. The system acts like a reserve currency system with the value of the reserve

currency not backed by anything of value, such as gold, but by a
national currency, the USD. As countries are not committed to
fixing their exchange rates to each other, in principle they can
choose to have autonomous monetary policy to deal with internal
economic matters such as unemployment and inflation. However,
partly for historical reasons and partly because the United States is
still the largest economy with the most mature financial system,
many countries continue to keep the vast majority of their foreign
reserves in USD. Central banks want to keep a large amount of USD
reserves not just because they need to defend their currency peg
when necessary, but also the citizens of their countries, such as
firms and households, need USD when they buy goods and services
through international trade and or buy financial assets through
international financial transactions. Their central banks need to
have sufficient amounts of USD to provide dollar liquidity to their
citizens. The historical reason for this entrenchment of the USD is
that, by 1973, when the Bretton Woods system ended, the USD was
the dominant invoicing, funding, investment, and reserve currency
of the world. As the USD was widely used and kept, it was very easy
to exchange into and out of the currency. The transaction costs of
exchanging USD were very low compared with those of other currencies. There was literally no rival. Figure 1.4 shows the average
transaction cost (measured by bid–ask spread) of exchanging
between currency-pairs among four currencies: USD, EUR, GBP,
and JPY during 2013–2017. It is clear that the average transaction
cost of exchanging with the USD is the lowest compared with that
of other currencies. The phenomenon that the transaction cost of
exchanging with a currency is lower when more people use it is
called network externalities. This, together with the fact that more
people use a currency when the transaction cost of using it is lower,
creates a positive feedback effect between the (larger) number of
people who use the currency and the (lower) transaction cost of
using it. This positive feedback effect partly explains the entrenchment of the use of the USD all over the world by 1973.

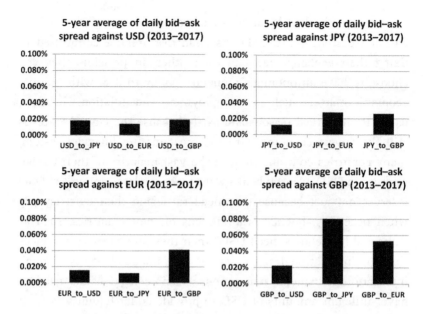

FIGURE 1.4 Average bid–ask spread of selected currency pairs, 2013–2017.
Source: Bloomberg

BOX 1.1   **How the Americans seized the opportunity in Bretton Woods**

The fact that the USD with its ties to gold was placed at the center of the post-World War II international monetary system (IMS) was not totally determined by economic reality but also by a power struggle between the declining British power and the ascending American power at the twilight of the war. The privileged position occupied by the USD anointed by the Bretton Woods conference in July 1944 was accepted by the participants only after some very heated arguments between the representatives of the Americans and those of the British. The American team was led by Harry Dexter White, the chief international economist at the Department of the Treasury of the United States at that time, while the British team was headed by none other than the iconoclastic economic thinker John Maynard Keynes. White represented the financial power of the United States, while Keynes represented the intellectual power of Britain.

BOX 1.1   **(cont.)**

White drafted the US blueprint for the International Monetary Fund (IMF) that competed with the plan drafted for the British Treasury by Keynes. However, the final compromise adopted at Bretton Woods mostly followed White's plan: White drafted a plan that would restore international stability after the war through the creation of the IMF and the World Bank. His plan defined the IMF and the World Bank as a promoter of economic growth through international trade with the financial plumbing based on the USD. In the end, White prevailed, not because of the superiority of White's intellectual power, but because of the strength of American economic and political power. Thus, the IMF was shaped primarily by White's plan rather than that of Keynes, and so the IMF became a dollar-based institution.

Where the two founding fathers of the IMF differed most was the degree of independence of the IMF and its power. To Keynes, the world needed an independent countervailing force to balance American economic power, a world central bank that could regulate the global supply of credit and its distribution. Keynes wanted to create an international reserve currency called the "bancor," to be issued by the IMF, which would act as a global central bank. White was opposed to the idea of a global central bank and that of the bancor. White wanted the IMF to be an adjunct to American economic power, an agency that could promote the balanced growth of international trade in a way that preserved the central role of the USD in international finance.[1]

Unfortunately, the Bretton Woods system contained a serious flaw. For international reserves to keep pace with the growth in world trade required an ever-expanding supply of dollars, which, as the economist Robert Triffin observed in the late 1950s, was incompatible with the preservation of a stable value for the dollar. This would cause a confidence problem regarding the exchange value of the USD. The way out of that dilemma was for the IMF to create an international credit instrument to supplement dollars in reserves. That instrument was finally created by the IMF in 1969. It was the special drawing right, or SDR, a fictitious currency composed of all major currencies at that

BOX I.I **(cont.)**

time, such as the USD, Deutsche Mark, Japanese yen, and British pound, for use as central bank reserves.

In fact, most people focus on the confidence problem raised by Robert Triffin, and ignore the problem of the dominance of the USD as a consequence of the Bretton Woods conference. This is a serious omission. The creation of the SDR came too late, as the USD was already entrenched in the IMS.

1 See Boughton 1998 and "Buttonwood" 2014. As an aside to the story of Harry Dexter White being cast as the hero of the US by orchestrating the dominance of the USD at Bretton Woods, there was a bizarre turn of events in the later years of his life: he was accused of being a spy for the Soviet Union during the McCarthy era. White had all along wanted to co-opt the Soviet Union into the IMF for the sake of world peace and prosperity. But, according to Boughton (1998), "White's intensely personal internationalism came under heavy criticism in the United States once the wartime military alliance with the Soviet Union against the Axis countries was no longer in force. During the investigations of the McCarthy era, attacks on his motives ranged from the questionable to the bizarre. His meetings with Soviet officials around the time of Bretton Woods were interpreted as espionage. His efforts during the war to hold the Nationalist government in China accountable for hundreds of millions of dollars in U.S. financial aid were interpreted as an effort to undermine Chiang Kai-shek in favor of Mao Tse-tung. His assistance in drafting a plan to limit the reindustrialization of Germany after the war was interpreted as part of a grand design to create an economic vacuum in Europe to be exploited by the Soviet Union." See also Steil 2013.

I.5 THE USD-BASED INTERNATIONAL MONETARY SYSTEM AND ITS PROBLEMS

The fact that the United States is the largest economy in the world with the most mature financial system implies that it has the deepest, broadest, and most liquid domestic financial market. This, together with the fact that the USD is fully convertible in the current account and the capital account, makes it very attractive to be used as a funding currency for firms that need to raise funds for their business and as an investment currency for financial institutions that invest on behalf of their clients, such as households that save for retirement. There are two more reasons why the USD is widely held all over the world. The first is that the United States is politically stable and militarily powerful, which makes the USD a safe-haven currency in times of turmoil in the world. The second is that the monetary policy of the United States is disciplined by the checks and balances set up in the system of governance of the country. It has a relatively independent central bank, the Federal Reserve System, whose mandates are to maintain stable price levels and economic growth. This system makes it harder for the executive branch of the government to influence the central bank to print or create money to finance fiscal expenditure or stimulate the economy to facilitate re-election yet gives the central bank the freedom to steer the course of the economy by monetary policy, such as influencing inflation and unemployment. This set of institutions wins the trust of other countries.

During 1996–2005, China's exports took off while the RMB was pegged to the USD. Like many other developing countries, China tried to maintain a stable exchange rate with the USD. As a result of such a policy, China's central bank accumulated huge amounts of USD assets. In its 2018 annual report, the State Administration of Foreign Exchange (SAFE) disclosed that China's total foreign exchange reserves grew from a value equivalent to USD 1.07 trillion at the end of 2006 to a value equivalent to USD 3.84 trillion by the end of 2014. The amount then began to fall. Still, by the end of 2018, the value of China's foreign reserve was equal to an enormous amount of USD 3.07 trillion, compared with USD 3.14 trillion at the end of 2017 (see Figure 1.5). Foreign analysts broadly agreed that as of 2014 about two-thirds of Chinese foreign exchange reserves are held in USD. The USD assets held by the central bank of China yield very low interest rates compared with the potential average return from investing in domestic real assets. Thus,

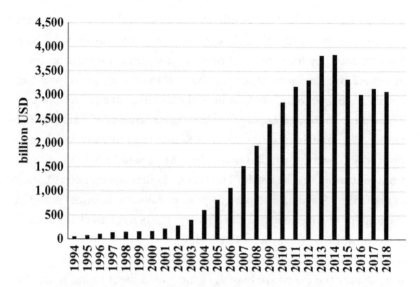

FIGURE 1.5 China's foreign exchange reserves, 1994–2018.
Source: State Administration of Foreign Exchange Annual Report (2018) [国家外汇管理局 《国家外汇管理局年报（2018）》 (in Chinese)

China paid a high price in buying an "insurance policy" to secure a stable exchange rate between the RMB and the USD. So, like many other developing countries that pegged their currencies to the USD, China was caught in "the dollar trap."

The global financial crisis in 2007–2009 sounded an alarm that the dollar-based system could be unreliable. For a period after the brokerage house Lehman Brothers went bankrupt in September 2008, there was a large-scale credit crunch in the banking system in the United States and Europe. They could not provide the necessary trade finance denominated in USD, euro, and other hard currencies to Asian countries and regions. This led to the collapse of trade in many Asian countries. Thus, countries and regions such as South Korea, Malaysia, Indonesia, China, and Hong Kong began to encourage settling bilateral trade using their own currencies, which was facilitated by bilateral currency swap agreements among the countries. For China, the natural response to this collapse of USD-based trade finance was to promote the international use of the RMB for trade settlement. Since 2009, the offshore RMB market in Hong Kong has rapidly developed into a platform for facilitating RMB trade settlement. By 2015, the percentage of trade with China settled in RMB reached 29.4 percent, which was a historical high even up to the time of writing.[13] As many as 36 countries had entered into bilateral currency swaps with China by March 2018.

Other signs that the incumbent major reserve currencies could be quite unreliable were found in the euro debt crisis and the downgrading of US Treasury bond rating. In 2011, because of the euro crisis, the market generally predicted that the euro would depreciate by a large margin and suspected even that the euro might eventually disintegrate. In the same year, Standard & Poor downgraded the rating of US Treasury bond from AAA to AA+.[14] These events showed that the expected values of these incumbent reserve currencies might not be always sound. They suggested that perhaps central banks of the world should consider making their portfolios of reserve currencies more diversified. The RMB, being the currency of the second largest and the fastest-growing country at that time, was an obvious candidate for adding into their diversified portfolios.

The fragility of the USD-based international monetary and financial system prompted China to seek independence from it. China felt the need to increase the use of its own currency in international transactions and establish its own system in international payments. Moreover, certain quarters within the Chinese government felt that it was a good idea to use capital account liberalization, which is a prerequisite for internationalization of the RMB, to create pressure for domestic financial sector reform. This is called *daobi* (倒逼), which literally means creating a pressure in the reverse direction. As a result of the confluence of the above-mentioned factors, there has been a series of measures aimed at RMB internationalization since 2010. The effects were dramatic. As of the end of 2014, the amount of RMB deposits in banks in Hong Kong reached RMB 1,003.6 billion (12 percent of total deposits). Offshore RMB centers emerged all over the world, including Hong Kong, Taipei, Singapore, and London. At the end of 2014, the outstanding amount of offshore RMB-denominated bonds (called dim sum bonds) issued in Hong Kong reached RMB 380.5 billion. In December 2015, RMB became the fifth most used payment currency in the world, and the second most used trade finance currency, according to SWIFT. In October 2016, RMB officially became one of the five currencies in the basket of the SDR.

However, in order for the RMB to be a significant international currency, it has to be largely convertible in the capital account (i.e., capital has to be largely free to move in and out of China) and China's financial market must be sufficiently deep, broad, and liquid. It is not clear whether and when this might happen. The further development of the financial market is hindered by the requirement for the state-owned banks to offer cheap credit to non-profitable state-owned enterprises (SOEs) to keep them afloat for social and political reasons. As for capital account opening, one obstacle is that China does not want to fully integrate its financial system with the rest of the world, partly because of the experience of the global financial crisis in 2007–2009 that the United States-based IMS is not always reliable, and partly because of ideology – a mistrust of the West. This is one obstacle to RMB internationalization. To overcome this obstacle, the Chinese government borrows a page from the playbook of Deng Xiaoping's "one country, two systems" idea. They decide to adopt the "one currency, two markets" approach, meaning that they create an offshore RMB market that is not completely integrated with the onshore one. The offshore RMB is called CNH, as distinct from the onshore RMB, which is called CNY. They facilitated the formation of offshore RMB centers in Hong Kong, Singapore, Taipei, London, and elsewhere. The CNH is a fully convertible currency in the offshore market. In the offshore centers, the markets for CNH-denominated bonds, loans, bank deposits, and financing of projects gradually develop. How effective this approach is going to be remains to be seen.

Moreover, capital account convertibility of the RMB (which is equivalent to free capital mobility except for some subtle differences) implies that its exchange rate would become less stable. This is due to the open-economy trilemma. It dictates that exchange rate stability cannot be achieved under free capital mobility if autonomy in monetary policy is to be maintained. Assuming that China always wants autonomy in monetary policy, there is a tradeoff between higher exchange rate stability and freer capital mobility. You cannot have both at the same time. To what extent is China willing to let its currency fluctuate according to market forces? If China is unwilling to let its currency fluctuate too much, then its degree of capital mobility would be limited. This is another obstacle to RMB internationalization. Faced with these challenges, the future of the internationalization of the RMB is unclear.

This book investigates the necessary conditions for RMB internationalization to succeed and the prospects of the initiative. In the following chapters, I shall tell my story, supporting my arguments with theory, and supporting my theory with evidence. I shall discuss the various factors that are important for RMB internationalization and assess the potential for China to satisfy the requirements. I shall also identify the impediments, the greatest of which is the Chinese system itself, which is essentially still a planned economy. Thus, RMB internationalization cannot move forward without further reforms. The two major reforms are capital account liberalization and financial sector liberalization. Currently, the country is characterized by capital controls and financial repression, both of which represent distortions to the economy, creating inefficiency. Reforms mean removal of distortions to the economy. According to economic theory, when there is distortion in one part of the economy, distortion in another part of the economy may be justified on the grounds of economic efficiency. This is called The Theory of the Second Best. Thus, when the country is under financial repression, it may be justified to have capital controls so as to maintain economic stability. In order to attain the "first best," however, both distortions need to be removed or relaxed, and this requires reforms in both parts of economy. In other words, both the capital account and financial sector need to be liberalized. We advocate that both reforms should be carried out in tandem in a gradual manner so as to exploit the synergy of the two reforms. In fact, we argue that RMB internationalization can be a catalyst for these reforms.

NOTES TO CHAPTER I

1 According to the website of the PBC, the China Foreign Exchange Trade System (CFETS) publishes the daily middle exchange rate of the renminbi against the USD for the permitted trading range of the day at 9:15 a.m. on each working day. As of 11 August 2015, the middle rate is based on three factors: the closing rate of the inter-bank foreign exchange rate market of the previous day; supply and demand in the market; and the price movements of major currencies. See www.pbc.gov.cn/goutongjiaoliu/ 113456/113469/2927054/index.html. According to the website of the PBC, "为增强人民币兑美元汇率中间价的市场化程度和基准性，中国人民银行决定完善人民币兑美元汇率中间价报价。自2015年8月11日起，做市商在每日银行间外汇市场开盘前，参考上日银行间外汇市场收盘汇率，综合考虑外汇供求情况以及国际主要货币汇率变化向中国外汇交易中心提供中间价报价。"

2 Indeed, after 11 August 2015, the RMB exchange rate was generally on a depreciating trajectory until the exchange rate reached its trough of about 6.96 yuan to the dollar around the end of 2016.

3 The trilemma has been challenged by researchers in recent years. See, for example, Rey 2015 and Han and Wei 2018. Nonetheless, there is still plenty of evidence to show that the theory is sound. See Chapter 5 for more discussion of the challenges.

4 See, for example, "CNH: 'Taken' – The RMB Episode," from the Development Bank of Singapore, 15 January 2016 (www.dbs.com/aics/ pdfController.page?pdfpath=/content/article/pdf/AIO/160115_insights_ defending_the_yuan.pdf).

5 In December 2015, the RMB exchange rate fixing mechanism became more transparent as the PBC officially published for the first time the composition of the reference currency basket. CFETS publicly released for the first time the CFETS RMB Index, which reflects the RMB exchange rates against 13 currencies traded at CFETS. The USD, the euro, and the Japanese yen had the highest weightings at 26.4 percent, 21.39 percent, and 14.68 percent respectively, followed by the Hong Kong dollar (6.55 percent) and the Australian dollar (6.27 percent). See Hong Kong Exchanges and Clearing Limited 2018.

6 Source: IMF Currency Composition of Official Foreign Exchange Reserves (COFER) (http://data.imf.org/?sk=E6A5F467-C14B-4AA8-9F6D-5A09EC4E62A4).

7 Sources: US Bureau of Economic Analysis (www.bea.gov/international/
index.htm#iip); US Department of the Treasury (www.treasury.gov/
resource-center/data-chart-center/tic/Pages/fpis.aspx#usclaims). The
shares of US Treasury, corporate bonds, and agency debts are calculated
using the data as of mid-2017 provided by the US Department of the
Treasury, so the shares do not add up to 100 percent.

8 Source: US Bureau of Economic Analysis (www.bea.gov/international/
index.htm#iip); US Department of the Treasury (www.treasury.gov/
resource-center/data-chart-center/tic/Pages/fpis.aspx#usclaims).

9 Calculated by the author, based on methodology suggested in Habib 2010 .

10 See, for example, Krugman, Obstfeld, and Melitz 2018: 55.

11 "The Use and Counterfeiting of United States Currency Abroad" (www
.treasury.gov/press-center/press-releases/Documents/counterf.pdf).

12 Board of Governors of the Federal Reserve System (US), "Liabilities and
Capital: Other Factors Draining Reserve Balances: Currency in
Circulation: Week Average [WCURCIR]," retrieved from FRED, Federal
Reserve Bank of St. Louis (https://fred.stlouisfed.org/series/WCURCIR),
6 June 2018.

13 Source: PBC – RMB trade settlement in 2015 (www.pbc.gov.cn/
diaochatongjisi/116219/116225/3004953/index.html); China Customs
Statistics – 2015 Total Trade (www.customs.gov.cn/publish/portal0/
tab49667/info785130.htm).

14 Source: Reuters, "S&P Lowers United States Credit Rating to AA+" (www
.reuters.com/article/us-usa-sp-downgrade-text/sp-lowers-united-states-
credit-rating-to-aa-idUSTRE7750D320110806).

2 China's Aversion to a Floating Exchange Rate

WHY DOES CHINA DESIRE A STABLE
EXCHANGE RATE?

International trade has been very important to China's economic development ever since the "reform and opening" policy was adopted in 1978. In the early years of its reform and opening, China had plenty of cheap labor but very little capital. Thus, it opened its door to inward foreign direct investment (FDI), which brought in capital and technological knowhow. Moreover, China had a huge amount of rural labor surplus (underemployed rural labor force) that had to be absorbed by the economy. According to official estimates, as of 2017, there were still 287 million migrant workers working in the urban area as a result of the rural labor surplus.[1] Thus, China needed to keep its labor employed by expanding external demand through exporting. Figure 2.1 shows the CNY/USD exchange rate over the period 1981–2018, where we can see the evolution of the exchange rate over the entire period from China's reform and opening to the present time. Before 1994, the CNY/USD official exchange rate was not market-determined; it was fixed by the Chinese government. Thus, a black market for foreign exchange existed. After 1994, the exchange rate began to be market-determined, and the black market disappeared. In order to sustain export promotion and inward FDI flows, during 1994–2005, China had been maintaining a relatively stable (and probably undervalued) exchange rate against the USD through foreign-exchange market intervention (at the level of 8.28 yuan to the dollar during 1997–2005). An undervalued and stable exchange rate sustained competitiveness in the export sector. At the same time, it made inward FDI attractive to foreign firms. In other words, China

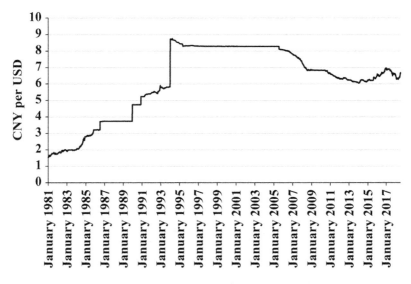

FIGURE 2.1 Historical CNY/USD exchange rate, 1981–2018.
Source: Bloomberg

adopted the dollar standard and made good use of it during this period. In 2001, China acceded to the World Trade Organization (WTO). This, together with its exchange rate policy of pegging to the USD, rapidly propelled China to the status of a major player in international trade. For one thing, China's processing trade and its engagement in the global value chain would not have been so successful had China not maintained a stable (and probably undervalued) exchange rate with the USD. The amount of processing trade of China as of 2001 and 2017 are USD 241 billion and USD 1,190 billion respectively, and their shares of total China exports are respectively, 47.4 percent and 29 percent.[2] Figure 2.2 shows that processing trade accounted for 50 percent or more of the total exports of China in most of the 1990s and 2000s. Its importance to China's exports was truly remarkable. A stable exchange rate against the USD has therefore become the cornerstone of China's export-oriented development strategy, at least during the period 1994–2005.

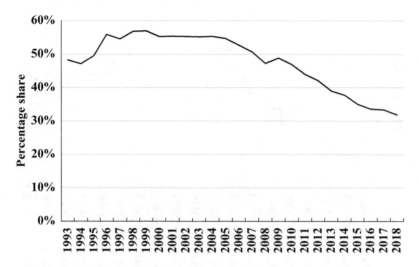

FIGURE 2.2 Share of processing exports in China's total exports, 1993–2018.
Data Sources: CEIC; General Administration of Customs

However, the success in export promotion inadvertently brought a huge current account surplus after China's accession to the WTO (in particular the bilateral surplus with the United States). Figure 2.3 shows the current account balance of China from 1982 to 2018. It can be seen that the current account balance was not high before 2001. The surplus never rose above USD 37 billion. However, it began to skyrocket after China's accession to the WTO in 2001. In 2005, China's current account surplus reached USD 132 billion, an annual increase of USD 63 billion from USD 69 billion in 2004. Its bilateral surplus with the United States reached USD 219 billion in 2005.[3] This prompted political pressure for the RMB to appreciate vis-à-vis the USD. Thus, in July 2005, the Chinese government allowed the yuan to gradually appreciate from the level of 8.28 yuan per dollar. By around July 2008, the exchange rate reached about 6.83 yuan per dollar, which amounted to a 21 percent appreciation from July 2005 to July 2008. Despite the large appreciation, China's current account surplus continued to grow rapidly, and it reached its peak in 2008, at

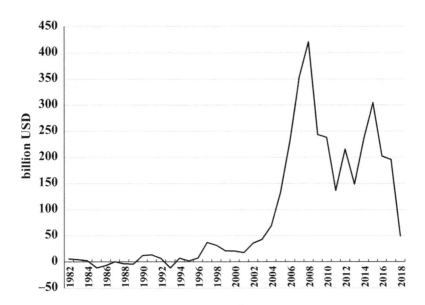

FIGURE 2.3 China's current account balance, 1982–2018.
Source: World Bank World Development Indicator – China's current account balance: https://data.worldbank.org/indicator/BN.CAB.XOKA.CD?locations=CN& name_desc=true.

USD 421 billion. In 2009, China decided to unofficially re-peg to the USD, due to the onset of the global financial crisis. In June 2010, in response to renewed external pressure, China announced that it had adopted a managed float exchange rate regime. From June 2010 to January 2014, the exchange rate appreciated further from 6.83 to 6.10 yuan per dollar. Since then, the bilateral exchange rate fluctuated. For example, in the year 2015, the yuan depreciated against the dollar by 4.4 percent, partly caused by the events on 11 August 2015, as described earlier. Nonetheless, even during the period 2005–2018, the RMB/USD exchange rate has never been fully flexible. It has always been managed so as to prevent it from excessive fluctuation or excessive appreciation or depreciation against the USD.

Another reason why a stable exchange rate with the USD is important to China is that its financial system is still too immature and weak to withstand large fluctuations in the exchange rate. Although there are still capital controls, they are not fully enforceable. Thus, the border is widely perceived to be "porous" rather than "impervious" to the flows of capital, both in and out. A managed exchange rate would anchor people's expectation that there would not be large depreciation or appreciation of the RMB. An expectation of future large depreciation of the RMB could trigger mass withdrawal of deposits from the banks to be exchanged to foreign currency and sent overseas (this is called "capital flight"). Moreover, firms that have large exposure to debts denominated in foreign currencies could go bankrupt because their revenue sources are in RMB but their liabilities are in foreign currencies (this is called "currency mismatch"). Banks that lend money to these firms would suffer losses. Given the immature financial system, serious capital flights can lead to serious strain in the banking system, bank runs, and even bankruptcy of banks. Thus, both capital flight and currency mismatch of firms' assets and liabilities can lead to bank runs and banking crisis under a large depreciation of the RMB.

Capital flights do not occur very often. But policymakers still want to prevent excessive capital outflows when the market expects the RMB to depreciate. Maintenance of a relatively stable exchange rate would minimize the chance of formation of depreciation expectations and the ensuing capital outflows, which policymakers regard as posing risks to the financial system.

The exchange rate policy of neighboring emerging economies might have also inspired China to adopt a stable exchange rate with the USD. The exchange rates of Taiwan, South Korea, and the Southeast Asian countries of Thailand, Malaysia, and Indonesia all closely tracked the USD. They all tried to avoid excessive appreciation or depreciation against the USD. Since this region is the largest trading partner of China, it is natural for China to maintain a stable exchange with these countries.

China might have also taken to heart the Japanese experience. It is interesting to note that the history of the development of China's banking and financial system is not unlike that of Japan. From the end of World War II to the mid-1980s, the Japanese banking system was characterized by the so-called convoy system whereby all the banks, including the least competitive ones, were under the protection of the Ministry of Finance (MOF). Moreover, banks were subject to the strict regulations of the MOF. It was unthinkable that a commercial bank would go bankrupt. Their profits were very much protected, and they had little incentive to develop skills and improve productivity. Because of the strict regulation, banks could not decide on the interest rate on time deposits. This sounds very similar to the financial repression policy implemented in the banking sector of China up till very recently. In the mid-1980s, the United States was running a large current account deficit with Japan. In response to that, the Plaza Accord was signed in September 1985, which compelled Japan to let the yen appreciate substantially against the USD. At the time of signing of the Accord, the USD/JPY exchange rate was 236.9 yen per dollar. A year later, the yen had appreciated to 154.8 yen per dollar, a 53 percent appreciation within a year. In response, there was an outcry in Japan, especially from the exporting sectors, for the government to implement policies to counter this effect. This led the Bank of Japan to reduce the key interbank lending rate from around 8 percent at the end of 1985 to about 3 percent by mid-1987. At the same time, realizing that the Japanese banking system was seriously outdated, the government began to deregulate the financial market. The most important development was the growth of the corporate bond market. The market soon became an important source of funding for the high-quality firms of Japan. In the meantime, the banking sector still absorbed the savings of most of the households in the form of deposits but lost an important group of high-quality borrowers. Therefore, the banks had to find alternative lending channels to make profits. They turned to the real estate sector. This eventually fueled the real estate bubble that ultimately burst and contributed to the disastrous "lost decade" of Japan between 1991 and 2002, during which the average annual growth rate was only 0.9 percent.[4]

The financial repression, followed by financial market liberalization and the sharp increases in real estate prices all sound similar to recent developments in China in around 2018. The export-dependence of the Chinese economy today is also quite similar to the experience of Japan in the mid-1980s. Thus, any sharp appreciation of the RMB with respect to the currencies of its main trading partners, notably the USD, would increase the risk of the financial market reform. Therefore, China treated Japan's exchange rate policy in the 1980s as a negative experience, which reinforced its determination to pursue its own policy of managed float with a view to guarding against excessive appreciation against the USD.

Using the terminology of W. Max Corden (2009), the exchange rate policy of China can be summarized by "exchange rate protection" and "exchange rate stability." Exchange rate protection is to maintain an undervalued exchange rate so as to sustain competitiveness in the export sector and to give employment to the urban workers and underemployed rural labor force. Exchange rate stability is to avoid having a fully floating exchange rate or sharp changes in fixed-but-adjustable exchange rates so as to protect the immature financial system. In addition, it is the general principle of the Chinese government to make changes gradually rather than sharply; it gives them more confidence that things will not get out of control. Besides, stability is generally preferred to fluctuation from the Chinese government's point of view, again because it makes both the government and the public feel a stronger sense of security.

One lesson about exchange rate regime and capital controls still fresh in the minds of policymakers in China is the Asian Financial Crisis. The crisis erupted on 2 July 1997 with the devaluation of the Thai baht. The initially planned 15 percent devaluation proved to be unsustainable as the currency was under severe speculative attacks, which plunged the currency value to a much lower level. The speculative attacks spread to the currencies of Thailand's neighbors, first Malaysia, then Indonesia, and then to South Korea. Other neighboring economies such as Hong Kong and Singapore were also severely hurt. In the eyes of the currency speculators, these economies all seemed to be vulnerable to the repercussions of the economic slowdown of their largest neighbor, Japan. Despite aid from the IMF (except Malaysia, which imposed capital controls instead of getting aid from the IMF), the currency crisis caused the four major crisis countries mentioned above to turn from growth rates of more than 6 percent in 1996 to severe contraction in 1998. The worst case was Indonesia. Its currency value tumbled by 85 percent from its original level by the summer of 1998. Most companies went bankrupt. Political unrest and ethnic violence ensued. There was mass unemployment and, in some areas, even basic foodstuff was unaffordable to the residents. All the above countries suffered, to different extents, mass bank failures and mass corporate bankruptcies triggered by severe currency depreciation due to the currency mismatch problem explained above. Many banks and corporations in these countries held large amount of debt denominated in foreign currencies, mostly USD, while their assets and revenue sources were mostly denominated in their domestic currencies, a case of currency mismatch. Thus, a large depreciation of the domestic currency sharply reduced the dollar value of their assets and they could not pay back their dollar debts, leading to bankruptcy. As is typical of a balance of payments crisis, there were mass capital flights from these countries as people withdrew their bank deposits, converted them into dollars and sent the money overseas.

China survived the Asian Financial Crisis of 1997–1998 relatively unscathed, mainly because capital flows both in and out of China were controlled at that time. One lesson that China learned from the Asian Financial Crisis was that, although capital controls helped it to survive the Asian Financial Crisis unscathed, it needed to prepare for the situation when it gradually opened its capital account or that capital controls gradually became less and less effective over time. When the capital account is more open and the country wants to maintain a stable exchange rate with a foreign currency, it needs to accumulate sufficient amounts of foreign exchange reserves to guard against the possibility of a balance of payments crisis when the currency is subject to speculative attack. In order to sustain a stable

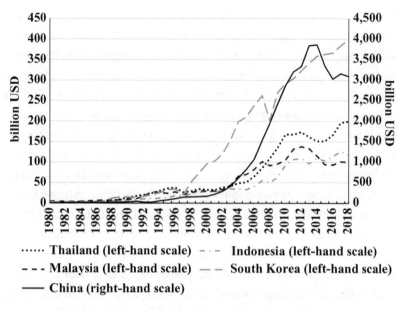

······ Thailand (left-hand scale)   **– · –   Indonesia (left-hand scale)**
– – – Malaysia (left-hand scale)   **— —   South Korea (left-hand scale)**
——— China (right-hand scale)

FIGURE 2.4 Foreign exchange reserves (excluding gold) of selected countries, 1980–2018.
Source: World Bank World Development Indicators: total reserves minus gold: https://data.worldbank.org/indicator/FI.RES.XGLD.CD

RMB–USD exchange rate, China realized that it must accumulate more foreign exchange reserves, especially USD reserves. Thus, the People's Bank of China increased its level of foreign exchange reserves from around 15 percent of GDP in 2000 to around 50 percent of GDP by 2009. Figure 2.4 shows the foreign exchange reserves of the Asian countries over time. It is clear that the amount skyrocketed after the Asian Financial Crisis.[5]

The policy of exchange rate stability, however, becomes an obstacle in RMB internationalization, which requires that China allows much freer capital mobility. This is because the open-economy trilemma dictates that exchange rate stability cannot be achieved under free capital mobility if autonomy in monetary policy is to be maintained. Assuming that China always wants autonomy in monetary policy, there is a tradeoff between higher exchange rate stability and freer capital mobility. This becomes a conundrum in RMB internationalization.

Is China's desire for exchange rate stability rational? Can the management of the exchange rate be justified? Below, we try to offer a defense of the case for China to manage its exchange rate by alluding to some recent research.

2.2 SOME DISCUSSION ABOUT EXCHANGE RATE MANAGEMENT

The foreign exchange market is a central component of the international capital market, and the exchange rates it sets would influence the profitability of international transactions of all types. Exchange rates therefore communicate important economic signals to households and firms engaged in international trade and investment. If these signals do not reflect all available information about market opportunities, a misallocation of resources will result. Studies of the foreign exchange market's use of available information are therefore important as they can help us to judge whether the international capital market is sending the right signals to markets. From the policy point of view, one main concern of Chinese policymakers is excessive exchange rate volatility. Below, we review some recent research work that throws light on whether exchange rates have been excessively volatile under the floating exchange rate regime.

2.2.1 Tests for the Economic Efficiency of the Foreign Exchange Market

If the foreign exchange market is economically efficient, exchange rates should be able to send the right signals to the market for it to allocate resources efficiently. If it is not, then government intervention may be warranted. There are two issues that are crucial in determining whether the foreign exchange market is economically efficient. First, in order for the foreign exchange market to be economically efficient, exchange rates must be determined by economic fundamentals. Otherwise, government intervention may be warranted. Second, if exchange rates are found to be excessively volatile beyond the levels justified by economic fundamentals based on credible economic models, they do not send the right signals to the market for the efficient allocation of resources. For example, a finding of excessive volatility would imply that the foreign exchange market is sending the wrong signals to investors who base their decisions on exchange rates. In that case, again, some government intervention, such as adopting a managed exchange rate regime, may be warranted.

One finding in the research on exchange rate determination is that statistical forecasting models of exchange rates based on standard "fundamental" variables like money supplies, government deficits, and output perform poorly even when actual values of future fundamentals are used to form exchange rate forecasts. For example, one influential study by Meese and Rogoff (1983a) showed that a naïve, "random walk" model, which simply takes today's exchange rate as the best guess of tomorrow's, performs better than a model based on economic fundamentals. This finding, which is sometimes called the "Meese and Rogoff puzzle," can be viewed as evidence that exchange rates have a life of their own, unrelated to the macroeconomic determinants. According to Cheung, Chow, and Qin (2017), the efforts to resolve the puzzle has so far been in vain. Attempts to resolve the puzzle include, for example, the works of Bacchetta, van Wincoop, and Beutler (2010), Meese and Rogoff (1983b), and Rogoff (1996). More recently, Rossi (2013) shows that, under the floating exchange rate regime, it is difficult to find a model that consistently outperforms the random walk specification for all exchange rates, for all periods, and for alternative evaluation criteria. Apparently, one reason for the robustness of the Meese and Rogoff puzzle is that it is difficult to find a commonly agreed framework to assess equilibrium exchange rates. More recent research has confirmed that while the random walk outperforms more sophisticated models for forecasts up to a year away, the models seem to do better at horizons longer than a year and have explanatory power for long-run exchange rate movements.[6] These findings can possibly justify some short-term management of the exchange rate by governments to prevent excessive short-term volatility.

Another line of research on the foreign exchange market examines whether exchange rates have been excessively volatile, perhaps because the foreign exchange market is "irrational," and "overreacts" to news. But how do we determine whether an exchange rate is "excessively volatile"? This is a difficult question to answer because, according to economic theory, market exchange rates should be more volatile relative to the economic fundamentals, such as national money supplies, outputs, government spending and taxes, even if they are economically efficient, because exchange rates must move quickly in response to economic news in order to send the correct price signals. Studies that attempt to find out whether exchange rates are excessively volatile produce inconclusive results, however. One difficulty is that it is hard to quantify the economic impacts of all the relevant variables, which can include social or political events. The ambiguous evidence on the excessive volatility of exchange rates indicates that market exchange rates might not be sending the right signals to the market for it to allocate resources efficiently. Thus, some government intervention in the foreign exchange market may be warranted. This can strengthen the case of countries like China to manage their exchange rate.

2.3   COMPARISON OF EXCHANGE RATE VOLATILITY ACROSS ASIAN COUNTRIES

Figure 2.5 shows the time trend of exchange rate volatility of a few Asian countries. Because of the Asian Financial Crisis, the exchange rate volatility of Indonesia, South Korea, and Thailand were quite high until 2003. It can be seen that China indeed has been having the lowest exchange rate volatility since 1999, i.e., just after the eruption of the Asian Financial Crisis. So, even by Asian developing-country standards, its exchange rate volatility has been distinctly lower than those of other countries. This can explain why it was criticized for lack of exchange rate flexibility. However, there is some sign that China has allowed higher exchange rate volatility in recent years, as

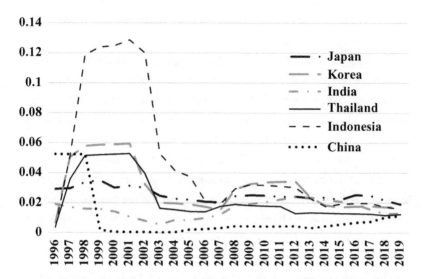

FIGURE 2.5 Exchange rate volatility against the USD, 1996–2019
Note: Exchange rate volatility is defined as the standard deviation of the
first difference in the monthly natural logarithm of nominal bilateral
exchange rate with the USD over the previous five years including the
current year.
Source: BIS – https://stats.bis.org/#df=BIS:WEBSTATS_XRU_CURRENT_
DATAFLOW(1.0);dq=M.CN+ID+IN+JP+KR+TH..A%3FstartPeriod=1992-01-01;pv=
1,2~4~1,0,0~name

shown in the figure. In fact, there seems to be a trend of convergence
in exchange rate volatility across all the countries. So, China's aversion to exchange rate flexibility has become less severe. This is favorable to RMB internationalization.

2.4   CONCLUSION

Maintaining a stable exchange rate with the USD has served China
well historically. However, its exchange rate policy was heavily scru-
tinized after China's current account surplus ballooned in 2005–2006.
China was accused by foreign countries of undervaluing its currency.
Later, in 2015–2016, China was blamed for letting its currency depreciate too quickly, causing global financial turmoil.

The exchange rate policy of China was (and still is) a conten-
tious topic a long time after 11 August 2015. Some economists

criticize China's intervention in the foreign exchange market as unwarranted.[7] In August 2019, President Donald Trump of the United States, in addition to engaging in a heated trade war with China, labeled China a "currency manipulator," the first time the United States had done so since 1994. However, the IMF did not hold the same view and refused to say that China manipulated its exchange rate. So, as of 2019, there is no consensus as to whether China indeed excessively managed its exchange rate.

In fact, adopting a managed exchange rate regime does not automatically imply that the country is a currency manipulator or that the managed exchange rate is economically inefficient. Cheung, Chow, and Qin (2017: chap. 4) demonstrate that it is hard to determine accurately the equilibrium exchange rate of a currency, as different models and different time horizons can be used, and the method of estimation can differ across studies.[8] Therefore, it is hard to determine whether the RMB is undervalued or overvalued. Consequently, it is hard to argue that China is a currency manipulator even if it manages the exchange rate of the RMB.

Regardless of whether China "manipulates" its currency, the debate goes on about whether China's exchange rate should be managed, and if so to what extent. The literature review in this chapter about the random-walk nature and excessive volatility of the market-determined exchange rate shows that a market-determined exchange rate is not necessarily efficient. Thus, from the point of view of both its own national interest and the interest of the rest of the world, China should not be faulted for its effort to reduce short-term or even medium-term volatility of its exchange rate per se. From the point of view of RMB internationalization, however, maintaining a stable exchange rate becomes a problem for China. This is because, in order to maintain exchange rate stability, China has to give up either autonomy in monetary policy or capital mobility, neither of which should be given up if it wants to achieve the internationalization of the RMB without undermining its ability to carry out monetary policy. In short, in order to internationalize the RMB, China must allow higher exchange rate flexibility.

NOTES TO CHAPTER 2

1 Source: National Bureau of Statistics – "2017年农民工监测调查报告" – Chinese Migrant Workers Investigation Report 2017 (www.stats.gov.cn/ tjsj/zxfb/201804/t20180427_1596389.html).

2 For data for 2001, see China Customs Yearbook 2001 (中国海关统计年鉴- 2001). For data for 2017, see China Customs Statistics (www.customs.gov .cn/customs/302249/302274/302276/1421284/index.html).

3 See Bosworth 2012.

4 See, for example, Shioji 2013 for the Japanese experience.

5 The literature on foreign reserves accumulation suggests that in order to explain the huge accumulation of foreign reserves by some countries after the Asian Financial Crisis based on the "precautionary saving" motive, the degree of risk aversion of these countries must be extremely high, which is quite implausible. Lee and Luk (2018) try to circumvent this problem by assuming that agents are uncertain about which model is the best for explaining the real world, and so they entertain a set of possible models and make decisions that serve them best under the worst-case scenario. This result may or may not be considered to be consistent with the behavior of China in this case.

6 See, for example, Chinn and Meese 1995, Mark 1995, and Corte and Tsiakas 2012.

7 See, for example, Prasad 2017a.

8 See also Cheung, Chinn, and Nong 2017.

3 Why Does China Want to Internationalize the RMB?

3.1 WHAT IS AN INTERNATIONAL CURRENCY? WHAT IS THE INTERNATIONALIZATION OF THE RMB?

Money has three functions: unit of account, medium of exchange, and store of value. Likewise, an international currency serves these three functions at the international level. As a unit of account for the public sector, it is used as a pegging currency by foreign central banks; for the private sector, it is used for trade invoicing and denomination of financial assets such as bank deposits, loans, bonds, and stocks. As a medium of exchange for the public sector, it is used as an intervention currency by foreign central banks in the foreign exchange market to influence exchange rates; for the private sector, it is used for settlement of international trade and international financial transactions. As a store of value for the public sector, an international currency (or an interest-bearing asset denominated in that currency) is used as foreign exchange reserves for foreign central banks; for the private sector, it is a financial asset for saving, such as in the form of bank deposits in foreign countries. These functions are summarized in Table 3.1. An international currency is widely used for the above three purposes. These three functions are interrelated. One function reinforces the other two. For example, if a currency is an invoicing currency for the trade of certain goods in a foreign country, it is usually also the settlement currency for the same goods in that country. If a currency is a major invoicing and settlement currency for a foreign country, then there is a strong demand for liquidity in that currency for international trade participants in that foreign country, which induces them to own bank deposits or purchase financial assets in that currency for saving purposes (i.e., store of value). When the

Table 3.1 *Roles of an international currency*

Function of money	Governments	Private actors
Store of value	International reserves	Cross-border deposits; cross-border securities
Medium of exchange	Vehicle currency for foreign exchange intervention	Invoicing trade and financial transactions
Unit of account	Anchor for pegging local currency	Denominating trade and financial transactions

Sources: Ito (2011) and Chinn and Frankel (2007), both of which are inspired by Kenen (1983).

firms and households in a foreign country have a strong demand for a currency for trade settlement and financial transaction, there is a need for the central bank of the country to keep a large amount of that currency as foreign exchange reserves so that it can provide liquidity of that currency to its firms and households in times of need. Thus, the currency becomes an important reserve currency for the foreign country. Furthermore, if a currency is the major invoicing currency for international trade and financial transactions, there is a strong incentive for the foreign central bank to peg its exchange rate to that currency to maintain exchange rate stability. The forward, futures, and options markets for the exchange between the two currencies would also be developed for hedging purposes.

The internationalization of the RMB is therefore the process of turning the RMB into a currency widely used internationally as a unit of account, medium of exchange, and store of value. There are multiple reasons that motivate China to try to make the RMB a major international currency. Basically, internationalization of the RMB is a long-term strategy of China in creating a stable international monetary environment for its economic development. Its goal is that Chinese citizens (households, firms, government) can use their own currency, the RMB, for trade, lending, borrowing, and investing internationally. In other words, it is hoped that Chinese citizens can use RMB for invoicing and settling trade in goods and services as well as invoicing and settling trade in financial assets and financial transactions, including borrowing and lending.

3.2 THE BENEFITS OF RMB INTERNATIONALIZATION TO CHINA

There are several benefits from achieving the above goals. First, the exchange rate risks in trade, investment, and financial transactions are minimized for Chinese citizens if they can use their own currency as a unit of account, medium of exchange, and store of value.

Second, there is less reliance on foreign currencies such as the USD and its associated institutions such as the payment system. The independence from foreign countries and foreign currencies, such as the United States and the USD, is a long-term development goal of China. In fact, the 2007–2009 global financial crisis made the need for such independence more urgent and concrete. During the crisis, there was a severe shortage of dollars in East Asia for trade finance, which contributed to the collapse of trade in the region. China believes that if more of its trade were to be settled in RMB, China's trade would suffer less under the shortage of the dollar or any other foreign currency. Moreover, the use of RMB for international payments would facilitate them to be handled by a payment system that is under the jurisdiction of China. The use of the USD for payments, on the other hand, requires the use of a payment system under the jurisdiction of US authority. For national security reasons, China clearly does not want a foreign authority to have too much information about and control over the flows of payments into and out of China, which the foreign country could possibly exploit for its own benefit. The Trump administration's confrontational approach to the US–China economic and trade relationship reminds China once again that the United States considers the rise of China as a threat and that the United States is trying to check China's technological and economic progress in an attempt to benefit the United States. This makes China's desire to be independent of the systems under US jurisdiction, including its payment systems, all the more urgent.

Companies that use the mainstream international banks for business would, by extension, almost certainly use the dollar payment system, and therefore are liable under American global jurisdiction. China learned a firsthand lesson of the risk of conducting business using the dollar payment system. In December 2018, Canadian police arrested the Chief Financial Officer, Meng Wanzhou, of the Chinese technology giant Huawei for possible extradition to the United States to face charges of violation of US laws. In January 2019, the US government formally leveled charges against Meng and Huawei for violating US sanctions against Iran by doing business with the country through a subsidiary named Skycom. US prosecutors accused Meng of lying about Huawei's relationship with Skycom and misleading the company's banking partners about the nature of Huawei's business in Iran. The company certainly did not violate Chinese or Canadian law even if it did business with Iran, as both countries did not impose sanctions on Iran. However, if it indeed did business with Iran, it might be found guilty under US laws if the company or its subsidiary had a banking partner that used the dollar payment system. China thinks that this extraterritorial legal reach of the US government renders China at the mercy of the United States. Thus, there is a strong desire for China to seek independence from the USD payment system.

In fact, many other countries are suspicious of the United States using the global reach of its legal system to gain economic advantage at the expense of foreign countries. *The Economist* magazine reported on 17 January 2019 that punishments by the US government of foreign companies that violated US sanctions could be disproportionately large, fueling suspicion that they were arbitrary and aiming at economic gains for the United States.[1] For example, in 2014, BNP Paribas, a French bank, was hit with a sanctions-related fine of USD 8.9 billion, which threatened the stability of the company. According to the magazine, Pierre Gattaz, head of BusinessEurope, the European

Union's main employer federation, said that "European companies are increasingly impacted by the extraterritoriality of US sanctions. Moreover, these are increasingly instrumentalised to promote economic interests."

For the above reasons, as part of the RMB internationalization initiative, China developed its own global payment system that provides funds clearing and settlement services to domestic and foreign participants in cross-border RMB payments. It culminated in the launching on 2 May 2018 of Phase 2 of the RMB Cross-Border Interbank Payment System (CIPS), with eligible direct participants engaged online simultaneously. As of the end of March 2018, a total of 31 domestic and foreign direct participants, as well as 695 domestic and foreign indirect participants had joined CIPS, expanding its actual business scope to 148 countries and jurisdictions. The payment system is regarded as the "superhighway" facilitating the international use of the RMB. Thus, CIPS is an important infrastructure of the RMB internationalization initiative.[2]

Third, being able to borrow internationally in China's own currency is an important benefit for China. For one thing, it can help China avoid the crises caused by the "original sin" problem explained below. For the long-term development of China, its firms should be able to borrow freely from foreigners so as to finance their business. It would be inefficient if Chinese firms can only borrow in China if there is a rich set of funding sources available in foreign countries. This would require that China opens its capital account. However, it would be much safer for Chinese firms to borrow internationally in RMB than in a foreign currency. This would reduce the risk of a mismatch between the currency denomination of the revenue source (which is RMB) and the currency denomination of the debt (which is a foreign currency) of the companies, which can result in bankruptcy of the firms in the face of a sharp depreciation of the RMB. Suppose the debts of a company are mostly denominated in USD but its revenues are mostly denominated in RMB, then a large depreciation of the RMB against the USD means that the domestic-currency value of the liabilities rises sharply while the domestic-currency value of the assets remains the same. This can lead to a sharp fall in the net worth and therefore bankruptcy of the firm. If a large number of firms have large exposure to foreign-currency debts while their revenues are denominated mostly in RMB, there would be widespread bankruptcy in the face of a "balance of payments crisis." A balance of payments crisis is often marked by a sharp depreciation of the currency and capital flight. The sharp depreciation is often caused by speculative attack of the currency as speculators believe that the currency is overvalued and that the central bank does not have enough foreign reserve to defend the currency. (That is, the central bank does not have enough foreign reserves to fill the payment gap in the balance of payments account at the pegged exchange rate, and therefore the currency has to depreciate.) A balance of payments crisis often causes banks to go bankrupt as depositors withdraw their money from the banks so as to exchange domestic currency for foreign currency and move the money out of the country, while bankrupt firms that borrowed from the banks default on their loans. Thus, the balance of payments crisis is often followed by a banking crisis. This kind of double-crisis would not occur if the domestic firms can borrow in their own currency. Barry Eichengreen and Ricardo Hausmann (1999) call the phenomenon that a less-developed country cannot borrow in its own currency "original sin." It should be recalled that it was this "original sin" that led to currency mismatch between the revenues and the debts of the firms in Asian countries such as Thailand and Indonesia in the face of a currency crisis and caused widespread bankruptcy and economic disasters in these countries during the 1997–1998 Asian Financial Crisis. If Chinese citizens can mostly borrow internationally in their own currency, they can avoid the original sin problem.

Fourth, when a currency becomes sufficiently international-ized, the country's citizens and government might be able to borrow abroad large amounts at low interest rates in the country's own currency. The United States is a case in point. The yields of US

Treasury securities are not impressive when compared with other financial instruments. Yet US Treasury securities are widely held by financial institutions and central banks around the world as it is considered safe and highly liquid. Gilmore and Hayashi (2011) and Hassan (2013) document that USD risk-free assets generally pay lower expected returns (net of exchange rate movements) than the risk-free assets of most other currencies. The reason behind this phenomenon is that when the currency of a country is widely used as an invoicing and settlement currency in international trade, it can also more likely be a funding currency, i.e., a currency chosen by borrowers to denominate their debts, such as bonds or loans. This is because the interest rate is more likely to be lower as the demand for holding safe assets denominated in that currency is boosted by the fact that it is used as a settlement currency (or payment currency) for trade in goods and services. Gopinath and Stein (2018) put forward a theory to support this view and use the theory to explain how the establishment of the Federal Reserve in 1913 helped to increase the use the USD as an invoicing currency, which in turn enhanced its development as a funding currency. This further paved the way for the USD to overtake the pound sterling as the dominant international currency later on (see also Eichengreen, Mehl, and Chiṭu 2018). As we discussed earlier, one can see how this advantage can translate into the ability of a country (such as the United States) to run persistent current account deficits year after year without triggering default. This is possible as long as the average interest rate on the country's foreign liabilities is substantially lower than the average return on the country's foreign assets. As explained above, this can happen if the currency is a widely held international currency so that the country can borrow in its own currency at low interest rates.

In 2017, the average interest rate the United States paid on its international liabilities was 7.5 percent while the average interest rate the United States received on its international assets was 14.6 percent.[3] The total value of the international liabilities of the United States in that year was USD 35.5 trillion, while the total value of the international assets of the United States was USD 27.6 trillion.[4] So, in that year, the total amount of interest payments was USD 2.7 trillion and the total amount of returns to international assets was USD 4 trillion. In other words, even though the United States owed foreigners USD 7.9 trillion more than foreigners owed the United States, the United States earned a net positive return of USD 1.3 trillion. Thus, the United States was like a shrewd businessperson who borrowed cheaply from the financial market and invested the proceeds smartly in assets that yield him much high returns, making lucrative profits. What is more striking is that the United States was in fact the largest debtor country in the world in 2017, and yet it made a huge amount of money in 2017 (USD 1.3 trillion) by paying a negative amount out of its own pocket (−7.9 trillion USD). (The USD 7.9 trillion, which has been borrowed from foreigners, has been used to finance the investment of the United States.) In the case of China, it was just the opposite. In 2017, the average interest rate Chinese citizens and government paid on their international liabilities was 8.9 percent while the average interest rate China received on its international assets was 4.2 percent.[5] The total value of the international liabilities of China in that year was USD 5.1 trillion, while the total value of the international assets of China was USD 6.9 trillion.[6] So, in that year, the total amount of interest payments was about USD 0.45 trillion and the total amount of returns to international assets was about USD 0.29 trillion. Thus, although foreigners owed China more than China owed foreigners by USD 1.8 trillion, China made a net loss of USD 0.16 trillion, a non-trivial amount. So, China acted like an incompetent investor who borrowed at high interest rates and invested the proceeds in assets that yielded low returns, resulting in a substantial loss. It lost USD 0.2 trillion in 2017 by paying USD 1.8 trillion out of its own pocket, which could have been used to finance China's own investment. The difference between the United States and China reveals the advantage of the issuing country of a major reserve currency over an emerging economy having a currency that is hardly used internationally. The US government can borrow very cheaply

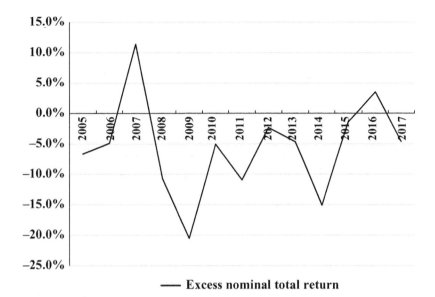

— **Excess nominal total return**

FIGURE 3.1 Excess return of Chinese overseas assets over its overseas liabilities, 2005–2017.
The real return curve is almost exactly the same as the nominal return curve and therefore it is not shown.
Source: Calculated by the author based on methodology suggested by Habib 2010.

(as reflected in the low yields of the US Treasury securities) as the United States is a major global reserve currency. US corporations can also borrow cheaply because the USD is the dominant global trade invoicing currency and funding currency.

The year 2017 is just an example. On average, the annual return of American overseas assets far exceeds its overseas liabilities, while it is the opposite for China. Figures 3.1 and 3.2 show the annual excess return of the two countries from 2005 to 2017. Figures 3.1 and 3.2 show that, for example, during the period 2005–2017, the excess return of American international assets over its international liabilities was 3 percent, while that for China was −6 percent. The difference is astounding.

Another way to look at a country's borrowing and lending is that they reflect assets-for-assets trade. When a country lends to

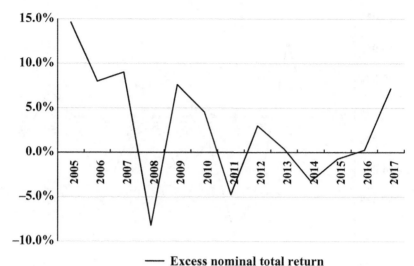

—— Excess nominal total return

FIGURE 3.2 Excess return of US overseas assets over its overseas liabilities, 2005–2017.
The real return curve is almost exactly the same as the nominal return curve and therefore it is not shown.
Source: Same as for Figure 3.1.

foreigners, it is exporting capital service. Conversely, when it borrows from foreigners, it is importing capital service. The interest rate at which the country lends to foreigners is the price of the capital service that it exports, while the interest rate at which the country borrows from foreigners is the price of the capital service that it imports. The ratio of the price of its exports of capital service to the price of its imports of capital service is the terms of trade in this assets-for-assets trade. Everything else being equal, the higher the terms of trade, the larger is the country's gains from trade. In the example of the United States given above, the terms of trade of the United States in 2017 was 14.6/7.5 = 1.95, whereas the terms of trade of China in 2017 was 4.2/8.9 = 0.47.[7] Thus, the terms of trade of the United States were more than four times those of China's. The gains from assets-for-assets trade for the United States must therefore be much higher than those of China (from a welfare point of view).

Thus, if the RMB becomes sufficiently internationalized, Chinse firms and companies will be able to borrow abroad large amounts at low interest rates in RMB, and this implies that China can run a current account deficit with less interest burden. Although China may not want to run persistent current account deficits year after year like the United States does, this advantage means that China gains more from assets-for-assets trade – its terms of trade are higher – and it benefits China whenever its firms, households, or government need to borrow overseas. A related point is that when the RMB becomes sufficiently internationalized, the exchange rate with the USD can fluctuate more than before without causing instability in the financial system. Since China does not need to intervene as much as before to stabilize the RMB exchange rate against the USD, China does not need to accumulate as much low-interest-bearing dollar-denominated assets such as US Treasury bonds as before. This means that it can earn higher average returns from its foreign assets. In this sense, it can decouple itself from the "dollar trap" that we discuss in Chapter 1.

Fifth, wide international use of the RMB would provide more business for the banking and financial sectors of China. Eichengreen, Mehl, and Chiţu (2018: 61) document the rivalry between countries over the international use of their currencies to benefit their banking business such as in trade financing. In the case of the RMB, when the currency is more widely used, it benefits the Chinese banks and financial institutions as the international demand for RMB assets would bring business to domestic financial institutions, which are the main sources of RMB liquidity, as payments in RMB have to be ultimately cleared and handled by Chinese banks and financial institutions.

Sixth is the ability to earn seigniorage from foreign countries (issuing RMB to foreigners in exchange for real goods). When foreigners trust the RMB, they are willing to hold the currency as a medium of exchange and store of value. Thus, they are willing to sell goods to China in exchange for the RMB. This is especially useful when foreign liabilities are denominated in the home currency and the home government prints or creates money to pay for sovereign debts. In this case, the seigniorage raised by "printing" of money to pay foreign creditors helps to avoid a default of the sovereign debt by the government. Even if the foreign debts are not sovereign in nature, but are incurred by commercial banks, defaults of the banks can be avoided as the central bank, being the lender of last resort, can "print" money and lend it to the commercial banks so that they can pay foreign creditors. In fact, this benefit is related to the third one mentioned above, i.e., being able to borrow overseas in China's own currency so that the double-crises caused by the "original sin" problem can be avoided.

Seventh is political influence. When a currency becomes a major reserve currency for another country, the issuing country of the currency can use it as leverage to exchange for favors from the foreign country. This is because the central bank of the issuing country can act as a lender of last resort to the foreign country in times of need, such as when the foreign central bank runs out of foreign reserves and needs to borrow from the issuing country to fill the payment gap in the balance of payments account, or when foreign commercial banks need the liquidity in the currency to pay its depositors so as to avoid a banking crisis, or when foreign firms are short of the currency for trade financing. When the RMB becomes a major reserve currency for a foreign country, it will become a closer ally of China. Consequently, RMB internationalization can give China greater international influence.

There is yet another, uniquely Chinese, reason for (certain quarters in) China to push for internationalization of the RMB. China is now faced with the difficult task of financial sector reform. The banking and financial systems have been controlled by the government through state-owned banks and financial institutions. This is a typical case of financial repression – the deposit interest rates are set artificially low so that loans could be extended to state-owned enterprises at low interest rates in order to achieve the government's economic, social, and political goals. However, China has come to a point where the financial sector and the sectors dominated by state-owned enterprises need to reform in tandem so as to allow the market to play a more dominant role in the financial system. This is necessary for a more efficient allocation of resources, which is in turn necessary for sustaining growth. But there are powerful vested interests resisting such reforms. Certain quarters within the Chinese government want to use the capital account liberalization and financial market liberalization that come with RMB internationalization to create pressure for domestic financial sector reform, pretty much like China's accession to the World Trade Organization (WTO) created pressure for domestic industrial sector reform back in 2001. Like accession to the WTO, RMB internationalization appeals to the masses in China as it is considered a recognition of China's status by the international community, which Chinese people believe they deserve. It confers prestige on its people. It is a matter of national pride. Thus, the liberal quarters of the government think that promoting RMB internationalization is a good tactic for pushing forward domestic financial sector reform. This motivation explains why China has stronger incentives to internationalize its currency than some other countries historically, such as Japan or Germany.

3.3   THE BENEFITS OF RMB INTERNATIONALIZATION TO THE REST OF THE WORLD

In an IMS where each country adopts a floating exchange rate regime, but there is only one single reserve currency, say the USD, the rest of the world other than the issuing country needs the reserve currency to serve as an international safe asset for store of value. However, there is potentially a long run problem with this arrangement. As the rest of the world grows more quickly than does the United States, their demand for foreign reserves will ultimately surpass the fiscal capacity of the United States to repay the dollar-denominated US government debt that it issued to meet this demand. This will cause the United States either to depreciate its currency over time so as to inflate away the debt, or to default. The anticipation of such an event can cause a confidence problem. A confidence problem of a similar nature under the gold exchange standard during the Bretton Woods era was pointed out by the economist Robert Triffin (1960). He argued that as central banks' demand for international reserve grew over time, their holdings of dollars would grow until they exceeded the value of the US gold stock, priced at the rate of USD 35 per ounce as promised by the United States. Thus, if all central banks simultaneously demand to redeem their dollars into gold from the US government, it would not be able to meet its obligation. This would lead to a confidence problem whereby central banks, knowing that their dollars might no longer be worth as much gold as promised, might become unwilling to accumulate more dollars and might even attempt to exchange the dollars they already held into gold from the US government. This would lead to the collapse of the system. This is called the Triffin dilemma. Indeed, faced with a run on the dollar, the Nixon administration first devalued the dollar in 1971 and eventually abandoned the peg of the dollar to gold in 1973.

Under today's IMS, the USD is the most important reserve currency, with about a 62 percent share of global foreign reserves, followed by the euro, with about a 20 percent share. However, the euro is arguably only a regional currency, as most of the countries that hold euro as foreign reserves are located near the eurozone. This means that the USD is the single dominant international reserve currency. But there is no reason why the world cannot accommodate more than one major reserve currency. Eichengreen, Mehl, and Chiţu (2018) envision such a multipolar world and argue that it is more stable than the current system, which has essentially one dominant reserve currency. The rationale is that, as the US GDP share of the world is set to fall continuously because of the fast growth of the developing countries, the fiscal capacity of the United States will eventually not be able to supply the assets for reserves and payments needed by the world. Some other currency(ies) is/are needed to fill the gap. The RMB is a potential candidate. Thus, if the RMB eventually becomes another major reserve currency beside the USD and euro, it could possibly lead to more stability in the IMS, as the rest of the world can benefit from diversification and a larger supply of reserve currencies.[8] One possible scenario is that the RMB becomes a regional reserve currency, being a major reserve currency for China's neighbors, namely the Southeast and Northeast Asian countries. During the global financial crisis of 2007–2009, there was a collapse of trade in Asia because of an acute shortage of the USD for trade financing. One can argue that if the RMB had been more widely used in Asia and if the Asian countries had been using RMB to finance some of their trade, the extent of trade collapse might have been less severe, and the economies of these countries could have suffered less, as trade was so important to them.

3.4 THE COSTS OF RMB INTERNATIONALIZATION TO CHINA

There are potentially three types of costs to China for internationalizing the RMB. First is that the demand for the RMB will be more volatile as foreign demand for RMB increases. As the demand for RMB in different countries may or may not be correlated, the variance of the aggregate demand for RMB overseas will increase. This larger fluctuation in the demand for RMB will lead to larger fluctuation in the RMB exchange rate. Given the open-economy trilemma, China cannot really control such a volatility of exchange rate if it wants to allow capital mobility and monetary autonomy.

The second cost is an increase in the average demand for the RMB. This will lead to the appreciation of the currency and undermine the export competitiveness of the country. This will make it more difficult for China to sustain its export-led growth strategy. China will have to transform its development strategy and find alternative sources of growth.

The third cost is the increase in international responsibilities. If other parts of the world are pegged to the RMB, China's monetary policy has to take care of their economies in addition to China's own domestic economy. For example, if China is in a boom but other countries pegged to the RMB are in a recession, China cannot increase interest rates too much lest these countries will be hurt. If the central banks of these countries run out of RMB and face a balance of payments crisis or a banking crisis, China may have to lend them RMB to avert a crisis or recover from a crisis.

3.5   WHY DID'NT JAPAN NTERNATIONALIZE ITS CURRENCY?

When one asks why China wants to internationalize the RMB, one should also ask why other large countries that had even more well-developed financial systems, such as Japan, did not internationalize their currencies. A comparison between China and Japan is quite meaningful, as the two countries share many similarities. Japan was the second largest economy in the world in the 1980s, and it was the second largest exporting country as well. Post-war Japan was under a rather controlled financial system, just like China has been under a system of financial repression. Were there some reasons why Japan did not internationalize its currency that China should know so that China should not waste its time repeating what Japan had done and did not succeed, or avoid the mistakes that Japan made?

3.5.1   *The History*

In fact, the yen did not play any international role before the 1970s. In 1970, the yen was not used to invoice any international trade, even that of Japan. Before 1975, the share of yen in global foreign reserves of central banks was negligible. The reason was that the institutions necessary to support the yen as an international currency were not well developed. According to Fukao (2003), post-war Japan was under a state-controlled trade system with extremely strict foreign exchange controls. It resembled financial repression in China in the recent past. The Japanese financial system was characterized by: (1) Prohibition of foreign transactions, with exceptions – foreign currency transactions by Japanese residents were restricted except where expressly authorized. This was lifted in 1980 to become "freedom of foreign transactions with exceptions." (2) Foreign exchange concentration – all foreign exchange receipts were centrally controlled and allocated by the government. The objective was to concentrate all foreign exchange for acquiring the parts, machinery, and technology from foreign countries for the manufacturing sector so as to boost economic growth. This policy of foreign exchange concentration was facilitated by a system of authorized foreign exchange banks, whereby only banks with express authorization were permitted to deal in foreign exchange.

According to Eichengreen, Mehl, and Chiţu (2018), the 1970s was the turning point in the financial development of Japan. The repurchase agreement (repo) market of government bonds and the market for certificates of deposit (CDs) helped to supply liquidity to the money market with market-determined interest rates. The collapse of the Bretton Woods system in 1973 made Japan rethink its reliance on the USD for international transactions and to contemplate using the yen instead. However, the transformation towards a more open financial system was very slow. The Ministry of Finance was very conservative; for example, it continued to restrict Japanese banks' foreign currency positions and imposed prudential measures to ensure systemic stability and exchange rate stability. In addition, exporting firms were opposed to the relaxation of capital controls for fear of inflows of capital which could push up the exchange value of the yen as well as increase exchange rate volatility and hurt exporting. Banks were afraid of foreign competition. Domestic politics was generally against currency internationalization while the government was at best neutral (see Frankel 2011). However, external pressure, notably that from the United States, tipped the balance in the other direction. The United States pressured Japan to liberalize its financial market and capital account. The Yen–Dollar Agreement of 1984 eventually led to the convertibility of the yen in the capital account. The creation of the market for bankers' acceptances and short-term treasury bills was pivotal for the internationalization of the yen, as acceptances were important for trade financing, while short-term treasury bills were important as vehicles of foreign reserves for foreign central banks.

Because of the above initiatives, the share of Japanese exports invoiced in yen rose from less than 30 percent in 1980 to nearly 40 percent in 1991. The share of imports invoiced in yen started from a much lower level than that of exports. It rose from less than 3 percent in 1980 to more than 15 percent in 1991. The share of yen in global central bank reserves rose from 4.1 percent in 1982 to more than 8 percent in 1991, probably due to the greater availability to foreign central banks of liquid yen-denominated assets and the appreciation expectation of the yen. The share of the yen in global gross foreign exchange turnover in 1989 was 27 percent (where the sum of the shares of all currencies is equal to 200 percent), according to the Bank for International Settlements.

However, the shares for the yen were still small when compared with the USD. In other words, despite the liberalization measures undertaken by the authorities, the yen still could not become a major international currency at its peak performance. The reasons were: (1) The markets for short-term debt instruments that were attractive to foreign investors were both small and illiquid compared with, say, the corresponding US debt instruments, due to taxation and other impediments to market expansion. (2) The Bank of Japan was reluctant to be the lender of last resort for other countries by entering into currency swap agreements with foreign central banks. (3) Large trading companies were willing to invoice their exports in dollar, partly because raw materials accounted for 40 percent – 50 percent of total imports, which was higher than in other industrialized countries, and they were almost all invoiced in USD. (4) Japanese trade was closely associated with the supply chains in East Asia, whereby Japanese manufacturers set up manufacturing bases and export platforms in East Asian countries. Since the final goods were mostly exported to the United States and Europe, they were invoiced in USD. In order to hedge against exchange rate risks, the intermediate goods were also invoiced in USD so as to avoid currency mismatch between the invoicing currency of the final goods and that of the intermediate goods. This last motivation is also documented in Ito, Koibuchi, Sato, and Shimizu (2010).

Unfortunately, the onset of the banking crisis of Japan and the "lost decade" led to the shrinking of the yen's market shares on almost all fronts. The yen's share of global foreign reserves fell gradually from 8.3 percent in 1991 to 4.8 percent in 1997. The share of Japanese exports invoiced in yen fell from 40 percent to about 30 percent during the 1990s. Japan's share of global GDP fell from 18 percent in 1994 to 8 percent in 2011. Its share of global exports fell from 10 percent in 1986 to 5 percent in 2010.

In September 1997, after the eruption of the Asian Financial Crisis, Japan proposed the creation of an Asian Monetary Fund, which, under the leadership of Japan, would provide emergency loans to Asian countries in need. The proposal was to set up a regional network funded by Asian countries to overcome current and future economic crises. Later, a report titled "Internationalization of the Yen for the Twenty-First Century" was published by the Japanese Ministry of Finance in 1999, suggesting that the yen should play a role in Asia the way the USD did in the Western Hemisphere and the euro played in Europe.[9] However, the weak economic growth of Japan led to the continued decline of the international use of the yen. The Asian Monetary Fund failed to materialize in the face of opposition from the United States, and China's reluctance to support it.

To summarize, the answer to the question "Why didn't Japan internationalize its currency?" is that it took time to liberalize Japan's financial system and open its capital account, and before these initiatives were completed the country's growth rate suffered severe decline due to domestic reasons and the international environment. Since financial development, capital account openness, and economic size are all important for currency internationalization, the Japanese yen could not become a major international currency.

3.6   CONCLUSION

RMB internationalization is part of the long-term development strategy of China. Its motivation is driven by the quest for independence in international monetary affairs, and further reform and opening. China wants to be able to borrow internationally mostly in its own currency. It wants to be independent from its reliance on foreign currencies and foreign countries, such as the USD and the United States. It also wants to have more political influence and more prestige. It is hoped that RMB internationalization can bring about these benefits. In this sense, it is a goal. On the other hand, RMB internationalization can create pressure to reform China's financial system, its exchange rate regime, and its system of capital controls to become more open and market-determined. In this sense, it is a tool. Many people think that reform and opening are more fundamental to the long-term development of China than attaining more independence in currency and international monetary affairs. From the point of view of these people, RMB internationalization should be treated more as a tool than as a goal. Moreover, RMB internationalization is ultimately determined by the market. It cannot be achieved by policy alone. The market will not be ready until China's financial market is sufficiently developed and open, and its institutions, such as the rule of law and an independent judiciary and indeed the whole system of governance, become more mature and well-developed. This can only be achieved by further reform and opening. Only under such circumstances can the RMB be a major international currency.

NOTES TO CHAPTER 3

1 See *The Economist* 2019.
2 For the announcement by the PBC of Phase II of CIPS, see www.pbc.gov
   .cn/english/130721/3533376/index.html.
3 Source: author's calculation, based on raw data provided by IMF –
   International Investment Position (http://data.imf.org/regular.aspx?key=
   61468209) and Bureau of Economic Analysis – International Transaction

(www.bea.gov/international/bp_web/tb_download_type_modern.cfm?
list=1&RowID=2).

4 Source: IMF – International Investment Position (http://data.imf.org/
   regular.aspx?key=61468209).

5 Source: author's calculation, based on raw data provided by: IMF –
   International Investment Position (http://data.imf.org/regular.aspx?key=
   61468209); China State Administration of Foreign Exchange – Balance of
   Payments (www.safe.gov.cn/wps/portal/sy/tjsj_szphb).

6 Source: IMF – International Investment Position (http://data.imf.org/
   regular.aspx?key=61468209).

7 To understand the calculation, recall that, in 2017, the average interest
   rate the US paid on its international liabilities was 7.5 percent and the
   average interest rate the US received on its international assets was 14.6
   percent, while the average interest rate Chinese citizens and government
   paid on their international liabilities was 8.9 percent and the average
   interest rate China received on its international assets was 4.2 percent.

8 Farhi and Maggiori (2018) argue that the IMS with more than one reserve
   currency may or may not be more stable than one with just one reserve
   currency, depending on the number of such currencies (larger is better) and
   whether the reserve currency-issuing countries have full commitment or
   limited commitment (full commitment is better).

9 Refer to the link: www.mof.go.jp/english/about_mof/councils/customs_
   foreign_exchange/e1b064a.htm.

4 China's Strategy of Internationalizing the RMB

China is probably the first country in history not considered one of the most advanced in its time to try to make its currency an international one. Historically, the financial market of a country that issues an international currency needs to be large, reliable, efficient, and liquid. This is because a currency that is widely used as a medium of exchange needs to have low transaction costs when exchanging with other currencies, to be widely held internationally so that it is easy for holders to find a counterparty to exchange the currency with other currencies, and to have a large variety of financial products for store of value. Thus, the issuing country needs to be economically large and have an open and well-developed financial market. All these factors together constitute what economists call "thick market externalities" in making a currency an international medium of exchange. These features are usually associated with a more developed country. China is special, however. It is a developing country that is expected to soon become the largest economy in the world. But its financial system is still immature compared with that of the most advanced countries, and still needs to improve on reliability, efficiency, breadth, depth, and liquidity. Moreover, its currency is still not fully convertible in the capital account. Market forces alone, therefore, would not be able to make the RMB a significant international currency. Thus, government policy is required. Borrowing a page from the playbook of Deng Xiaoping's "one country, two systems" idea, the Chinese government has decided to adopt the "one currency, two markets" approach, meaning that they have created an offshore RMB market which is not completely integrated with the onshore one. The offshore RMB is called CNH, as distinct from the onshore RMB, which is called CNY. They facilitated the formation of offshore RMB centers in such cities as Hong Kong, Singapore, Taipei, and London. The CNH is a fully convertible currency in the offshore market. In the offshore centers, the markets for CNH-denominated bonds, loans, bank deposits, and other financial instruments have gradually developed. In addition to the establishment of the offshore RMB centers, trade settlement in RMB is allowed and even encouraged. China has also entered into bilateral currency swap agreements with 35 countries as of 2017. The capital account is gradually being liberalized, through schemes such as Qualified Foreign Institutional Investor (QFII), Qualified Domestic Institutional Investor (QDII), RMB-Qualified Foreign Institutional Investor (RQFII), Shanghai–Hong Kong Stock Connect, Shenzhen–Hong Kong Stock Connect, Bond-Connect, Mutual Fund Connect, Shanghai Free Trade Zone (FTZ) , Shenzhen Qianhai FTZ, and so on. In November 2017, China announced that it would begin allowing foreign securities, fund management, and futures firms to have 51 percent ownership in their Chinese subsidiaries. The overall picture, however, is that China has been very slow in opening its financial market. At the same time, China is gradually building up its international interbank payment system, called the Cross-Border Interbank Payment System (CIPS), which clears and settles RMB-denominated payments and trade. When the system becomes mature, China's international payment process can be more independent from the West. This is part and parcel of the RMB internationalization strategy.

One important factor that determines thick market externalities is capital account openness. In Chapter 5, we shall discuss in detail the importance of capital account openness for the thick market externalities of a currency, which in turn is important for creating a positive feedback effect or snowballing effect for a currency to become a trade settlement currency. Suffice it to say here that even as of 2017, China's capital account was still considered rather closed by international standards, being more closed than that of Thailand and South Korea, not to mention those of the United States and Japan.

Another important factor that determines the thick market externalities of a currency is financial development. In Chapter 6, we shall discuss in more detail the level of financial development of China. Figure 6.1 in Chapter 6 indicates that China's level of financial development as recent as 2017 was still quite low. It was behind not only those of the developed countries such as the United States and Japan, but also other emerging markets such as Thailand and South Korea. It was only higher than those of countries such as Indonesia and India.

Since an international currency must be widely used not only for trade invoicing and settlement but also as a funding and investment currency, it is hard to imagine how a currency such as the RMB can become an international currency through market forces alone given that China's financial market is still immature and capital mobility in and out of the country is still quite tightly controlled. Given that financial development and capital account liberalization take time, the only way to make the RMB more widely used internationally at this point is to make use of government policies. Thus, the Chinese government has taken the following steps to facilitate RMB internationalization: (i) encouraging the RMB to be used to settle trade and denominate offshore financial instruments; (ii) facilitating the formation of offshore RMB centers in places such as Hong Kong, Singapore, Taipei, and London; (iii) supplying trading partners with RMB liquidity (e.g., establishing currency swap lines with foreign central banks and allowing them to participate in the onshore foreign exchange market) so that both sides do not have to use a third currency such as the USD for trade settlement; (iv) gradually relaxing capital controls and making the RMB more convertible in the capital account; (v) further development of the onshore financial market.

Such policies have turned out to be tremendously successful. More and more trade was settled in RMB, peaking in 2015 (approximately 21 percent of China's trade by the end of 2016). More and more RMB deposits were held in banks in various offshore centers, peaking in 2014. The issuance of offshore RMB bonds (dim sum bonds) and the creation of offshore RMB loans in various offshore centers grew rapidly. The foreign exchange turnover share of RMB increased rapidly (reaching 4 percent – out of a total of 200 percent – in 2016).[1]

This chapter emphasizes the history of RMB internationalization starting from the early 2000s. For the most recent developments concerning capital account liberalization, financial liberalization and the offshore market, the reader should refer to Chapters 5, 6 and 7.

4.1 OFFSHORE RMB CENTERS

Policy measures were taken to encourage the development of offshore RMB markets which are closely linked but not fully integrated with the onshore RMB market. Offshore centers should be located in well-developed international financial centers with mature financial markets and free capital mobility. The offshore RMB should be fully convertible in both the current account and the capital account, meaning that it can be freely tradable in the foreign exchange market and freely usable for trade invoicing, trade settlement, and denominating financial instruments.

It is no coincidence that Hong Kong was chosen to be the first offshore RMB center. Under this "one currency, two markets" model for the RMB, there is a firewall between the onshore and offshore RMB markets, making control easier in case the offshore market encounters turmoil and gets out of hand. In the same way, under the "one country, two systems" model for the Hong Kong Special Administrative Region (SAR), there is a firewall between the SAR's and the Mainland's jurisdictions. Freedom in the Hong Kong SAR is not allowed to spill over to the Mainland, which has its own pace of development. The SAR is useful as a window or portal to the rest of the world, which is open to the influences of foreign cultural, political, and economic forces. That way, China can exchange with the rest of the world in a controlled manner, which makes her feel more secure. In the same way, the offshore RMB market in Hong Kong is useful as a place where China can exchange (its currency) with the rest of the world in a controlled manner. It is a place where RMB is freely convertible and usable, but the RMB there is not completely free to flow back onshore, nor is the onshore RMB completely free to flow out to the offshore market. The firewall allows the Mainland to reform its financial market and liberalize its capital account at its own pace.

Thus, the Chinese government implemented a number of policy measures to facilitate the establishment of an offshore RMB market, which was to be located in a number of RMB centers in various parts of the world. The first RMB center chosen was Hong Kong, followed later by Taipei, Singapore, London, and so on.

4.1.1   Settlement and Clearing of Offshore RMB Payments

Before the functioning of the Cross-Border Interbank Payment System (CIPS) (which will be discussed in detail in Chapter 7), there are two major channels through which an offshore company carries out cross-border settlement and clearing of RMB funds:

1. through an offshore official RMB clearing bank, with which the offshore company has an account;
2. through an onshore commercial bank acting as correspondent of an offshore commercial bank, with which the offshore company has an account.

4.1.1.1   Correspondent Banking Relationships

Basically, offshore banks need access to clearing balances with onshore banks in order to facilitate RMB transactions in the offshore market. "Correspondent banking relationships" allow offshore banks to open RMB accounts at banks in Mainland China. When a foreign company wants to pay a Chinese company, money is taken out of an account at its local bank (which is in local currency) and an equivalent amount of money is put in the Chinese company's account in the Mainland (in RMB). The money from the payer's account goes to an internal account of the foreign bank. The money to the Chinese company comes from an account this foreign bank holds with a bank in China – the foreign bank's correspondent account, at its correspondent bank, the bank in China.

4.1.1.2   Official Clearing Banks

Clearing generally refers to the activities involved in confirming, monitoring, and ensuring that sufficient collateral or margin is provided where required, until a trade is actually settled (i.e., monies exchanged between transacting parties). The first milestone in the development of the offshore RMB market is the establishment of a clearing bank in Hong Kong. The offshore RMB market began to form in February 2004 when the Bank of China (Hong Kong) (BOCHK) was appointed the RMB clearing bank in Hong Kong, the first of its type outside of China. This meant BOCHK could accept RMB deposits from banks in Hong Kong and place them with the PBC's Shenzhen sub-branch. In turn, BOCHK could clear and settle RMB transactions in the Hong Kong offshore market. On account of its clearing bank status, BOCHK was granted a quota to transact directly within China's onshore interbank foreign exchange (FX) market, enabling it to square foreign currency positions arising from participating bank transactions. Participating banks in Hong Kong would hold accounts with BOCHK for the purpose of clearing RMB transactions.

The second milestone is the beginning of RMB trade settlement. In July 2009, BOCHK signed the "Clearing Agreement Between the People's Bank of China and Bank of China (Hong Kong) Limited in Relation to Renminbi Business" with the PBC to provide the participating banks with clearing services for trade settlement. Corporations in Hong Kong, Macau, and ASEAN countries are eligible to use RMB as the settlement currency for cross-border trade transactions. In July 2010, BOCHK signed the revised "Settlement Agreement on the Clearing of Renminbi Businesses" with the PBC. Following the revision of the Settlement Agreement, the scope of the RMB business clearing service has been extended from Hong Kong, Macau, and ASEAN countries to other regions in the world.[2]

In subsequent years, the Chinese authorities have designated official RMB clearing banks in many other countries. By the end of 2016, the PBC had established RMB clearing arrangements in 23 countries and regions, covering Southeast Asia, Europe, the Middle East, America, Oceania, and Africa.[3] Table 4.1 shows the list of offshore RMB clearing banks as of 23 October 2019. It can be seen that there

Table 4.1 *Offshore RMB clearing banks*

Asia

Country or region	Time of designation	Name of RMB clearing bank
Hong Kong	Dec. 2003	Bank of China (Hong Kong) Co. Ltd
Macau	Sept. 2004	Bank of China, Macau Branch
Laos	June 2012	Industrial and Commercial Bank of China, Vientiane Branch
Taiwan	Dec. 2012	Bank of China, Taipei Branch
Singapore	Feb. 2013	Industrial and Commercial Bank of China, Singapore Branch
Cambodia	Mar. 2014	Industrial and Commercial Bank of China, Phnom Penh Branch
South Korea	July 2014	Bank of Communications, Seoul Branch
Australia	Nov. 2014	Bank of China, Sydney Branch
Malaysia	Jan. 2015	Bank of China (Malaysia), Berhad Branch
Thailand	Jan. 2015	Industrial and Commercial Bank of China (Thai)
Japan	Oct. 2018	Bank of China, Tokyo Branch

EMEA (Europe, Middle East, and Africa)

Country or region	Time of designation	Name of RMB clearing bank
United Kingdom	June 2014	China Construction Bank (London)
Germany	June 2014	Bank of China, Frankfurt Branch
France	Sept. 2014	Bank of China, Paris Branch
Luxembourg	Sept. 2014	Industrial and Commercial Bank of China, Luxembourg Branch
Qatar	Nov. 2014	Industrial and Commercial Bank of China, Doha Branch
Hungary	June 2015	Bank of China, Hungarian Branch
South Africa	July 2015	Bank of China, Johannesburg Branch
Zambia	Sept. 2015	Bank of China (Zambia)
Switzerland	Nov. 2015	China Construction Bank, Zurich Branch
Russia	Sept. 2016	Industrial and Commercial Bank of China (Moscow)
United Arab Emirates	Dec. 2016	Agricultural Bank of China, Dubai Branch

Table 4.1 (*cont.*)

North and South America

Country or region	Time of designation	Name of RMB clearing bank
Canada	Nov. 2014	Industrial and Commercial Bank of China (Canada)
Chile	May 2015	China Construction Bank, Chile Branch
Argentina	Sept. 2015	Industrial and Commercial Bank of China (Argentina)
United States	Sept. 2016	Bank of China, New York Branch
United States	Feb. 2018	J.P. Morgan Chase Bank, N.A.

Source: PBC, updated as of 23 October 2019.

are 27 clearing banks in total, with 11 in Asia, 11 in Europe, Middle East, and Africa, and 5 in North and South America. After the establishment of clearing banks in Hong Kong and Macao in 2003 and 2004, there was a big time-gap before the next wave of establishment of clearing banks in other parts of the world, starting in 2012. This pattern verifies our view that China actively pushed for RMB internationalization after the 2007–2009 global financial crisis, which revealed the vulnerability of the dollar-based IMS.

The primary purpose of the clearing banks is to facilitate cross-border RMB payments between the onshore and offshore RMB markets, and within the offshore market itself. Like BOCHK, the clearing banks in other parts of the world are permitted to maintain onshore RMB balances to facilitate RMB transactions on behalf of their offshore participating banks. They also have more direct access to RMB liquidity from the PBC and are permitted to transact directly within China's onshore interbank foreign exchange market, subject to a quota. The primary benefit of using an official offshore clearing bank rather than an onshore correspondent bank is that it can provide a more direct method of effecting payments (for example, a reduction in settlement delays). Over time, this could improve the efficiency and/or lower the transaction costs of such payments. The official status of these clearing banks also means that they play an important symbolic role in establishing recognized offshore RMB centers, especially by raising awareness and confidence among firms in these foreign countries about their local financial sectors' capacity to facilitate RMB transactions.[4]

However, as will be explained in Chapter 7, with the introduction and operation of CIPS, the importance of the clearing banks is going to diminish, as offshore participating banks can directly send payments to onshore banks through CIPS without going through the offshore clearing banks.

A clearing/payment center can be defined as a country/region/city where a clearing bank exists. Figure 4.1 shows that, as of June 2018, Hong Kong is still by far the most important offshore RMB clearing/payment center (offshore location where RMB payments take

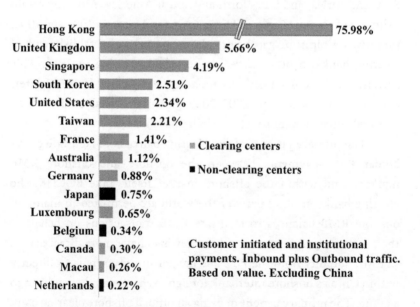

FIGURE 4.1 Top 15 offshore RMB economies (in terms of payment) by weight as of June 2018.
Source: SWIFT RMB Tracker

place), accounting for almost 76 percent of all customer-initiated and institutional payments going through SWIFT. Note that any inbound or outbound payment associated with a payment center must be cleared and settled in that center as well.

Because of the overwhelming importance of Hong Kong as an offshore RMB center, we mainly focus on Hong Kong in the following discussion about the offshore RMB market. In fact, we can treat any new developments of the offshore RMB market in Hong Kong as pilot schemes that would be replicated elsewhere in the world. Thus, we can assume that the types of RMB business that take place in Hong Kong also take place in other RMB centers, but on a smaller scale or with a time lag.

4.1.2 RMB Bank Deposits

Offshore RMB deposits in offshore participating banks are a funding source for companies to borrow RMB to invest directly onshore. It is a channel for Chinese firms to borrow internationally in their own currency. RMB deposits in Hong Kong started to exist in 2004, when the BOCHK was designated as the sole RMB clearing bank in Hong Kong. Figure 1.2 shows the monthly RMB bank deposits in Hong Kong from 2004 to 2019 in billion USD as well as the proportion of RMB deposits in the total deposits in Hong Kong. It shows that August 2015, around the time of the central parity reform of the RMB exchange rate formation mechanism, marked the beginning of a steep decline in both the absolute amount of RMB deposits in Hong Kong as well as the proportion of RMB deposits in total Hong Kong deposits, indicating a significant setback of the Hong Kong offshore market. Table 4.2 shows similar information as in Figure 1.2 on an annual basis in more recent years. At the end of 2011, 2012, 2013, 2014, 2015, 2016, 2017, and 2018 the amount of RMB deposits in banks in Hong Kong (excluding certificates of deposit) was 9.56 percent, 9.04 percent, 12.01 percent, 12.44 percent, 9.46 percent, 5.21 percent , 5.26 percent, and 5.23 percent respectively of the total value of deposits in the city, peaking at 12.44 percent in 2014. It shows a dramatic fall in 2015.

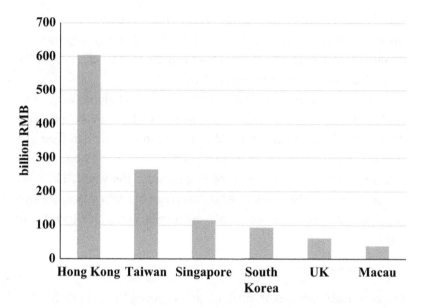

FIGURE 4.2 Offshore RMB deposits by region as of 2019 Q2 (excluding certificates of deposits).
Sources: CEIC; PBC

Figure 4.2 shows the amount of RMB deposits in various countries/regions as of the end of the second quarter of 2019. It can be seen that the amount of RMB deposits in Hong Kong was still the largest among them, signifying the dominant position of Hong Kong as an offshore RMB center.

4.1.3   Dim Sum Bonds and RMB Loans

A dim sum bond is any RMB-denominated bond issued outside of Mainland China. Their existence allows domestic and foreign entities to borrow offshore RMB by issuing bonds and then use the money to invest directly in the Mainland of China. In fact, many entities that issued dim sum bonds are Chinese companies. When Chinese firms issued dim-sum bonds in Hong Kong, they were borrowing internationally in their own currency, which is one of the goals of RMB internationalization. The first dim sum bond was issued in July

Table 4.2 *RMB deposits in Hong Kong, 2011–2018 (excluding certificates of deposit)*

	2011	2012	2013	2014	2015	2016	2017	2018
Amount at the end of the year (billion yuan)	589.00	603.00	860.50	1003.60	851.10	546.70	559.10	615.00
Percentage of total deposits in Hong Kong	9.56	9.04	12.01	12.44	9.46	5.21	5.26	5.23

Source: CEIC.

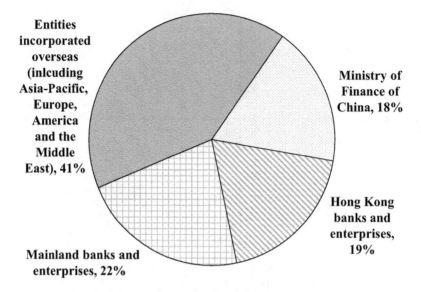

FIGURE 4.3 Outstanding RMB bonds issued in Hong Kong by type of issuer as of the end of October 2015.
Source: Hong Kong Monetary Authority

2007 by China Development Bank. In June 2009, China allowed financial institutions in Hong Kong to issue dim sum bonds. HSBC was the first institution that issued these. In August 2010, McDonald's was the first corporation that issued dim sum bonds. In October 2010, the Asian Development Bank (ADB) raised a RMB 1.2 billion 10-year bond, and became the first supranational agency which issued dim sum bonds and also the first issuer listed in the Hong Kong Stock Exchange.[5] Figure 4.3 shows the outstanding amount of RMB bonds issued in Hong Kong by the type of issuer as of the end of October 2015. It shows that there was a variety of entities that issued dim sum bonds in Hong Kong, including the central government agency (Ministry of Finance), Hong Kong-based banks and companies, Mainland-based banks and companies, and overseas corporations. Figure 4.4 shows the scales of RMB financing activities in Hong Kong over time, which include the outstanding amount of dim sum bonds and outstanding amount of RMB loans in Hong Kong over the

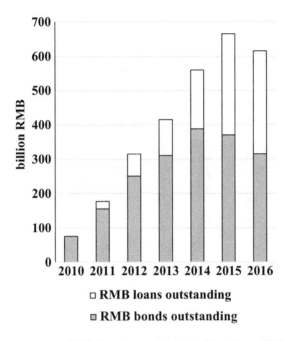

FIGURE 4.4 RMB financing activities in Hong Kong, 2010–2016.
Source: Hong Kong Monetary Authority

years 2010 through 2016. The outstanding amount of dim sum bonds issued in Hong Kong in 2010 through 2016 in billion RMB were 55.8, 146.7, 237.2, 310.0, 380.5, 368.0, and 318.8 respectively, peaking in 2014 at 380.5 billion yuan. Figure 4.5 shows the amount of dim sum bonds issued in Hong Kong over these years. The amounts issued in 2010 through 2017 in billion RMB were 35.8, 107.9, 112.2, 116.6, 197.0, 75.0, 52.8, and 20.6 respectively, peaking in 2014 at 197.0 billion yuan. On the other hand, Figure 4.6 shows the global amount of CNH bonds (dim sum bonds) issued over time. It clearly shows an inverted-U shape peaking in 2014. All these charts show that the amount of offshore RMB bonds issued and outstanding in Hong Kong as well as at the global level, all peaked in 2014, the year before the central parity reform of the RMB exchange rate formation mechanism that took place on 11 August 2015. It is quite clear that the event fundamentally changed people's expectation about the

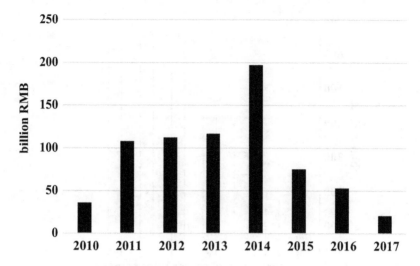

FIGURE 4.5 Amount of RMB bonds issued in Hong Kong, 2010–2017.
Source: Hong Kong Monetary Authority

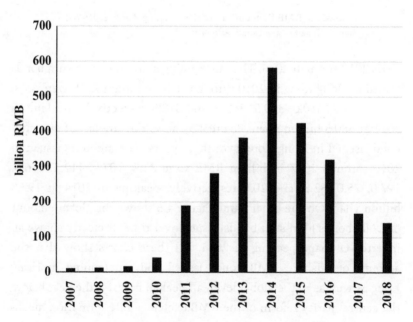

FIGURE 4.6 Amount of global CNH bonds issued, 2007–2018.
Source: Bloomberg

exchange rate of the RMB from unidirectional appreciation to uncertainty, thus dampening the enthusiasm in keeping RMB as a store of value. This in turn affected people's interest in investing in RMB-denominated assets such as dim sum bonds.

4.1.4 RMB Trade Settlement

By promoting RMB trade settlement as one of the first steps to push for RMB internationalization, China seemed to have heeded the advice of Eichengreen (2011), who points out that "the logical sequencing of steps in internationalizing a currency is: first, encouraging its use in invoicing and settling trade; second, encouraging its use in private financial transactions; third, encouraging its use by central banks and governments as a form in which to hold foreign reserves." Indeed, RMB trade settlement was a milestone in RMB internationalization, as it led to a rapid expansion of the offshore pool of RMB in Hong Kong and elsewhere. The offshore RMB foreign exchange market was formed soon after. Since the announcement of a pilot scheme for RMB trade settlement in mid-2009, the Chinese authorities have been gradually easing restrictions on the use of RMB outside Mainland China. Since mid-2010, the original RMB trade settlement scheme has been expanded to encompass all trade between China and the rest of world.[6] This has enabled the creation of a pool of RMB outside the Mainland and the development of an offshore RMB market. Hong Kong became the primary destination for RMB trade settlement and offshore RMB business. A sizable offshore RMB market was created in Hong Kong. The "one currency, two markets" model became a non-trivial reality. The offshore RMB became fully convertible outside Mainland China. It is another policy experiment of China. This time, the experiment was to find out to what extent RMB could be used outside China without fully opening its capital account.[7]

Table 4.3 shows the amount of RMB trade settlement and the percentage of trade with China settled in RMB over the years. In 2011, 2012, 2013, 2014, 2015 and 2016, 2017, and 2018 the percentages of

Table 4.3 *RMB trade settlement handled by Hong Kong, 2011–2018*

	2011	2012	2013	2014	2015	2016	2017	2018
Amount of global RMB trade settlement in the year (trillion yuan)	2.09	2.94	4.63	6.60	7.23	5.23	4.36	5.11
Percent of trade with China settled in RMB	9.00	12.00	18.00	25.00	29.00	21.00	15.70	16.60
Percent of RMB trade settlement handled by banks in Hong Kong	91.00	89.00	83.00	95.00	95.00	87.00	90.00	82.00

Source: CEIC.

FIGURE 4.7 Cross-border RMB trade settlement, 2012–2019 (quarterly).
Primary sources: CEIC; PBC

trade with China settled in RMB were 9 percent, 12 percent, 18 percent, 25 percent, 29 percent, 21 percent, 15.7 percent, and 16.6 percent respectively (peaking at 29 percent in 2015), of which 91 percent, 89 percent, 83 percent, 95 percent, 95 percent and 87 percent, 90 percent, and 82 percent respectively were handled by Hong Kong banks. The dominance of Hong Kong in trade settlement is clear. Figure 4.7 shows the amount and percentage of trade with China settled in RMB by quarter from 2012 Q1 to 2019 Q3. Unsurprisingly, the amount and percentage both peaked in the 2015 Q3, when the central parity reform of the RMB occurred. As of 2019 Q3, the share of trade with China settled in RMB was 19.2 percent, much lower than the 32.8 percent registered in 2015 Q3.

Although RMB trade settlement reached more than 30 percent in the third quarter of 2015, one note of caution is in order. The fact that RMB was the settlement currency in an international transaction did not necessarily mean that it was an invoicing currency in that same transaction. A settlement currency serves as a medium of exchange, while an invoicing currency serves as a unit of account. For most currencies, the settlement currency is almost always the invoicing currency, as the determination of an invoicing currency is usually driven by market forces – the buyer and the seller negotiate the invoicing currency and they naturally settle trade with the invoicing currency. For RMB, the situation was quite different. In 2012, of all merchandize trade settled in RMB, only 56 percent was invoiced in RMB (see Li 2013).[8] Although there are no data to prove it, it is likely that most of it involved (Mainland) China–Hong Kong trade. Therefore, even as recently as 2013, it is likely that only a very small fraction of China's trade with foreign countries (which do not include Hong Kong) was invoiced in RMB. According to our research, as of 2017 Q2, RMB invoicing in the total exports of Japan, Australia, Thailand, and Indonesia were approximately 1.5 percent, 0.5 percent, 0.3 percent, and 0.5 percent respectively, whereas RMB invoicing in the total imports of these countries were 0.9 percent, 0.6 percent, 0.8 percent, and 0.6 percent respectively.[9] These are really small numbers, given that trade with China constituted a rather large percentage of the trade of each of these countries. Thus, one suspects that the percentage of trade with China not involving Hong Kong that was invoiced in RMB could be really low. This could indicate that RMB trade invoicing beyond Hong Kong–Mainland trade still has a long way to go.

Why is RMB trade invoicing harder to realize than RMB trade settlement? The main reason is that, for foreigners, accepting RMB invoicing is a deeper commitment than accepting RMB settlement, as they have to bear the exchange rate risk. Whether a currency is used for trade invoicing is more determined by economic fundamentals. For example, theory and evidence suggest that producer currency pricing (PCP), whereby traded goods are invoiced in the exporting country's currency, is usually adopted for differentiated goods as the seller has more market power, whereas local currency pricing (LCP), whereby traded goods are invoiced in the importing country's currency, is usually used for less differentiated goods as the seller has less market power. Furthermore, vehicle currency pricing, whereby traded goods are invoiced in a vehicle currency, which is often the dominant global currency, is likely to be adopted for homogeneous goods such as oil and commodities, as thick market externalities for the currency (network externalities of a widely used currency) and coalescing effect (firms trying to invoice in the same currency as their competitors) are important for determining the invoicing currency of a homogeneous good. By the same logic, one conjectures that the degrees to which the exports and imports of a country are invoiced in its own currency increase as the thick market externalities and coalescing effect of the currency become stronger. On the other hand, whether a currency is used for trade settlement may be determined by short-term considerations, such as the expected appreciation of the currency. For this reason, the long-term prospect of RMB trade settlement business is not guaranteed once people stop expecting RMB to appreciate. This point is verified by Figure 4.7, which shows that the total amount of trade with China settled in RMB declined sharply after the third quarter of 2015, the quarter in which the reform of the central parity formation mechanism of the RMB took place, leading to sharp depreciation of the RMB. It is apparent that after 11 August 2015 the market turned from expecting the RMB to appreciate to expecting it to depreciate, thus leading to sharp declines in RMB trade settlement.

Table 4.4 summarizes the indicators of the various types of offshore RMB business in Hong Kong over the years 2010 through 2018, including bank deposits, trade settlement, bonds, and loans. The inverted-U shape of the trend is quite clear.

4.2   BILATERAL CURRENCY SWAP AGREEMENTS BETWEEN CENTRAL BANKS

Foreign central banks have cooperated with China in a number of initiatives that support the development of the offshore RMB market, including bilateral currency swap agreements. Under these agreements, foreign central banks can swap their local currency for RMB

Table 4.4 *Offshore RMB business in Hong Kong, 2010–2018*

	2010	2011	2012	2013	2014	2015	2016	2017	2018
					billion yuan				
RMB customer deposits	314.9	588.5	603	860.5	1003.6	851.1	546.7	559.1	615.0
RMB certificates of deposit outstanding	6.8	73.1	117.3	200.1	154.7	159.3	78.3		
Totals	321.7	661.6	720.3	1060.6	1158.3	1010.4	625.0		
RMB trade settlement handled by banks in Hong Kong (amount during the year)	369.2	1914.9	2632.5	3841.0	6258.0	6833.0	4542.1	3926.5	4208.9
RMB bond issuance (amount during the year)	35.8	107.9	112.2	116.6	197.0	75.0	52.8	20.6	
RMB bonds outstanding	55.8	146.7	237.2	310.0	380.5	368.0	318.8		
RMB loans outstanding	1.8	30.8	79.0	115.6	188.0	297.4	294.8	148.7	

Source: Hong Kong Monetary Authority.

with the PBC for mutually agreed purposes. This enables foreign central banks to provide RMB liquidity to the offshore market during times of market stress or, in some cases, simply to promote the development of the offshore RMB market. By providing an assurance that market participants can approach their local central bank to access RMB liquidity if required, central bank swap lines support the development of the local RMB market.

Generally, a swap line allows a central bank in one country to exchange a currency, usually its domestic currency, for a certain amount of foreign currency. The recipient central bank can then lend this foreign currency on to its domestic banks, on its own terms and at its own risk. At the start of a swap, central bank 1 sells a specified amount of currency A to central bank 2 in exchange for currency B at the prevailing market exchange rate. Central bank 1 agrees to buy back its currency at the same exchange rate on a specified future date. Central bank 1 then uses the currency B it has obtained through the swap to lend on to local banks or corporations. On the specified future date that the swap unwinds and the funds are returned, central bank 1, which requested activation of the swap, pays interest to central bank 2.[10]

In 2008, China began to sign bilateral currency swap agreements with foreign central banks. By the end of 2016, 36 central banks or monetary authorities had signed bilateral currency swap agreements with the PBC. The total amount of agreements exceeded RMB 3.3 trillion yuan. In 2016, under the bilateral currency swap agreements signed by the PBC and foreign counterparties, the amount of actual utilization of RMB by foreign central banks or monetary authorities was RMB 127.8 billion yuan, while the amount of actual utilization of foreign currency by the PBC was equivalent to RMB 66.4 billion yuan. In other words, the rate of utilization was less than 10 percent. By the end of 2016, the cumulative amount of actual utilization of RMB by foreign central banks or monetary authorities reached RMB 365.53 billion yuan and the balance stood at RMB 22.15 billion yuan. By contrast, the cumulative amount of actual utilization of foreign currency by the PBC was equivalent to RMB 112.84 billion yuan, and the balance was RMB 7.76 billion yuan.[11] Table 4.5 shows the list of countries which had signed bilateral currency swap agreements with PBC as of May 2018. By that time, the total amount of swap lines was about 3.1 trillion yuan and the number of central banks/monetary authorities was 33. Judging from the rate of utilization, the swap agreements do not seem to be very useful in boosting the international use of the RMB. However, they do serve the function of providing assurance of the availability of RMB liquidity in case there is a need. In case there is a shortage of the USD for trade financing, such as during the global financial crisis of 2007–2009, the countries can bypass the USD and use the RMB or other local currencies to settle trade.

4.3   LIBERALIZATION OF CAPITAL FLOWS

Capital account liberalization is one of the most important measures that need to be taken in order to increase the international use of the RMB, as it increases foreigners' access to the onshore capital market and domestic citizens' access to foreign capital markets, thus increasing the financial integration of China with the rest of the world. A number of measures of liberalization of capital inflows and outflows were implemented over the years.

4.3.1   Qualified Foreign Institutional Investor (QFII)

In 2002, the China Securities Regulatory Commission (CSRC) and the People's Bank of China (PBC) jointly issued the Provisional Measures on Administration of Domestic Securities Investment of Qualified Foreign Institutional Investors, initiating the pilot QFII scheme allowing foreign investors to enter China's capital market directly. The QFII includes asset management companies, insurance companies, securities firms, commercial banks, and others such as pension funds, charity foundations, endowment funds, and sovereign wealth funds.

Table 4.5 *Bilateral currency swap agreements between PBC and foreign central banks as of May 2018*

North and South America		EMEA (Europe, Middle East, and Africa)				Asia	
Country	RMB (bn)	Country	RMB (bn)	Country	RMB (bn)	Country	RMB (bn)
Canada	200.0	European Central Bank	350.0	Hungary	10.0	Hong Kong	400.0
Argentina	70.0	England	350.0	Morocco	10.0	South Korea	360.0
Chile	22.0	Switzerland	150.0	Pakistan	20.0	Singapore	300.0
Suriname	1.0	Russia	150.0	Belarus	7.0	Australia	200.0
TOTAL	293.0	Qatar	35.0	Kazakhstan	7.0	Malaysia	180.0
		UAE	35.0	Iceland	3.5	Thailand	70.0
		South Africa	30.0	Tajikistan	3.0	New Zealand	25.0
		Egypt	18.0	Albania	2.0	Mongolia	15.0
		Nigeria	15.0	Serbia	1.5	Sri Lanka	10.0
		Turkey	12.0	Armenia	1.0	TOTAL	1,560.0
				TOTAL	1,210.0		

Source: People's Bank of China.
Total Volume: RMB 3,063.0 billion.

4.3.2 *Qualified Domestic Institutional Investor (QDII)*

Started in 2006, the QDII scheme enables domestic Mainland Chinese institutional investors with a QDII license and quota approved by the relevant Mainland regulatory authority to invest in offshore markets. Each QDII is granted a specific quota by the State Administration of Foreign Exchange (SAFE).

4.3.3 *The RMB Qualified Foreign Institutional Investor (RQFII)*

Starting from 2011, offshore RMB could be used to make investments in Mainland China, primarily via the RQFII program. The RQFII regime is a modified version of the QFII regime, which is designed to facilitate the use of RMB held outside the Mainland of China for investment in the Mainland securities market. This allows approved foreign investors to buy and sell designated assets in China's onshore equity and bond markets. The RQFII program can thus be thought of both as being part of China's broader capital account liberalization process and as an initiative that is designed to encourage broader participation in the offshore RMB market.

Importantly, the RQFII program is only available to investors with operations in a jurisdiction that has been granted an RQFII quota by the Chinese authorities. However, once a firm has acquired a quota, it is able to offer RMB investment products to a broad range of investors, including those located outside its original jurisdiction. For example, some Hong Kong-domiciled firms have partnered with US- and Europe-domiciled financial institutions to launch exchange-traded funds on foreign stock exchanges, including the New York Stock Exchange and the London Stock Exchange. This allows investors without an RQFII quota to gain exposure to China's equity and bond markets.

The RQFII program is in addition to the Qualified Foreign Institutional Investor (QFII) program, which had been in place since 2003. The QFII program permits approved foreign investors to use foreign currency to invest in designated Chinese financial assets. Unlike the RQFII program, the QFII program has no jurisdiction-specific quotas.

From an investor's perspective, however, the RQFII program has several potential advantages over the QFII program – among them, greater discretion in portfolio allocation and less restrictive rules regarding the repatriation of funds offshore. The RQFII program also permits authorized investors to invest part of their RQFII quota in China's fixed-income interbank bond market, whereas QFII-approved investors must apply for an additional quota to access this market.[12]

The RQFII regime has been expanded to countries/regions such as Hong Kong, Singapore, UK, France, Korea, Germany, Qatar, Australia, Switzerland and Luxembourg, Canada, Thailand, and the United States. By the end of 2016, 18 countries or regions had been granted RQFII quotas, with a total amount of RMB 1.51 trillion yuan (see Figure 4.8). On 25 September 2020, SAFE announced that QFII and RQFII would be combined on 1 November 2020, and more investment options would be offered, as the benefits of these programs have been eroded by the success of the Stock Connects and Bond Connect programs described below.

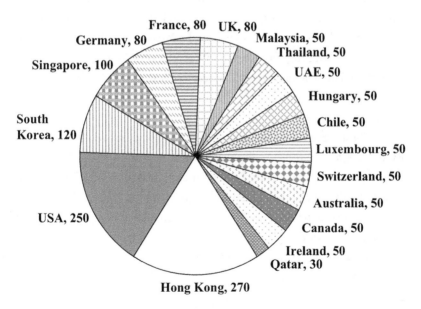

FIGURE 4.8 Allocation of RQFII quotas as of end of 2106 (in billion yuan).
Source: People's Bank of China (2017)

4.3.4 Stock Connects

The Stock Connect is a unique collaboration between the Hong Kong, Shanghai, and Shenzhen Stock Exchanges that allows international and Mainland Chinese investors to trade securities in each other's markets through the trading and clearing facilities of their home exchange. As of 30 August 2019, the net amount of northbound investments from Hong Kong to Mainland China through Stock Connects in 2019 was about USD 17 billion.[13]

The Shanghai–Hong Kong Stock Connect program, which began operating in November 2014, allows offshore investors to purchase approved (RMB-denominated) stocks listed on the Shanghai Stock Exchange (SSE) – known as "northbound" trading. Similarly, eligible Mainland investors are able to purchase (Hong Kong dollar-denominated) stocks listed on the Hong Kong Stock Exchange (HKEx) – known as "southbound" trading. In other words, the Stock Connect program provides an additional avenue through which off-shore (onshore) investors can buy and sell Mainland Chinese (Hong Kong) equities in addition to the RQFII and QFII programs, and there-fore is an additional link between the offshore and onshore RMB markets. Mimicking the Shanghai–Hong Kong Stock Connect, the Shenzhen–Hong Kong Stock Connect scheme, which connects the Shenzhen Stock Exchange (SZSE) and HKEx, was officially launched in December 2016.

The primary advantage of the Stock Connect program over the RQFII program is that it is open to all foreign investors, whereas the RQFII program is restricted to financial institutions domiciled in countries that have been granted RQFII quotas (although once an institution obtains an RQFII quota, it can use this to set up RMB products elsewhere). Moreover, gaining an RQFII license and quota for individual institutions is a comparatively lengthy process.[14]

Nevertheless, the RQFII program is likely to continue to be used as it has some advantages over the Stock Connect program. Importantly, institutions with an RQFII quota can invest in

Mainland fixed-income assets and a broader range of Mainland stocks. In addition, while Stock Connect investors are subject to an aggregate daily quota (for the market as a whole) and execution queues, RQFII investors can transact subject only to their own individual quotas. The two programs are nonetheless partial substitutes. Since Hong Kong has exhausted its aggregate RQFII quota, some Hong Kong-based entities have reportedly requested to be allowed to transfer stocks bought under the RQFII program to the Stock Connect program in an attempt to free up space in their existing RQFII quotas.

4.3.5   Chinese Interbank Bond Market (CIBM) Direct

At the end of 2018, the Chinese bond market was already the third largest in the world (USD 11.17 trillion in 2018 Q4), after those of the United States and Japan.[15] The liberalization of the domestic bond market through the CIBM Direct scheme, announced in February 2016, was a further step in opening up Chinese financial markets to international investors and encouraging them to invest in RMB-denominated assets. The CIBM Direct scheme created a route for international investors to access onshore bonds, complementing long-established QFII and RQFII schemes. Under this scheme, foreign institutions can trade bonds directly through banks holding a Type A license in Mainland China (there are only six such foreign banks as of April 2019).

4.3.6   Bond Connect

Bond Connect is a mutual market access scheme that allows investors from Mainland China and overseas to trade in each other's bond markets through a connection between the related Mainland China and Hong Kong financial infrastructure institutions. Northbound Trading commenced on 3 July 2017, allowing overseas investors from Hong Kong and other regions to invest in the China interbank bond market (CIBM) through mutual access arrangements in respect of trading, custody, and settlement. As of late 2019, Southbound Trading was still to be explored at a later stage.

4.3.7 *Other Schemes*

There are other schemes of smaller scale, such as

- Mutual Recognition of Funds (MRF), launched in July 2015. Under the scheme, eligible Mainland and Hong Kong funds can be distributed in each other's market through a streamlined vetting process.
- Shanghai FTZ, launched in September 2013. The zone is used as a testing ground for a number of economic and social reforms.
- Shenzhen Qianhai FTZ.
- Qualified Foreign Limited Partner (QFLP), launched in 2010. It provides foreign investors with a channel to access the onshore unlisted equity market.
- RMB-Qualified Foreign Limited Partner (RQFLP), launched in 2012.
- Qualified Domestic Limited Partner (QDLP), launched in 2012. It allows onshore investors to access a wider range of offshore products or assets (including, in particular, equity investments in overseas unlisted entities and overseas regulated commodities markets).
- Qualified Domestic Investment Enterprise (QDIE), launched in 2014. It is similar to QDLP but is more far-reaching.

It is noteworthy that the last four schemes were all first launched in Shanghai, signifying that Shanghai aspired to be the pioneer in spearheading capital account opening in the Mainland.

However, the more capital account opening schemes there are, the more it shows that the capital account of China is quite closed. This is because each scheme represents what type of capital flows are allowed, and, in China, what is not explicitly stated as allowed cannot be taken for granted as being allowed. Those transactions that are not included in the officially permitted schemes are not considered to be permissible by the authority, although they are not explicitly treated as impermissible either. They are in the gray area and can be subject to the discretion of the authority, depending on the circumstances being considered.

4.4 THE BELT AND ROAD INITIATIVE

According to the Chinese government, the aim of the Belt and Road Initiative (BRI) is to promote the connectivity of Asian, European, and

African continents and their adjacent seas through the construction of infrastructure and implementation of measures to facilitate trade and investment. It will enable China to further expand and deepen its opening-up, and to strengthen cooperation with countries in Asia, Europe, and Africa and the rest of the world.

There has been a lot of discussion about the Belt and Road Initiative (BRI) being potentially a big boost to RMB internationalization. What is the reasoning behind this anticipation? As far as I can tell, the potential to leverage the use of RMB for (i) trade invoicing, trade settlement, and invoicing of outward direct investments and (ii) issuance of RMB-denominated international debt securities (bonds) to fund the infrastructure projects, can potentially enhance the internationalization of the RMB. First, as far as trade invoicing and settlement are concerned, the Chinese exports associated with Chinese outward direct investments (ODIs) are more likely to be invoiced in RMB than ordinary exports from China, as they are bought by Chinese-affiliated companies. Chinese imports from these Belt and Road (B&R) countries are also more likely to be invoiced in RMB if they are related to the Chinese ODIs in these countries, or if China is a large buyer (e.g., resources or energy). The large amount of Chinese ODIs in the B&R countries also enhances the bilateral trade flows between China and these countries (as foreign direct investment and trade are complementary to each other, as many studies have shown), further increasing RMB trade invoicing. Furthermore, the infrastructure projects serve to reduce trade costs between the B&R countries and China, further increasing their bilateral trade flows with China and RMB trade invoicing. Second, as far as the issuance of international debt securities is concerned, the BRI can facilitate the issuance of RMB-denominated bonds as it involves the financing of many Chinese ODIs, whose currency habitat is RMB. Moreover, the large amount of RMB trade invoicing and trade settlement in the BRI make it more attractive to use the RMB as a funding currency, thus incentivizing companies to issue debts in RMB. (See, for example, Gopinath and Stein (2018) for the experience of the United States in 1913, as explained in Chapter 3.) Hopefully, the BRI can stimulate the formation of a larger and more liquid offshore RMB capital market. The offshore RMB centers such as Singapore, London, and Hong Kong can play an important role in RMB debt securitization and project financing. The upshot is that the BRI can stimulate the formation of a larger and more liquid offshore RMB capital market to increase the offshore market thickness of RMB. This would facilitate the further development of the offshore RMB market and enhance RMB internationalization. However, as we shall show in Chapter 8, the effect of the BRI on RMB internationalization is probably too small without the concurrent onshore capital account liberalization and onshore financial market liberalization, which are still the two crucial factors for successful RMB internationalization.

4.5   MEASURING THE DEGREE OF RMB INTERNATIONALIZATION

What is the degree of RMB internationalization today? How do we measure it? There is no one single commonly adopted measure for the degree of internationalization of a currency. By and large, there can be five indicators, namely the use of the currency in the following dimensions: (i) denomination of international debts; (ii) denomination of international loans; (iii) foreign exchange turnover; (iv) the use in global payments; and (v) the use as foreign exchange reserves.

Figure 4.9 shows that the percentage of outstanding global international debt securities denominated in RMB is about 0.4 percent, as of mid-2019, compared with about 47 percent for the USD. Thus, the share of the USD was about 110 times that of the RMB in this regard, which indicates that a lot of work needs to be done to promote the use of RMB for denominating bonds and other debt instruments outside of China. On the other hand, Table 4.6 shows that the relative importance of the RMB along the dimensions of foreign exchange turnover, use in global payments, and use as foreign exchange reserves shows more promising signs. They all indicate similar magnitudes in the three dimensions. For example, as a global

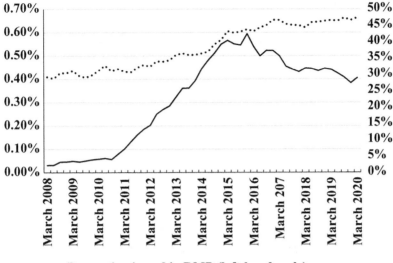

——— Proportion issued in RMB (left-hand scale)

····· Proportion issued in USD (right-hand scale)

FIGURE 4.9 Proportion of global international debt securities outstanding denominated in RMB and USD as of mid-2019.
Source: Primary data from *BIS*. https://stats.bis.org/#ppq=SEC_OUTST_IDS_BY_CUR;pv=15~8~0,0,0~both

payment currency, the RMB is about 1.22 percent versus 45.78 percent for the USD. The share of the RMB as foreign exchange reserves is about 2 percent in 2019 Q2. The RMB's share was boosted in October 2016 by the inclusion of the RMB into the basket of five currencies in the SDR. Before 2016 Q4, the share of the RMB was negligible. So, this dimension is less market-determined, and therefore should be given less weight. Figure 4.10 shows that the percentage of global trade of goods settled in RMB was around 1.5 percent in mid-2019. This proportion is quite similar to those of the other dimensions mentioned above.

How is the progress of RMB internationalization over time? The Standard Chartered Bank has constructed a "RMB Globalization Index" (RGI), which summarizes the degree of internationalization of the RMB in each month.[16] Figure 4.11 shows the values of the index

Table 4.6 *The relative importance of the USD, EUR, JPY, and RMB in the international monetary system, in percentage, 2016–2019 Q2*

	Currency Year reported	USD	EUR	JPY	RMB
Foreign exchange market turnover share[1]	2019 (April)	44.15	16.14	8.40	2.16
Global payments share[2]	2020 (May)	45.78	33.69	4.27	1.22
Foreign exchange reserves share[3]	As of 2019 Q2	61.6	20.3	5.4	2.0

Sources: BIS; SWIFT; IMF.

[1] From BIS triennial survey 2019. Normalized so that the total is equal to 100 percent.

[2] Payment shares as an international payments' currency, as reported by SWIFT. Live and delivered, MT 103 and MT 202 (customer-initiated and institutional payments), excluding payments within eurozone. Messages exchanged on SWIFT. Based on value.

[3] From IMF COFER.

over time. The index is based on four components of the offshore RMB markets: CNH deposits, trade settlement and other international payments, dim sum bonds and certificates of deposit issued, and FX turnover. It can be seen from Figure 4.11 that the index peaked around August 2015, the time of the central parity reform, after which the index has been flat through late 2019. It shows just how fragile the sustainability of the use of the currency is in the international market. As part of the exercise in calculating the RGI, the bank also calculated the market shares in September 2019 of the offshore centers: Hong Kong 67.6 percent, United Kingdom 14.1 percent, Singapore 6.7 percent, United States 4.6 percent, and Taiwan 3.5 percent. Thus, Hong Kong still gets the lion's share of the global offshore RMB business. What is a bit surprising is that the UK, and not the other two Asian centers, occupies the second position. This apparently reflects the

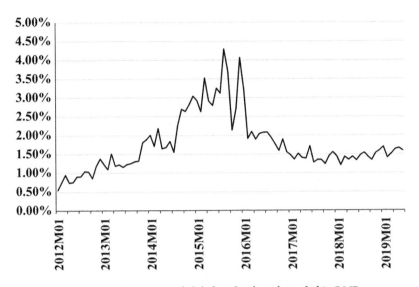

FIGURE 4.10 Proportion of global trade of goods settled in RMB, 2012–2019.

Source: Primary data from PBC; Bloomberg; IMF International Financial Statistics

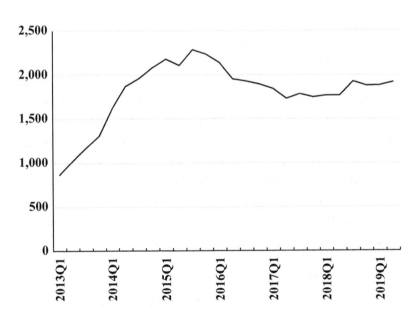

FIGURE 4.11 The RMB Globalization Index, 2013–2019.

Source: Standard Chartered Bank

special relationship between the UK and China. According to the Standard Chartered Bank's RGI website, until July 2011, the market share of Hong Kong had been 100 percent. This is not surprising given that the offshore RMB spot exchange rate started to exist only in July 2010. According to Standard Chartered Bank, Hong Kong's market share then began to fall continuously to 60.2 percent in October 2015, when it bottomed out, and then rose continuously (but mildly) again through late 2019. So, the second half of 2015 was indeed the watershed in the development of the offshore markets, in the sense that they were badly damaged and needed to be rebuilt, or that the euphoria before then was a bubble that popped when the appreciation expectation of the RMB was reversed.

One might ask: Was the central parity reform in August 2015 just an exogenous policy measure unrelated to the economic conditions at that time, or was it introduced due to some deeper problem in the economy of China? In 2014, the growth momentum of China began to weaken. By late 2014, there were already some signs of capital outflows from China, signifying that the market was beginning to be less bullish about the Chinese economy. The exchange value of the RMB then began to be under pressure to fall. However, the PBC intervened to prevent it from falling. In August 2015, the PBC apparently thought that it was time to allow the RMB to depreciate according to the market so as to stimulate exporting. This also served the purpose of demonstrating to the IMF that the RMB exchange rate was market-determined, thus strengthening the case for including the RMB in the basket of currencies in the SDR. This move seemed to aim at killing two birds with one stone. Viewed in this light, the setback to the offshore RMB markets that occurred in late 2015 was indirectly caused by the weakening of China's economy.

4.6 CONCLUSION

The strategy of launching RMB internationalization pursued by China is essentially "one currency, two markets," which means that a firewall is built between the onshore market and the offshore market so that China's financial market reform and capital account opening can be carried out in a controlled manner. The spirit is not unlike that of "one country, two systems," whereby China allows a part of its territory (i.e., Hong Kong) to adopt a more open system, while keeping the rest of the country more tightly controlled. This is because China needs a window to the rest of the world but is not ready to fully open itself. Thus, the offshore markets, especially Hong Kong, become an important facilitator of the use of the RMB outside China. It should be noted that the international use of the RMB started from a very low base. So, initially the growth rate of the degree of RMB internationalization was very fast. However, eventually it will flatten out if no further major liberalization measures are undertaken to allow the offshore markets to expand, as the process of RMB internationalization is ultimately determined by market forces, which are in turn influenced by capital account opening and the financial development of China.

It is likely that China is going to continue to rely on a "one currency, two markets" strategy for RMB internationalization. In that case, Hong Kong is probably going to be the largest beneficiary of this policy. As it continues to get the lion's share of the global RMB business, Hong Kong's status as a premier international financial center is helped by RMB internationalization, even if the RMB is only slowly moving up the rank of international currencies at the global level. As the RMB becomes a more globalized currency, Hong Kong's share of the global RMB business is almost certainly going to fall, as RMB businesses will spread to other RMB centers all over the world due to international competition. However, the absolute value of Hong Kong's RMB-related activities will almost certainly continue to grow, given that the total amount of RMB businesses is set to increase. Moreover, as China's financial development and capital account opening will take time, Hong Kong will probably continue to play an important role in RMB internationalization for some time.

NOTES TO CHAPTER 4

1 Note that the sum of the FX turnover shares of all currencies is equal to 200 percent.

2 Source: Bank of China (Hong Kong) website (www.bochk.com/en/rmb/clearing/service.html).

3 See People's Bank of China 2017.

4 See, for example, Nixon, Hatzvi, and Wright 2015 and King & Wood Mallesons 2014.

5 See, for example, "Internationalization of the Renminbi": Wikipedia 2021c.

6 Relevant events of "mid-2010": On 17 June 2010, the PBC, MOF, MOFCOM, GAC, SAT, and CBRC jointly issued the Notice on Expanding the Pilot Program of RMB Settlement of Cross-Border Trade Transactions, to expand the scope of the pilot program (PBC Document 2010 No. 186). On 19 July 2010, the PBC and the HKMA signed the Supplementary Memorandum IV of Cooperation on the Pilot Program of RMB Settlement of Cross-Border Trade Transactions. The PBC and BOC (Hong Kong) Ltd. signed the revised RMB Clearing Agreement. On 17 August 2010, the PBC issued the Notice Concerning the Pilot Program on Investment in the Interbank Bond Market with RMB Funds by Three Types of Institutions Including Overseas RMB Clearing Banks (PBC Document 2010 No.217). On 31 August 2010, the PBC issued the Administrative Rules for RMB Bank Settlement Accounts of Overseas Institutions (PBC Document 2010 No.249). See People's Bank of China 2017.

7 See Nixon, Hatzvi, and Wright 2015.

8 See Li 2013.

9 Sources: websites of Australian Bureau of Statistics, Bank of Indonesia, Ministry of Finance of Japan, and Bank of Thailand.

10 Source: Steil 2019.

11 See People's Bank of China 2017.

12 See Nixon, Hatzvi, and Wright 2015.

13 See Hong Kong Stock Exchange website (www.hkex.com.hk/eng/InvestChinaA/index.htm).

14 See Nixon, Hatzvi, and Wright 2015.

15 Source: BIS/BNP Paribas (https://securities.bnpparibas.com/insights/china-interbank-bond-market.html).

16 See www.sc.com/en/trade-beyond-borders/renminbi-globalisation-index/.

5 The Importance of Capital Account Liberalization

In order to understand what the capital account of a country is, we need to have some basic knowledge about the balance of payments accounts of a country.

5.1 THE BALANCE OF PAYMENTS ACCOUNTS

Table 5.1 shows the simplified balance of payments accounts of a country.

The balance of payments accounts of a country record the international transactions of a country. By convention, receipts from foreigners are recorded as credits and payments to foreigners are recorded as debits. As shown in the Table 5.1, the balance of payments accounts consist of the current account and the capital account. The current account records payments to and receipts from: imports and exports of goods and services, factor income arising from services provided by factors of production to foreign countries (e.g., 1. wage income; 2. investment income such as (a) dividends and interests in portfolio investments in stocks and bonds and (b) earnings in foreign direct investments) and inward and outward unilateral transfers. The capital account records payments to and receipts from: the purchase or sale of foreign assets, such as money, stocks, bonds, and factories. It reflects the flows of capital in and out of a country. It can be divided into two sub-accounts: (1) the official capital account, which records transactions undertaken by the domestic and foreign central banks; (2) the non-official capital account, which records transactions undertaken by the private sector and other entities in the domestic and foreign countries.

Note that the definition of the capital account described above is different from that of the IMF, which adopts a narrow definition of

Table 5.1 *The simplified balance of payments accounts of a country*

Current account

(1) Exports	Goods
	Services
	Factor income receipts from foreigners
(2) Imports	Goods
	Services
	Factor income payments to foreigners
(3) Net unilateral inward transfers	

Balance on current account = (1) – (2) + (3)

Capital account

(4) Net acquisition of financial assets from foreigners	Official (i.e., central bank) reserve assets
	Non-official (i.e., private sector and other entities) assets
(5) Net incurrence of liabilities to foreigners	Official (i.e., central bank) reserve assets
	Non-official (i.e., private sector and other entities) assets

Net financial outflows = (4) – (5)

Statistical discrepancy

Net financial outflows, less balance on current account, i.e., (4) – (5) – [(1) – (2) + (3)]

the capital account. The IMF splits what I refer to as the capital account into the financial account and the capital account, with most of the items in what I refer to as the capital account being included in the financial account. Based on the definition of the capital account in this book, capital account liberalization means that domestic citizens are freer to purchase foreign assets and foreign citizens are freer to purchase domestic assets, and that there are freer capital flows in and out of the country. Therefore, what I refer to as capital account liberalization in this book is the same as "financial account liberalization" in the terminology of the IMF.

The current accounts of most countries are quite open, in the sense that goods and services are free to flow in and out of the country. However, the capital accounts of some countries, especially developing ones, are not very open, in the sense that capital flows in and out of the country are substantially controlled. In the case of China, anyone can exchange RMB into foreign currencies for all the RMB earned in transactions under the current account. Thus, we say that the RMB is fully convertible in the current account. However, people cannot freely convert all RMB earned in transactions under the capital account (e.g., investments in financial assets) into foreign currencies. Thus, we say that the RMB is not fully convertible in the capital account.

5.2 CAPITAL ACCOUNT OPENNESS OF CHINA

Anyone who has some experience of doing business with China or investing in China can feel that capital flows are quite tightly controlled. For example, as of the time of writing (late 2019), each domestic citizen is only allowed to exchange RMB into USD 50,000 worth of foreign currency per year and move it out of the country. Foreigners who earn RMB from investment may not freely convert it into foreign currency and move it out of the country. Moreover, there are restrictions for anyone to move RMB in and out of China. We shall rely on two objective measures to gauge the extent of capital controls and the degree of convertibility of the RMB: one is a de jure measure and the other is a de facto measure.

5.2.1 De Jure Capital Account Openness

To appreciate the degree of openness of the capital account (or degree of freedom of capital mobility) of China compared with other countries, we can refer to Figure 5.1, which shows the Chinn–Ito Index (KAOPEN) of openness of the capital account in seven countries. The index is normalized to between zero and one.[1] The higher is the index, the more open is the capital account of the country. KAOPEN is based

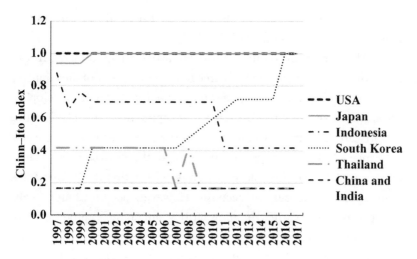

FIGURE 5.1 Chinn–Ito Index normalized to the range between 0 and 1,
1997–2017.
Reference: Chinn and Ito (2006)
Data source: http://web.pdx.edu/~ito/Chinn-Ito_website.htm

on the binary dummy variables that codify the tabulation of restric-
tions on cross-border financial transactions reported in the IMF's
Annual Report on Exchange Arrangements and Exchange
Restrictions (AREAER) in the section, "Summary Features of
Exchange Arrangements and Regulatory Frameworks for Current
and Capital Transactions in Member Countries." Based on this index,
China's capital account was very closed as of 2017. When compared
with emerging markets such as Thailand, India, Indonesia, and South
Korea, China had the lowest capital account openness, which was the
same as those of India and Thailand, but lower than those of South
Korea and Indonesia.[2] AREAER reports whether a country imposes
restrictions on each of a set of items of capital account transactions.
Any measure of capital account openness calculated based on this
kind of criterion is referred to as de jure capital account openness, as it
is concerned with what are stipulated in the laws.

Table 5.2 shows the capital account items for which transactions were restricted by China as documented by the IMF. A "Yes"

Table 5.2 *Comparison of capital account items for which transactions were restricted, 2013–2018*

	United States	Japan	China					
	2018	2018	2018	2017	2016	2015	2014	2013
Controls on payments for invisible transactions and current transfers	No	Yes	Yes	Yes	Yes	Yes	Yes	Yes
Proceeds from exports and/or invisible transactions								
Repatriation requirements	No	No	Yes	Yes	Yes	Yes	Yes	Yes
Surrender requirements	No	No	No	No	No	No	No	No
Capital transactions								
On capital market securities	Yes	Yes	Yes	Yes	Yes	Yes	Yes	Yes
On money market instruments	Yes	No	Yes	Yes	Yes	Yes	Yes	Yes
On collective investment securities	Yes	No	Yes	Yes	Yes	Yes	Yes	Yes
Controls on derivatives and other instruments	Yes	No	Yes	Yes	Yes	Yes	Yes	Yes
Commercial credits	No	No	**Yes**	**Yes**	**No**	**No**	**No**	**No**
Financial credits	No	No	Yes	Yes	Yes	Yes	Yes	Yes
Guarantees, sureties, and financial backup	Yes	No	Yes	Yes	Yes	Yes	Yes	Yes
Controls on direct investment	Yes	Yes	Yes	Yes	Yes	Yes	Yes	Yes
Controls on liquidation of direct investment	No	No	Yes	Yes	Yes	Yes	Yes	Yes
Controls on real estate transactions	Yes	No	Yes	Yes	Yes	Yes	Yes	Yes
Controls on personal capital transactions	No	No	Yes	Yes	Yes	Yes	Yes	Yes

Table 5.2 (cont.)

Provisions specific to	United States 2018	Japan 2018	China 2018	2017	2016	2015	2014	2013
Commercial banks and other credit institutions	No	No	Yes	Yes	Yes	Yes	Yes	Yes
Institutional investors	Yes	No	Yes	Yes	Yes	Yes	Yes	Yes

Source: IMF Annual Report on Exchange Arrangements and Exchange Restrictions (AREAER) (www.imf.org/en/ Publications/Annual-Report-on-Exchange-Arrangements-and-Exchange-Restrictions/Issues/2019/04/24/Annual-Report- on-Exchange-Arrangements-and-Exchange-Restrictions-2018-46162).

means there is control on that item. A comparison with the United States and Japan in 2018 is also listed in the table. Specifically, as recently as 2018, there are still many types of transactions that were restricted by China while they were allowed in other countries, such as the United States and Japan. It can be seen that by this criterion, China's controls on capital flows were basically unchanged from 2013 through 2018 (except capital transactions "commercial credits"). As of 2018, there were only two items on which the United States, Japan, and China all impose controls (i.e., capital transactions "on capital market securities" and "controls on direct investment"). But there were seven items on which both the United States and Japan did not impose controls while China did.

However, the data contained in the AREAER report sometimes give a picture quite different from what one observes in reality about the amount of capital flows into and out of a country. For example, in 2016, the KAOPEN index (which is based on AREAER) of Thailand is 0.18 while that of Indonesia is 0.41. But the total sum of international assets and international liabilities (called the gross international investment position [IIP]) of Thailand as a percentage of GDP was twice that of Indonesia (see Figure 5.1). Another example is the change over time in the capital account openness of Thailand, whose KAOPEN index shows that its capital account openness was flat from 1996 till 2007, then it fell sharply from 2007, and then it was sustained at that low level through 2016, whereas the gross IIP to GDP ratio shows that it became more and more open from 1997 through 2017. Thus, there are limitations to the use of the de jure measure of capital account openness that makes use of the data contained in AREAER. An alternative measure of capital account openness is based on the actual amount of international assets and liabilities relative to the size of the economy. Such a measure is called de facto capital account openness.

5.2.2 De Facto Capital Account Openness

Figure 5.2 shows the capital account openness over time of a few countries as measured by the "gross international investment

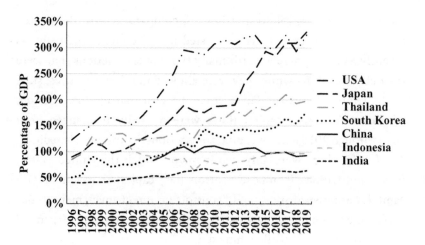

FIGURE 5.2 Gross international investment position as a percentage of GDP (de facto measure of capital account openness), 1996–2019.
Sources: IMF International Investment Position (http://data.imf.org/regular.aspx?key=61468209); World Bank Data Bank (https://data.worldbank.org/indicator/NY.GDP.MKTP.CD)

position," which is defined as the sum of the absolute values of foreign assets and foreign liabilities divided by the GDP of the country. Some argue that this is a more reasonable measure of capital account openness than the de jure measure, as the latter fails to capture the degree of enforcement of the laws and the relative importance of each capital control measure. Nonetheless, based on the de facto measure of capital account openness, China's capital account was again quite closed from 2004 through 2018. In 2018, China's capital account was not only much less open than those of developed countries such as the United States and Japan, but also those of some other emerging markets such as Thailand and South Korea. China was only more open than Indonesia and India.

It can be seen that the openness of the United States increased rapidly during 2002–2007, a period of increased financial globalization, but then the rise in the openness to capital flows came to a halt by 2008, during the global financial crisis. It became almost unchanged from 2009 to 2016. The openness of Japan also rose rapidly during 2001–2007, the years before the onset of the global financial crisis. However, unlike the United States, Japan's openness rose rapidly during 2012–2016, and it reached the same level as that of the United States in 2016. The openness of China was almost unchanged during 2004–2018 (the period for which data are available). By 2018, China's openness was only about one-third that of the United States and Japan. Figure 5.2 therefore shows clearly that China's capital account is still quite closed. In fact, if one takes into account the fact that most of the foreign assets of China consist of central bank foreign reserves, one can say that China's de facto capital account openness should be even lower than what the gross international investment position indicates. This is because the accumulation of foreign reserves by the PBC does not reflect the commercial decisions of market players in the private sector, which is what the de facto capital account openness measure is supposed to capture.[3]

5.2.3 Why Is Capital Account Liberalization Necessary for RMB Internationalization?

As mentioned in Chapter 3, an international currency in general serves three functions: unit of account, medium of exchange, and store of value. These three functions are interrelated and mutually reinforcing. Regarding the "medium of exchange" function, the use of a currency for international payments (such as for settlement of trade and financial transactions) is an important indicator of its international use. Empirically, when a currency is widely used as a medium of exchange, it is also widely used as a unit of account as well as a store of value (such as bank deposits and central bank reserves). Thus, the determinants of the use of RMB for international payments are by and large also the determinants of the internationalization of RMB. Below, I use trade settlement to illustrate my point.

There is a rich economics literature studying the factors that determine the use of a currency for trade invoicing/settlement. According to the theory, after controlling for other relevant factors, a currency's share in trade invoicing/settlement in a certain sector at the global level is mainly affected by two factors: "thick market externalities" and the "coalescing effect." "Thick market externalities" (also known as "network externalities") affect the invoicing share of a currency in all sectors or industries. That a currency has a thick market means that a large amount of the currency is being held and traded internationally. Having a thicker market implies that it is easier to exchange in and out of the currency as it is easier to find buyers or sellers of the currency. The issuing country of a currency with a thick market usually has a broad, deep, liquid, and open financial market (otherwise the currency would not have been widely held and traded). This increases the benefits of holding assets denominated in the currency. "Coalescing effect" affects the invoicing share of a currency in a certain sector. (Thus, a currency can have a strong coalescing effect in one sector but a weak coalescing effect in another sector.) It is determined by the pressure for each seller to invoice in the same currency as the majority of the other competitors in the same sector or industry. By and large, the size of a country tends to increase the coalescing effect of its currency in all sectors. There can be two reasons. First, since the country is a large market, in order to maintain their competitiveness in the market, foreign producers have incentives to invoice in the currency of that country so as to maintain stable prices for the local customers in the face of exchange rate fluctuations. Second, foreign producers selling to that country aim to limit the movements of their prices relative to those of local producers, who have competitive advantage in the market and invoice in their own currency. Below, we provide a more detailed explanation of these two factors and other miscellaneous factors that determine the global invoicing share of a currency in international trade.

Thick market externalities. Matsuyama, Kiyotaki, and Matsui (1993) and Rey (2001) analyze the "medium of exchange" function of an international money (i.e., for trade settlement) and conclude that "thick market externalities" are very important in the making of a vehicle currency.[4] The idea is that countries converge towards using one single currency for trade invoicing due to network externalities.

The rationale is that as each firm has an incentive to adopt the currency used by a majority of other firms, once a currency becomes sufficiently widely used, its role as a vehicle currency is self-reinforcing. Following Kindleberger (1981), Krugman (1984) draws an analogy between the use of a currency for settlement of trade and the use of a language for communication. He argues that what makes English the world's *lingua franca* is not its simplicity or internal beauty, but its wide use. As a language becomes more widely used, it is more attractive for outsiders to use it as well, as they can use it to communicate with more people in the world. Likewise, a firm is more willing to use a currency for trade settlement if other firms are already using it.

The network externalities become self-reinforcing as more firms use that currency for invoicing. In other words, as more firms use that currency for invoicing, the pool of firms using that currency increases, and so it becomes more attractive for outsiders to use it. As more outsiders use the currency, the pool of firms using it increases further, and so the snowballing effect goes on. A currency with strong network externalities usually possesses a few competitive advantages over other currencies, such as lower transaction costs, higher degree of convertibility, more open financial asset transaction, and more accessible financial services offered. Thus, the magnitude of the thick market externalities of a currency is affected by the openness of the capital account, degree of financial development (i.e., the depth, breadth, and liquidity of the financial market), as well as the economic size of the issuing country.

The above effect is called "externalities" because when a person uses a currency as a medium of exchange, it does not only benefit herself, but also benefits all others who use that currency, as the network of people using the currency has become larger. It is called "thick market externalities" because the externalities arise from the fact that the market of the currency has become "thicker" (i.e., the number of people using the currency increases). Thus, it can also be called "network externalities."[5]

The self-reinforcing mechanism may also be applied to the adoption of a reserve currency. Chinn and Frankel (2007) find that there is a statistically significant non-linear positive relationship between the currency share in official reserves and the GDP share of the issuing country. They call this the "tipping phenomenon." Suppose there are two currencies in the world: the leading (incumbent) currency (with a larger but unchanged GDP) and the challenger currency (with a smaller but increasing GDP). The tipping phenomenon says that the challenger currency's share in official reserves is a convex function of the GDP share of the issuing country of this challenger currency. In other words, because of the self-reinforcing mechanism (or positive feedback effect), the positive impact of the challenger's GDP share on its reserve-currency share accelerates as the GDP share increases and gets closer and closer to challenging the leading currency, until the tipping point finally occurs. As the GDP share of the challenger country increases beyond the tipping point, its reserve-currency share quickly balloons while that of the incumbent currency quickly shrinks.

Coalescing effect. Bacchetta and van Wincoop (2005) and Goldberg and Tille (2008) analyze the "unit of account" function of money (i.e., for trade invoicing). In particular, Goldberg and Tille argue that exporting firms have the incentive to mimic the choice of the invoicing currency of their competitors in the same market so as to minimize price volatility and maximize profits. They call this the "coalescing effect" and use it to explain why there is one single vehicle currency used in the world to invoice homogeneous commodities such as oil. Goldberg and Tille argue that the size of the issuing country is important for the coalescing effect of a currency, as foreign producers selling to that country aim to limit the movements of their prices relative to those of local producers, who dominate the market and invoice in their own currency. As a result, foreign producers also tend to use the country's currency as the invoicing currency.

Other factors. In addition to thick market externalities and the coalescing effect, other authors such as Swoboda (1968; 1969) emphasize the role of low transaction costs, such as the bid–ask spread of a currency in the use of the currency for financial transactions.

What do the above theories imply about the prospects of the RMB as an international currency? As explained above, the three functions of an international currency – unit of account, medium of exchange, and store of value – are interrelated and mutually reinforcing. Thus, factors that determine the use of the RMB as a payment (i.e., settlement) currency would more or less also determine the use of the RMB as an invoicing currency in international trade and financial transactions and as a reserve currency for central banks. So, we can conclude from the above theories that the prospect of the internationalization of the RMB depends largely on (1) China's capital account openness; (2) China's financial development; (3) China's share of the GDP of the world; (4) the stability of the exchange rate of RMB. It is widely predicted that China's GDP share will rise and even surpass that of the United States sometime in the future. The last two decades or so show that China has been maintaining a stable and mildly appreciating exchange rate for its currency against the USD and other hard currencies, such as the euro, GBP, and JPY. However, China's capital account openness and financial development are more difficult to predict. The major theme of this chapter is to discuss the history, the current status, and the future of capital account opening of China and how it affects the prospects of RMB internationalization, while Chapter 6 discusses similar topics concerning China's financial development.

Intuitively, the reason why capital account opening is conducive to internationalization of a currency is that a fully open capital account implies that the currency is fully convertible, and capital is fully mobile internationally. This free mobility of capital allows home and foreign investors to move capital freely across the border so as to seek higher returns and diversify their risks, which in turn leads to a large volume of foreign exchange turnover (i.e., a thick market for the currency), which lowers the transaction costs (bid–ask spread) of converting into and out of the currency. This decrease in transaction costs raises the appeal of the currency as a settlement and invoicing currency. The freedom of capital movement also increases the appeal of the currency as an investment currency for store of value both onshore and offshore. With capital mobility, further financial development (broader, deeper, and more liquid financial market) would make the currency even more attractive as an investment currency, which would further reinforce its appeal as an invoicing and settlement currency.

Just how much more important is a more open and developed financial market than a larger size of China's GDP in making the RMB an international currency? This seems to be a difficult question to answer. Nonetheless, we have tried to answer this question quantitatively using econometric analysis. Chapter 8 is devoted to a detailed analysis of this question. It is shown there that if China's GDP increased to that of the United States in 2016 while its financial openness and development were both unchanged (and the GDP and financial openness and development of other countries and everything else are unchanged as well), the share of the RMB in international payments would only increase from 1.6 percent to about 2.4 percent. On the other hand, if China's financial openness and development reaches those of Thailand in 2016 (which seems possible for China to achieve) while its GDP remains unchanged, RMB's share in international payments would increase from 1.6 percent to about 4.2 percent. Thus, the effect of increasing China's financial development and openness to that of Thailand in 2016 is about 1.8 times the effect of increasing China's GDP to that of the United States in 2016. Although the real world is a lot more complicated and many factors are interacting with each other, this rough counterfactual thought experiment demonstrates how much China is behind in the state of its financial development and openness compared with the more developed countries and how much more important financial development and openness are compared with the size of its economy if China really wants to make RMB an international currency, or even a

regional currency in East Asia. Thus, both theoretically and empirically, it can be shown that capital account opening, together with
financial development, is crucial in the internationalization of
the RMB.

One important question we ask is: Should China open its capital
account just because it wants to internationalize the RMB? This is a
controversial question. There are some observers, practitioners, and
scholars who strongly advocate pushing for RMB internationalization
and use it as a tool to push forward the capital account opening and
financial sector reform that are required for RMB internationalization
to succeed. They argue that financial development, capital account
opening, exchange rate flexibility, and interest rate marketization are
crucial for the next stage of China's development. Yet these reforms
are met with strong domestic resistance by vested interests, and so it
is necessary to use RMB internationalization to *daobi* domestic financial reform and opening. Along this line of logic, they further argue
that China need not follow the conventional wisdom concerning the
sequence of liberalization, namely financial sector reform should
precede capital account opening. Instead, the two sets of reforms can
proceed gradually and interactively in tandem, with RMB internationalization as a catalyst.[6] On the other hand, there are also people who
argue that RMB internationalization should not be an independent
goal to be pursued by China but should only be treated as a natural
outcome of capital account opening, the extent of which should be
considered in the broader context of China's economic development.[7]
This latter group of thinkers also point out the importance of the
correct sequence of liberalization, namely that a capital account
should not be opened too much until the financial sector is well
developed, and that China's financial market still has a long way to
go before it can attain a similar level of development to those of the
developed countries. Thus, RMB internationalization, and by extension, capital account liberalization, should be subordinate to financial
sector development, according to this view. Although I understand
the logic of the second group of thinkers, I actually agree more with

the first group and believe that it is a good idea to pursue RMB internationalization as a tool to force domestic capital account opening and financial development. This is because external commitments (i.e., commitments to become more open to the rest of the world) have historically been very effective in pressuring China to open up, and there is no question that China needs to be more open at its current stage of development.

A related question is: Is capital account opening beneficial to China for its own sake, regardless of the push for RMB internationalization? In order to answer this question, we should identify the benefits and costs of capital account liberalization, which I shall do below.

5.2.4   The Benefits of Capital Account Liberalization

Capital account liberalization is equivalent to opening a country to international trade in financial assets. International trade, broadly defined, is beneficial to a country for many reasons. There are three types of gains from trade between countries:

1. Goods and services of one country for goods and services of another country. This is contemporaneous trade. It is based on comparative advantage and economies of scale and is reflected in the gross flows of imports and exports in the current account.
2. Goods and services of one country for financial assets (i.e., claims for payments in the future) of another country. This is called intertemporal trade. It is based on differential returns to investment in different countries. The differential returns to investment can be due to intertemporal comparative advantage and intertemporal preferences. Everything else being equal, countries that have more highly productive investment opportunities (i.e., have stronger comparative advantage in producing future output relative to current output) than the average or whose patience is lower (i.e., stronger preference for current consumption relative to future consumption) than the average would be net borrowers, and they will be net importers of goods and services but net exporters of financial assets. These countries will run current account deficits.

3. Financial assets of one country for financial assets of another country. It is motivated by the desire for risk diversification or risk sharing. This kind of trade is reflected in the gross financial inflows and outflows in the capital account of the country.

Capital account liberalization is concerned with lowering the barriers to the second and third kind of trade above. In fact, the gains from trade go beyond the "static" gains explained above and there are "dynamic gains" from trade that can arguably be even more important than the static gains. Dynamic gains from trade can take many forms, but one that I want to emphasize here is how domestic firms' exposure to competition from foreign firms or foreign products today can increase their efficiency tomorrow. This is because subjecting domestic firms to foreign competition can motivate them to learn and innovate so as to survive and win. In principle, this should apply to trade in goods and services and trade in financial assets. In reality, however, opening the country to trade in goods and services is relatively less risky than opening the country to trade in financial assets, especially regarding short-term capital flows. In other words, current account liberalization is less risky than capital account liberalization. The reason is that the market for goods and services is fundamentally different from the financial market, as we shall see below.

Kose, Prasad, Rogoff, and Wei (2009) find that opening the financial markets to entry by foreign companies helps to discipline domestic firms and make them more efficient through competitive pressure and through imitation. First, given that foreign investors are more experienced and seasoned, they are more skillful in picking the well-managed firms and distinguishing the good firms from the bad ones, thus allowing foreign investors to come would strengthen the market mechanism of rewarding the good firms and punishing the poor ones. Second, foreign financial institutions such as banks can bring in state-of-the-art management and technology and provide new products and services – this would increase the efficiency of domestic firms as they have to compete with the foreign firms. Moreover, domestic firms can imitate and learn from the foreign firms. Third, bringing in foreign firms as shareholders can make them serve as "strategic investors" to improve the profitability of the firm, as they would have incentives to improve the efficiency of the company such as management, organization, and corporate governance. Prasad and Rajan (2008) find that liberalizing capital outflows can create competitive pressure on domestic financial institutions, such as banks, as they have to provide comparable returns to investment as those of foreign financial products so as to attract domestic investors to stay.

The opposite of capital account opening is capital controls, and they can lead to many problems. The main problem is that, by imposing onerous restrictions on international transactions, they lead to inefficient allocation of capital. This reduces the level of GDP, GDP growth, and welfare. Moreover, like any government intervention programs, they can breed corruption.

It should be noted that even those who advocate capital account liberalization do not suggest that opening the financial market to foreign competition would automatically lead to improvement in the performance of the financial sector. First, certain preconditions have to be met before capital account liberalization becomes useful to the economy. For example, there needs to be a good regulatory framework, which includes a set of laws that are enforced by an effective law-enforcement agency and the court system, as well as a set of effective regulatory agencies such as a securities and futures commission and a banking regulatory authority (see, further, Prasad and Rajan 2008.) Second, only certain types of capital inflows might be productive. In developing countries, the composition of capital inflows affects the risk of capital account opening. For example, having a sufficiently high proportion of capital inflows through equity portfolio investment and equity direct investment (equity finance) rather than through bond issuance and bank loans (debt finance) is preferred as it lowers the probability of default. This is because in equity finance the investors have to bear the risks when the performance of the firm fluctuates, while in debt finance the firm's committed amounts of payments to the investors do not fall with poor performance of the firm. This makes it more painful for the firm in bad times – painful enough to cause it to default. Thus, when opening a country to capital inflows, it is necessary to seek an optimal proportion of debt-to-equity finance, perhaps through trial and error.

5.2.5 The Costs of Capital Account Liberalization

Capital account opening is not non-controversial even among well-respected economists. For example, Dani Rodrik (1998), Jagdish Bhagwati (1998), and Joseph Stiglitz (2000) are against it. They argue that developing countries should keep or reinstate restrictions on capital mobility to be able to exercise monetary autonomy while enjoying stable exchange rates. The fact is capital account liberalization carries non-trivial risks especially for emerging economies with an immature banking and financial sector. The Asian Financial Crisis in 1998 is a case in point. The open capital accounts of some Asian economies allowed foreign capital to pull out en masse abruptly due to a change in the outlook of these economies. This led to speculative attack on their currencies, leading to a balance of payments crisis and a banking crisis and widespread bankruptcies. In fact, China took pride in its policy of capital controls during the Asian Financial Crisis as it could maintain a stable exchange rate and serve as a stabilizing force at that time.

Dani Rodrik (1998), in a paper titled "Who Needs Capital-Account Convertibility?," used the Asian Financial Crisis as an example to illustrate why capital account liberalization was more harmful than productive to developing countries. He observed that in 1996, five Asian economies (South Korea, Indonesia, Malaysia, Thailand, and the Philippines) received net private capital inflows amounting to USD 93 billion. One year later (in 1997), they experienced an estimated outflow of USD 12.1 billion, a turnaround in a single year of USD 105 billion, amounting to more than 10 percent of the combined GDP of these economies, causing economic disasters in these countries. It is not clear that even a country with strong financial institutions, such as the United States, could withstand a shock of such magnitude relative to its GDP.

Rodrik (1998) pointed out that the Asian Financial Crisis was just one example of many other major debt crises that have hit developing countries from time to time, such as the generalized debt crisis of 1982 and the Mexican crisis of 1994–1995. He argued that these examples illustrated that "there is a compelling case for maintaining controls or taxes on short-term [international] borrowing." He furnished a few arguments in favor of controlling capital flows. First, capital account liberalization can interfere with the domestic goals of controlling inflation and maintaining the exchange rate at a competitive level. Second, the financial market is fundamentally different from the market for goods and services, in several dimensions. For example, (i) asymmetric information combined with moral hazard due to implicit insurance of government bailout results in excessive lending for risky projects; (ii) a mismatch between short-term liabilities and long-term assets leaves financial intermediaries vulnerable to bank runs and financial panic, a problem that is particularly severe in cross-border transactions where there is no international lender of last resort; (iii) investors are myopic, and are prone to panics, herd behavior, and contagion from one market to another. Finally, Rodrik noted that he could not find any compelling evidence that capital account openness was correlated with successful economic performance.

Baghwati (1998) pointed out that the IMF had no intention of making capital account convertibility an obligation when it was first established, and that its move in that direction later was due to ideology (free market is always good) and special interests (financial institutions in the United States and the US Treasury). He argued that short-term capital flow was the culprit of both the Mexican crisis in 1994 and the Asian Financial Crisis in 1998, and that in general the gains from capital account opening were quite small. He noted that both China and Japan achieved rapid growth without capital account convertibility. Moreover, Western Europe's post-World War II return to prosperity was achieved also without capital account convertibility. Hence, he concluded that "the weight of the evidence and the force of the logic point towards restraints on capital flows."

Stiglitz (2000) pointed out that, during the Asian Financial Crisis, unemployment increased threefold to fourfold in South Korea and Thailand, and even more in Indonesia, and real wages fell by 10 percent in South Korea, and by about a quarter in Thailand and Indonesia. He attributed the occurrence of these events as the existence of the negative externalities of short-term capital flows, in the sense that the private benefits to the owners of short-term capital was much higher than the social benefits due to the potentially destabilizing effects it created. The existence of the negative externalities of short-term capital flows implies that some form of government intervention to restrict them is welfare enhancing, e.g., imposing a tax on short-term capital flows. Thus, he argued against full capital account liberalization. Stiglitz further pointed out (2002: 99) that countries in East Asia had no need for additional capital given their high savings rates, but capital account liberalization was pushed on these countries in the late 1980s and early 1990s. He believed that capital account liberalization was the single most important reason for the outbreak of the Asian Financial Crisis. He argued that few country could have withstood the sudden change in investor sentiment that reversed the huge inflow to a huge outflow of capital. In the case of Thailand, the reversal amounted to 7.9 percent of GDP in 1997, 12.3 percent of GDP in 1998, and 7 percent of GDP in the first half of 1999.

There is an additional cost to opening the capital account, which is that the exchange rate would likely become more volatile. This is due to the open-economy trilemma, which we mention without explaining in Chapter 1. Here, we will explain its theoretical basis in more detail. In order to do so, we first need to describe the balance sheet of the central bank and the principle of uncovered interest parity.

5.3   THE OPEN-ECONOMY TRILEMMA

5.3.1   Simplified Central Bank Balance Sheet

A simplified balance sheet of the central bank is presented in Table 5.3.

Table 5.3 *The simplified balance sheet of the central bank*

Assets	Liabilities
Foreign exchange reserves (e.g., foreign government bonds denominated in foreign currency)	**Currency in circulation** (C) **Reserves deposited by commercial banks** (R)
Domestic assets (e.g., domestic government bonds denominated in domestic currency)	**Other liabilities** (e.g., deposits from other government departments)
Other assets (e.g., gold and loans to commercial banks)	

The sum of currency in circulation (C) and reserves deposited by the commercial banks (R) is called the monetary base (MB). Any increase in the monetary base increases the supply of money in the economy, as banks can leverage the increase in the monetary base to create credits in the banking system. Assuming that the net worth of the central bank is constant in the face of changes in assets and liabilities, any change in the assets side of the balance sheet must be accompanied by an equal change in the liabilities side. Whenever the central bank buys assets (either foreign exchange reserves or domestic assets), it pays for them by issuing money, thus injecting money into the economy. The injection of money into the economy (by increasing the currency in circulation or reserves deposited by commercial banks) increases the monetary base. This action expands the assets and liabilities sides of the balance sheet of the central bank by equal amounts, and the money supply increases as a consequence. Conversely, whenever the central bank sells assets, members of the public pay money to the central bank, thus reducing the amount of money held by the public. Such an action shrinks the balance sheet of the central bank and the money supply falls as a result.

5.3.2   The Uncovered Interest Parity

The uncovered interest parity is a market equilibrium condition which would hold under free capital mobility. Thus, it is expected to hold reasonably well when capital control is minimal. The condition states that the rate of return to domestic currency time deposits should be equal to the expected rate of return on foreign currency time deposits when the proceeds from investing in the two deposits are converted into the same currency, after risk and liquidity factors have been taken into account. More precisely, the interest rate on domestic time deposits is equal to the interest rate on foreign time deposits plus the expected rate of appreciation of the foreign currency with respect to the domestic currency plus the risk-cum-liquidity premium on domestic currency deposits.[8] Any deviation from the condition will lead to arbitrage, which will restore the condition through adjustment in the exchange rate.[9] In the above discussion, "time deposit" can be replaced by any safe interest-bearing asset such as a government bond. Mathematically, the uncovered interest parity condition can be stated as the following equation.

$$R = R^* + \hat{E}^e + \rho$$

where R is the interest rate on domestic time deposit (or government bond); R^* is the interest rate on foreign time deposit (or government bond); $\hat{E}^e$ is the expected rate of appreciation of the foreign currency with respect to home currency; ρ is the (constant) risk-cum-liquidity premium on domestic currency deposits.[10]

For simplicity of exposition, let us assume that the risk-cum-liquidity premium on domestic currency deposits is not only constant but zero. (Maintaining the assumption of a constant but non-zero risk-cum-liquidity premium does not change our conclusion, but only makes the analysis more complicated.) Under a fixed exchange rate, due to uncovered interest parity, the domestic-currency rate of return to foreign currency deposits (when all proceeds are converted into the domestic currency) is just the foreign interest rate, as the expected rate of appreciation of the foreign currency with respect to the domestic currency is zero (since investors expect the exchange rate to be fixed in the future). Thus, under a fixed exchange rate regime, the central bank's duty is to keep the domestic time deposit rate equal to the foreign time deposit rate of the same maturity, say one year. When the domestic deposit rate falls below that of the foreign one, the domestic central bank has to reduce the money supply by selling foreign reserves and buying domestic currency so as to support the value of the domestic currency relative to the foreign currency. The reduction of the money supply would at the same time raise the domestic interest rate back to the level of its foreign counterpart.

Box 5.1 explains the theoretical basis of the trilemma.

BOX 5.1   The theoretical basis of the open-economy trilemma

The open-economy trilemma states that out of the three "desirable" goals of monetary policy autonomy, exchange rate stability, and freedom of capital flows, it is impossible to achieve all three at the same time (i.e., only two goals can be achieved at any one time [see Figure Box 5.1A]). Of course, the principle applies only when each goal is required to be achieved perfectly. In other words, it would be possible

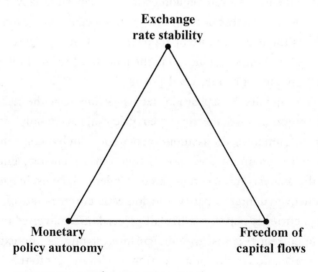

FIGURE BOX 5.1A The open-economy trilemma.

BOX 5.1 **(cont.)**

to achieve all three goals if some of them are achieved partially. Another way to understand the trilemma is that, when one goal (e.g., exchange rate stability) is to be maintained, there is a tradeoff between the other two goals (i.e., free capital mobility and autonomy in monetary policy)—if you have more of one, you will have less of the other.

Some real world examples can illustrate the validity of the trilemma clearly. Hong Kong is adopting a currency board system such that the Hong Kong dollar is linked to the USD at a fixed exchange rate of HKD 7.8 = USD 1 (with allowance for deviation of 0.64 percent each way, i.e., the allowable range is 7.75 to 7.85 Hong Kong dollars to 1 US dollar). At the same time, Hong Kong allows free capital mobility. Thus, according to the trilemma, Hong Kong completely loses monetary policy autonomy, which is indeed true. For example, during the Asian Financial Crisis of 1997–1998, the Hong Kong Monetary Authority (HKMA) could not fight the recession by increasing money supply since the commitment to honor the fixed exchange rate prevented the HKMA from increasing the supply of HKD, as this would amount to the HKMA issuing HKD to purchase USD reserves in the foreign exchange market, which would lead to a depreciation of the HKD with respect to the USD. This would violate the fixed exchange rate commitment.

The theoretical basis

Suppose a country wants to maintain a fixed exchange rate, and that there is a negative demand shock which lowers the aggregate demand. Typically, such a shock would lower GDP, lower the interest rate, and create pressure for the currency to depreciate. In order to stabilize the exchange rate, the central bank has to intervene in the foreign exchange market by selling foreign reserves (the foreign currency that the central bank owns) and buying domestic currency. The effect of this is a reduction in the amount of domestic currency in circulation or the amount of reserves deposited by the banks. As the central bank takes domestic currency out of circulation (or reduces the amount of

BOX 5.1 **(cont.)**

reserves deposited by the banks), its liabilities fall, and so the money supply is reduced. Such a reduction in money supply is necessary to keep the interest rate at the old level. If the central bank wants to exercise monetary autonomy, it has to carry out "sterilization" of the foreign exchange intervention. To sterilize, it has to buy domestic assets (e.g., government bonds) to increase the money supply back to the old level. However, this means that the domestic interest rate falls. If there is free capital mobility so that "uncovered interest parity" holds, then there will be capital outflow, as the expected return to foreign currency deposits is larger than that of domestic currency deposits, given that the fixed exchange rate regime is common knowledge to all players and is credible to the market. This capital outflow is accompanied by the selling of home currency and the buying of foreign currency, which nullifies the intervention of the central bank in the foreign exchange market. To curb this capital outflow, the government must do one of the following two things: The first option is to impose capital control so that conversion between currencies is not free. So, free capital mobility cannot be achieved. In that case, the uncovered interest parity does not hold. The second option is to forego monetary autonomy by selling domestic assets (e.g., government bonds) so as to reduce the money supply and raise the interest rate back to the previous level. So, autonomy in monetary policy cannot be achieved. To summarize, in order to maintain the exchange rate fixed in the face of a negative demand shock, the country has to give up either capital mobility or monetary policy autonomy.

In recent years, there have been some empirical studies that throw doubts on the validity of the open-economy trilemma. For example, Rey (2015) points out that, in the face of global financial integration, peripheral countries (countries other than the United States) are faced with a dilemma rather than a trilemma. Based on her finding about the "global financial cycles," characterized by large common movements in asset prices, gross flows, and leverage across countries, she concludes that whenever capital is freely mobile, the global financial cycle that originates from the center country (the United States) constrains national monetary policies of the peripheral countries regardless of the latter's exchange rate regime. Thus, governments of the peripheral countries are faced with the dilemma between choosing monetary autonomy and capital controls, rather than a trilemma. Independent monetary policies are possible if and only if the capital account is managed directly or indirectly. Han and Wei (2018), on the other hand, find some empirical evidence of a "2.5-lemma," or something between a trilemma and a dilemma. They find that, without capital controls, a flexible exchange rate regime offers some monetary policy autonomy when the center country tightens its monetary policy, yet it fails to do so when the center country loosens its monetary policy. On the other hand, capital controls help to sustain the monetary autonomy of the peripheral country in the face of monetary policy shocks from the center country regardless of whether the shock is tightening or loosening. Despite these empirical findings, we continue to maintain that the fundamental idea of the trilemma is theoretically sound and empirically well-supported. An implication of the trilemma is that there is more scope for addressing shocks with monetary policy in a country with a more flexible exchange rate, or with stronger controls on capital flows, than for a country with a more rigid exchange rate and open capital markets. This implication is much less controversial among economists.

5.3.3 What is "Sterilization"?

"Sterilization" is the buying or selling of domestic assets by a central bank following foreign exchange market intervention by the central bank. It changes the size of the assets side of the central bank balance sheet, which automatically changes the money supply (the liabilities side of the balance sheet). The purpose of carrying out foreign exchange intervention followed by sterilization is to affect the exchange rate without affecting the money supply. However, empirical evidence suggests that sterilized foreign exchange intervention is usually not very effective in affecting the exchange rate when capital mobility is high, as private sector arbitrage in the foreign exchange market would offset the effect on the exchange rate by the foreign exchange market intervention of the central bank. In other words, when the uncovered interest parity condition is satisfied (as arbitrage is possible due to free capital mobility), a central bank cannot affect the exchange rate without affecting the money supply. Conversely, if there is no free capital mobility, it is possible for a central bank to affect the exchange rate without affecting the money supply. Thus, the futility of sterilized intervention in the foreign exchange market is another way to prove the open-economy trilemma, as it proves that the exchange rate cannot be controlled (to be fixed) when there is free capital mobility and autonomy in monetary policy. That said, some scholars argue that sterilized foreign exchange intervention can still be effective as it signals to the market in which direction the central bank wants the exchange rate to go, thus it influences the market's expectation about what the exchange rate would be in the future.

5.3.4   Why RMB Internationalization Would Lead to Higher Exchange Rate Volatility

The reason why we expect that the RMB exchange rate would become more volatile as China's capital account becomes more open is based on the assumption that China would not give up any monetary policy autonomy, which is highly plausible. According to the open-economy trilemma, this means that the tradeoff is just between capital mobility and a stable exchange rate. As capital controls are relaxed, the exchange rate would become more volatile.

5.3.5   Evidence for the Open-Economy Trilemma

The balance sheet of the central bank as well as the description of how monetary policy and sterilization are carried out given above are highly simplified, especially in the case of China. The conduct of monetary policy in China is complicated, and there are multiple tools to influence money supply. So, given the simplicity of our model, is there any evidence for the validity of the open-economy trilemma in

China? The answer is yes. In fact, Wu (2015) found evidence of it based on the observation that as China tried to carry out foreign exchange market intervention and sterilization at the same time in an attempt to counter the effect of capital inflows on exchange rate stability, it could not attain exchange rate stability and monetary autonomy at the same time. In other words, sterilization could not be fully successful – capital inflows followed by foreign exchange market intervention to maintain exchange rate stability would sacrifice monetary autonomy even under sterilization.

Besides, we have carried out some simple statistical analyses and found evidence that an increase in capital mobility in a month is significantly and positively correlated with an increase in exchange rate volatility in that month, one month later, and two months later. The correlation coefficient in each case is significantly different from zero. This means that when capital controls are relaxed in a certain month, the exchange rate tended to become more volatile in that month, one month later, and two months later. This is consistent with the finding of Wu (2015) above, that an increase in capital mobility caused the central bank to intervene, but then it could not fully insulate the positive effect of the capital flows on exchange rate volatility as it attempted to maintain control over the money supply. We used data of monthly gross capital flow (a measure of capital mobility) and monthly exchange rate volatility from January 2010 through January 2018. Monthly gross capital flow is defined as the sum of the absolute change in assets and absolute change in liabilities during a month in the financial account of China's balance of payments accounts. Monthly exchange rate volatility is defined as the standard deviation of the first differences in the natural logarithm of the daily exchange rates over a month. The reader is referred to the Appendix to this chapter for details of the analysis.

As explained in Chapter 2, China has a fear of floating due to the concern over capital outflows when the exchange rate is expected to depreciate. This fear of exchange rate instability causes policy swings between looser capital controls when the market exchange rate is relatively stable, but tighter capital controls when the market exchange rate shows signs of instability due to expectations of depreciation of the RMB. This is demonstrated in the aftermath of the central parity reform on 11 August 2015, when the authority tightened capital controls in the face of a market expectation of depreciation of the RMB. This type of policy swing can be explained by the open-economy trilemma: in order to maintain monetary autonomy, it is necessary to tighten capital controls so as to stabilize the exchange rate when it is relatively volatile; but it is not a problem to loosen capital controls when the exchange rate is relatively less volatile.

In Chapter 4, we documented the various schemes of relaxing capital controls in China over time. Below is a timeline of the major events.

5.4 TIMELINE IN RELAXING CAPITAL CONTROLS IN CHINA

On 1 December 1996, China accepted the obligations of Article VIII of the IMF Articles of Agreement on current account convertibility.

Starting from 2001, prompted by the occurrence of the Asian Financial Crisis, China entered into bilateral currency swap agreements with a number of countries, including Thailand, Japan, South Korea, and Malaysia.

In 2002, the Qualified Foreign Institutional Investor (QFII) scheme was introduced.

In October 2003, China initiated the reform of an improvement in the RMB exchange rate regime and a gradual implementation of RMB financial/capital account convertibility at the third plenary session of the 16th Central Committee of the Communist Party of China.

In February 2004, Bank of China (Hong Kong) (BOCHK), the sole clearing bank for offshore RMB business in Hong Kong, began to offer RMB clearing services in relation to deposits, exchange, remittance, and bank card to some participating banks in Hong Kong.

In October 2005, the first "panda bonds" (i.e., RMB-denominated bonds issued onshore by a non-Chinese entity) were issued, making it the first time international institutions were allowed to issue onshore debt instruments denominated in RMB.

In 2006, the Qualified Domestic Institutional Investor (QDII) scheme was introduced.

In 2007, the first dim sum bond, a bond issued outside of Mainland China but denominated in RMB, was issued in Hong Kong.

Starting from 2009, with a view to internationalizing the RMB, China entered into bilateral currency swap agreements with monetary authorities in Hong Kong and other regions and countries.

On 6 July 2009, the pilot scheme for RMB cross-border trade settlement was jointly launched by authorities in the Mainland of China and Hong Kong, under which the Mainland designated enterprises in Shanghai, Guangzhou, Shenzhen, Dongguan, and Zhuhai to be allowed to use RMB as the settlement currency when trading with designated non-Mainland enterprises in Hong Kong, Macau, and ASEAN member countries.

In January 2011, approved Mainland companies were allowed to conduct outward direct investment (ODI) in RMB.

In 2011, the RMB Qualified Foreign Institutional Investor (RQFII) scheme was introduced.

In 2014, Shanghai–Hong Kong Stock Connect was introduced.

In 2014, the Chinese government officially announced pushing for the internationalization of the RMB

On 1 October 2016, the RMB was included in the basket of currencies that constitute the SDR

In 2016, Shenzhen–Hong Kong Stock Connect was introduced.

In 2017, Bond Connect was introduced.

On 1 May 2018, the daily quotas for the Northbound and Southbound investments for both Shanghai–Hong Kong and Shenzhen–Hong Kong Stock Connects were quadrupled.

On 17 June 2019, Shanghai–London Stock Connect was launched.

On 25 September 2020, SAFE announced that QFII and RQFII would be combined on 1 November 2020 and more investment options would be offered, as the advantage of these programs has been eroded by the success of the Shanghai–Hong Kong and Shenzhen–Hong Kong Stock Connects as well as the Bond Connect programs.

One piece of encouraging news about the capital account opening of China is that foreign ownership of Chinese stocks and bonds has accelerated in recent years. According to Lardy and Huang (2020), "A steady increase in foreign ownership of Chinese stocks and bonds reflects China's deepening integration into global financial markets. At the end of 2013, foreign owners held a total of RMB 744 billion of these assets. By the end of the first quarter of 2020, this figure had grown to RMB 4.2 trillion."

5.5   WHY PUSH FOR RMB INTERNATIONALIZATION NOW?

It is widely recognized among economists that financial market liberalization should precede capital account liberalization, as an economy with a stronger financial system can better deal with the sudden reversal of short-term capital flows than one with a weak financial system. The banks in the former system would have better risk management, are more well-regulated (such as having a higher capital requirement), have better deposit insurance, and the country would also have a better set of bankruptcy laws to deal with failing firms in a fair way. Since China does not have a very strong financial system, it should be very cautious when opening the capital account. Given that there are so many risks associated with capital account liberalization at this stage of China's development, why does the Chinese government still push for the internationalization of the RMB? The answer to this question is, first, that internationalization of the RMB is a popular goal among the Chinese people, as they feel that a great country like China should have a great currency that is recognized internationally for trade and investment. A second answer to this question is a bit more subtle. It is that the external commitment necessary for gaining international recognition serves as a pressure to force domestic reforms. The application of this principle to the present case is that internationalization of RMB requires capital account liberalization, which in turn puts pressure on financial sector reforms (*daobi*). In the current context, it means that offering a commitment to foreign countries or seeking external recognition creates a pressure that comes back to force domestic reform. People who buy into this second motivation are in fact more interested in financial sector reform than internationalization of RMB. According to this line of thinking, financial market reform in China is met with so much resistance by the vested interests that capital account liberalization is a necessary tool to force the reform. The mechanism by which this occurs is that capital account opening leads to foreign competition that disciplines the domestic banks and stimulates efficiency improvement, technology spillovers from foreign firms and strategic partners who emphasize the profit motive. The third reason, as we have alluded to before, is that China desires to be independent from foreign countries and the associated institutions such as the United States, the USD-based IMS, and the US-dominated international payment system. We shall leave the detailed discussion about the international payment system to Chapter 7.

Why is financial sector liberalization so important at this juncture? This is because China has arrived at a stage of development where capital misallocation becomes a core issue that prevents the sustenance of further, fast economic growth, and capital misallocation is caused by an inefficient financial system that is not sufficiently market-oriented. The lending rate is kept below the market rate, and there is credit rationing, in favor of SOEs. The preferential access of SOEs to capital is at the expense of the mostly privately owned small and medium-sized enterprises, which have become the main driver of economic growth and innovation at the current stage of development. Under financial repression, the suppressed deposit rate and the guaranteed profits of the large state-owned banks hurt the SMEs, as banks do not have the incentives to take the risk to lend to them by charging them higher interest rates so as to compensate for their higher risks compared with SOEs or larger private companies.

Historically, using *daobi* to force domestic reform has been very common in China. I can give a couple of examples. First, in order to join the WTO, a country has to commit to a schedule of tariff bindings (i.e., committing to a tariff rate no higher than a certain level for each sector), offer "most-favored nation" status to all other member countries of the WTO (i.e., giving the same treatment to all foreign countries), phase out import quota and export subsidies, and give "national treatment" to all members of the WTO (i.e., committing to giving foreign companies the same treatment as domestic firms). China's accession to the WTO in 2001 had the effect of speeding up domestic industrial enterprise reform by allowing foreign goods to be imported into China subjected to very low trade barriers. Such foreign competition served to discipline domestic firms and forced them to become more efficient and innovative in order to survive.

The second example of *daobi* is that, in order for the RMB to be included in the currency basket that constituted the SDR, the RMB had to be "freely usable" and its exchange rate had to be "market-determined." To achieve this goal, China gradually liberalized its capital account, encouraged RMB trade settlement, opened the domestic capital market to foreign investors, and let the RMB exchange rate move more freely according to market forces. On 1 October 2016, the RMB was officially included in the SDR basket. The weights of the five currencies in the SDR basket are USD 41.7 percent, euro 30.9 percent, Chinese yuan 10.9 percent, Japanese yen 8.3 percent, and pounds sterling 8.1 percent. The former governor of PBC, Zhou Xiaochuan, frequently cited the inclusion of the RMB into the SDR basket as an achievement of China though by itself inclusion of the RMB in the basket does not make the RMB a more international currency in any significant way. The SDR is a fictitious currency that is used to lend to member countries of the IMF to ease temporary balance of payments problems. Being included in the SDR basket does not mean that the RMB would be used more often in international commerce. However, the road leading to RMB inclusion in the basket had forced China to liberalize the financial market and the capital account as China had to take measures to satisfy the "freely usable" criterion of the IMF.

Using *daobi* to force domestic financial sector reform must be carried out with caution, however, as a weak financial system cannot deal with the large-scale short-term capital movements that might come with too much opening of the capital account before the financial system is strong enough. The capital account and the financial system should be liberalized in tandem, but in a gradual and interactive fashion so as to exploit the synergy between the two kinds of liberalization. In fact, this is more or less what Zhou Xiaochuan, the former governor of the PBC, suggested in an interview in October 2017 with *Cai Jing*, a Chinese online business magazine:

> 对外开放、汇率制度改革、减少外汇管制要整体推进，不管各自速度如何，整个大方向是要往前的。这就需要注意时间窗口，有些改革遇到了合适的时间窗口就可以加速推进，有些改革没有时间窗口就可能稍微缓一些

> Opening to foreign countries, exchange rate system reform and reduction of capital controls should be pushed forward collectively. Regardless of the speed of each of these three individual reform items, the overall direction is for all three of them to move forward. In order to implement this approach, one has to pay attention to the windows of opportunity. When a window of opportunity arrives for an item of reform to be pushed forward, it can be accelerated, while [the] other [two] reform items can be allowed to go more slowly if their windows of opportunity have not yet arrived.

RMB internationalization can conceivably serve as a catalyst for this strategy of reform.

The rationale behind the gradualist approach is that there is a positive feedback between capital account liberalization and financial liberalization: a more open capital account forces the financial sector to be more liberalized, while a more liberalized financial sector in turn makes further capital account liberalization feasible. In addition, capital account liberalization cannot be too much ahead of financial sector liberalization; otherwise, the financial system cannot withstand the interest rate and exchange rate movements caused by short-term capital flows. This explains why the two types of reforms should be carried in tandem in a gradual and interactive fashion.

How does capital account opening force financial sector liberalization? The mechanism is as follows. Capital account liberalization means that the currency has to be largely convertible in the capital account, which requires a sufficiently high degree of capital mobility, which requires domestic interest rates to be market-determined, which requires the banking system to be competitive and robust, which requires that (1) the banking system must have a set of safeguards similar to the ones established in the developed countries; (2) commercial banks should not be required to carry out policy lending to SOEs. The set of safeguards normally includes deposit insurance, reserve requirements, capital requirements and asset restrictions, bank examination, the central bank serving as the lender of last resort, and possibly a set of macro-prudential measures to control the flows of short-term capital.

How does a more liberalized financial sector make further capital account liberalization feasible? This is simply because a more robust financial system can better withstand the effects caused by the flows of short-term capital such as interest rates movement and exchange rate volatility.

Thus, with the above two effects feeding on each other, the capital account becomes more open gradually and the financial market becomes more developed gradually, which creates the conditions for the RMB to become more internationalized.

Because of the open-economy trilemma, as China opens the capital account, it must tolerate higher exchange rate volatility if it wants to retain monetary autonomy. This means that there has to be a change in the policy to allow the exchange rate to be more flexible. This should include allowing the market to play a large role as well as having less intervention by the central bank. Alternatively, in case the authority wants to maintain a certain degree of exchange rate stability, it may have to weigh whether it wants to sacrifice some monetary autonomy or use discretionary measures to limit capital flows. The latter will hurt RMB internationalization.

5.6 CONCLUSION

There are net gains from capital account opening for China due to intertemporal trade, diversification of portfolio, and dynamic gains from trade through opening the financial market to foreign participation and competition and allowing domestic residents to invest abroad. China's capital account is too closed, and it is tip-toeing towards gradual opening. As China opens its capital account, it must live with a more volatile exchange rate, due to the open-economy trilemma. The financial sector should get prepared for exchange rate volatility by establishing a robust banking and financial system. Thus, financial sector reform should in principle precede capital account liberalization. However, the special circumstances of China justifies undertaking financial sector liberalization and capital account liberalization in tandem in a gradual, interactive fashion, as suggested by the former governor of the PBC. Earlier in this chapter, I ask the question: Is capital account opening beneficial to China for its own sake, regardless of the push for RMB internationalization? My answer is yes. The capital account of China is too closed and needs to be opened up, but it needs to be done in conjunction with further financial development. Gradual capital account opening in tandem with gradual reform of the financial sector so as to exploit the synergy between the two would be beneficial to the development of the Chinese economy, regardless of the push for RMB internationalization.

Where do all these discussions about capital account opening leave us? The answer is that the capital account should be further opened up (in tandem with financial sector liberalization), but there should be an optimal degree of capital account liberalization for China, and that optimal level should increase over time as the financial market becomes more mature. Moreover, even when the financial market becomes more mature, the capital account should not be too open. Short-term capital movements should still be controlled. However, controls of short-term capital flows or any other forms of capital controls should be rules-based rather than discretion-based, and both the rules and their implementation should be transparent so that market participants can formulate their investment plans under a fair set of laws and rules. For example, short-term capital inflows/outflows can be controlled by a "Tobin tax" (see Tobin 1982) that is established by law rather than by administrative measures, relatively stable over time, openly announced, and openly enforced.

The recent history of China's capital account liberalization, however, has revealed a recurring problem: In every step of capital account opening, the authority would introduce some accompanying conditions that would leave room for some discretionary administrative intervention when they feel that there is a need. As a result of this approach, capital mobility is not governed by rules but by discretion. The discretion also breeds corruption. This lack of commitment to capital mobility hurts capital account liberalization. One possible motivation for this half-hearted approach to capital account opening is that the authority is concerned with exchange rate volatility. The open-economy trilemma dictates that as long as the authority is too concerned about exchange rate stability, it is hard for them to discard discretionary capital control measures. The consequence is that, when the market exchange rate is relatively stable, capital controls becomes looser, but when the market exchange rate shows signs of instability, the controls becomes tighter. Because of its uncertainty, these kinds of policy swings impede RMB internationalization.

In order to overcome the lack of commitment to capital mobility, some external force may be helpful. To the extent that capital account opening and financial market reforms are to be furthered in China at the current stage of its development, RMB internationalization can facilitate both reforms because the external commitments required for RMB internationalization can create a pressure that can help to push forward both reforms.

APPENDIX TO CHAPTER 5 EVIDENCE FOR OPEN-
ECONOMY TRILEMMA IN CHINA

WITHOUT MOVING AVERAGE ADJUSTMENT

See Figure Appendix 5.1.

Table Appendix 5.1 *Testing the trilemma: the results without moving average adjustment*

Correlation coefficient	No time lag	1-Period lag	2-Period lag
2010M01–2018M06	0.3069	0.2968	0.3435
p-value	0.0017***	0.0026***	0.0005***

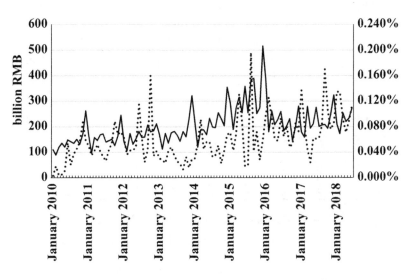

—— **Gross capital flow (left-hand scale)**

······ **Exchange rate volatility (right-hand scale)**

FIGURE APPENDIX 5.1 Monthly gross capital flow and exchange rate volatility.

3-MONTH MOVING AVERAGE

See Figure Appendix 5.2.

Table Appendix 5.2 *Testing the trilemma: the results with 3-month moving average*

Correlation coefficient	No time lag	1-Period lag	2-Period lag
2010M01–2018M06	0.4656	0.4831	0.5063
p-value	0.0000***	0.0000***	0.0000***

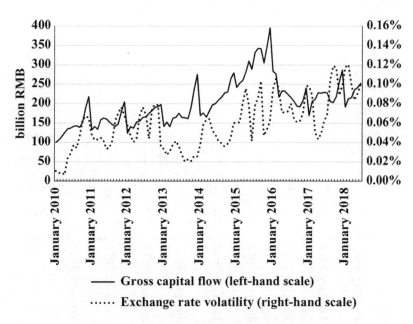

FIGURE APPENDIX 5.2 Monthly gross capital flow and exchange rate volatility (3-month moving average).

5-MONTH MOVING AVERAGE

See Figure Appendix 5.3.

Table Appendix 5.3 *Testing the trilemma: the results with 5-month moving average*

Correlation coefficient	No time lag	1-Period lag	2-Period lag
2010M01–2018M06	0.4734	0.5006	0.5226
p-value	0.0000***	0.0000***	0.0000***

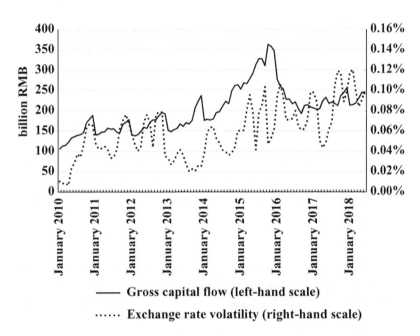

—— Gross capital flow (left-hand scale)

······ Exchange rate volatility (right-hand scale)

FIGURE APPENDIX 5.3 Monthly gross capital flow and exchange rate volatility (5-month moving average).

DEFINITIONS OF VARIABLES

Capital mobility: The sum of the absolute change in assets and absolute change in liabilities over a month in the financial account (by IMF's definition) of the balance of payments accounts of China. *Exchange rate volatility*: The standard deviation of the first differences in the natural logarithm of daily exchange rates over a month.

DEFINITION OF "LAG"

We interpret the "lagged-correlation" as the "correlation between capital mobility and lagged exchange rate volatility." Hence, in the above tables: "1-period lag" shows the correlation coefficient between the gross capital flow in each month and the exchange rate volatility in the later month (e.g., gross capital flow in 2010M1 with exchange rate volatility in 2010M2); "2-period lag" shows the correlation coefficient between the gross capital flow in each month and the exchange rate volatility two months later (e.g., gross capital flow in 2010M1 with exchange rate volatility in 2010M3).

INTERPRETATION OF THE RESULTS

From the above tables, it is clear that capital mobility is very significantly correlated with exchange rate volatility of the same period, as well as one period later and two periods later. The correlation coefficient in each case is significantly different from zero (the p-values are all less than 0.01). We interpret the result as supporting evidence of the existence of the open-economy trilemma in China.

NOTES TO CHAPTER 5

1 According to the link "data description" under the "Trilemma Indexes" in http://web.pdx.edu/~ito/trilemma_indexes.htm (which is linked to the file "Notes on the Trilemma Measures"), the Chinn–Ito index is normalized between zero and one.

2 See IMF Annual Report on Exchange Arrangements and Exchange Restrictions (AREAER) (2016) (www.imf.org/en/Publications/Annual-Report-on-Exchange-Arrangements-and-Exchange-Restrictions/Issues/2017/01/25/Annual-Report-on-Exchange-Arrangements-and-Exchange-Restrictions-2016-43741).

3 He and Luk (2017) point out that FX reserves accounted for more than two-thirds of China's foreign assets as of 2011. Although that proportion has fallen rapidly to about 41 percent in 2018, it is still very high.

4 A vehicle currency is defined as a currency used for invoicing trade when the issuing country is not one of the trading partners.

5 Positive (negative) externalities are the benefits (costs) spilled over to the rest of society as a person takes a certain action.

6 See, for example, Ma, Jun and Xu Jiangang《人民幣走出國門之路》商務印書館 2012 (in Chinese).

7 See, for example, Yu 2012.

8 There is a risk premium as different currency deposits (or government bonds) carry different default risk. For example, it is generally true that the default risk for the deposits or government bonds of a more developed country is lower than that of a less-developed country. There is a liquidity premium because different currencies have different liquidity. For example, it is often argued that the USD is the most liquid of currencies because it is easy to find people willing to trade other currencies for the USD. The greater liquidity of the USD means that people are more willing to hold the dollar even if a time deposit (or government bond) denominated in dollar yields a lower expected rate of return than that denominated in another currency, such as Indonesian rupiah. For the purpose of our current discussion, the risk-cum-liquidity premium can be assumed to be constant.

9 By assuming that foreign exchange risk (i.e., the volatility of the exchange rate) does not play any role in the holding of foreign currencies, we implicitly assume that the "speculative motive" for holding foreign currencies is by far more important than the "hedging motive," as speculators are assumed to be risk-neutral (i.e., they only care about the expected value and not the variance of the exchange rate), while the hedgers are risk-averse (i.e., they dislike exchange rate volatility). There are possibly other factors that can lead to deviation from the uncovered interest parity condition. For example, Sarno, Valente, and Leon (2006) argue that there can be deviation from uncovered interest parity if the Sharpe ratio, which measures the excess return per unit of risk, is too small, as there is not enough incentive for arbitrage to take place. If the Sharpe ratio is large enough, then arbitrage begins to occur, and the uncovered interest parity condition should be able to explain the reality better. So, the Sharpe ratio is like inverse transaction costs. We abstract from this factor by assuming that transaction costs are sufficiently small.

10 This equation is an approximation of the following more accurate equation: $1 + R = (1 + R^*)(1 + \hat{E}^e)(1 + \rho)$ when R, R^*, $\hat{E}^e$, and ρ are all small (e.g., less than 10 percent).

6   The Importance of Financial Sector Reform

The financial market is probably the most important market of an economy, as it is responsible for the allocation of capital, which has a first order effect on the economic efficiency of the entire economy. The function of the financial market is for the allocation of savings from the saving-surplus economic units efficiently to the final users, who are the saving-deficit economic units, either for investment in real assets (also called capital formation) or for consumption. The saving-surplus units are usually households, while the final users are usually firms (though they can be households, for example, in the case of mortgages), who use the funds for capital formation. The saving-surplus units are the ultimate lenders and the final users are the ultimate borrowers. The financial market consists of financial intermediaries that purchase direct claims from the ultimate borrowers and sell indirect claims to the ultimate lenders. By transforming the direct claims into indirect claims, the financial intermediaries provide many services to society. For example, they lower the transaction costs between the ultimate borrowers and the ultimate lenders, provide information to the ultimate lenders, transform the short-term or small-denomination lending from the ultimate lenders, who are usually households, into long-term or large-denomination loans to the ultimate borrowers, who are usually firms. Different financial intermediaries therefore provide different kinds of financial products to suit the needs of different types of ultimate lenders and ultimate borrowers. The financial intermediaries include such institutions as commercial banks, investment banks, insurance companies, mutual funds, pension funds, and other asset management companies. Financial markets can be classified according to maturity: the money market (short-term financial instruments – from overnight to, say, one year) and the capital market (long-term financial instruments – more than, say, one year). The money market is mainly used to bridge short-term needs that arise because of uncertainties. The capital market, because of the long term of maturity of the products, is mainly used for borrowing for investment in real assets (i.e., capital formation). The financial market includes the markets for debt instruments (such as bonds and bank deposits, which carry fixed-interest payments regardless of the financial circumstances of the firms) and equity instruments (such as stocks, which carry payments that depend on the financial circumstances of the firms).

As a financial market matures, more financial products would be developed, providing more variety in terms of expected rate of return, risk, term to maturity, and liquidity. Moreover, more types of financial institutions would emerge as the financial market develops. Thus, the more mature is a financial market, the more variety of financial products and more types of financial institutions there are. They would in turn lead to larger quantities of aggregate savings and aggregate capital formation of the economy, and more efficient allocation of capital from the savers to the final users. Therefore, a more mature financial market would be broader (have a larger variety of financial assets), deeper (have a larger quantity of transactions in each type of financial asset), and more liquid (it is easier to convert each financial asset into cash because it is easier to find buyers). Furthermore, a well-developed financial market should always provide incentives for firms to carry out continual innovations, giving birth to both new financial products and new financial intermediaries to cater to the evolving needs of the savers and borrowers. These continual innovations are essential for the maintenance of the efficiency of the financial market in allocating resources. By and large, given adequate regulations, the freer is a financial market, the more efficient it is in allocating resources at any point in time (this is called static efficiency) and in providing incentives for new financial products and new financial institutions to emerge so as to cater to the evolving needs of society (this is called dynamic efficiency). The empirical literature has provided rather convincing evidence about the positive impact of financial development to economic growth (see, for example, King and Levine 1993).

To understand China's current level of financial development, we must put the state of the Chinese financial market in historical perspective. First, China is still a developing country, meaning that its development started later than the more developed countries. Second, since the Communist Party took over the governance of the country, from 1949 to 1978, the country was essentially under a centrally planned system, with state-owned enterprises dominating the economy. The Marxist–Leninist ideology has a bias against the development of the financial sector. Third, financial development, more than the development of any other markets in the economy, hinges on contract enforcement, the rule of law, an independent judiciary, free flow of information, a free market, and a government with lots of checks and balances, just to name a few things. Being a developing country with 30 years of history of a centrally planned economy, China carries a heavy historical baggage with regard to financial development. For these reasons, China's financial markets were very underdeveloped and financial development was very slow in the first 40 years of the People's Republic. For example, the Shanghai Stock Exchange and Shenzhen Stock Exchange were established only in 1990, while the modern Tokyo Stock Exchange was reopened in 1949 after World War II. The Chinese Interbank Bond Market (CIBM) was started by the PBC only in 1997, and no important development occurred until 2015, while the Japanese bond market began to take off in around the mid-1980s. In 1980, the People's Insurance Company of China resumed its business, becoming the first operating insurer after more than 20 years of business suspension due to domestic political struggle. The company had been operating as a subsidiary of the People's Bank of China until 1984 when it gained independence as a state-owned company, but still reported to the PBC.

What is China's level of financial development? To answer this question, we can refer to the IMF Financial Development Index of

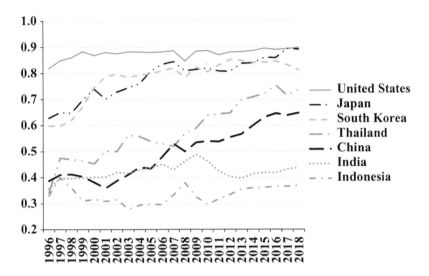

FIGURE 6.1 IMF Financial Development Index, 1996–2018.
Source: IMF Financial Development Index Database (http://data.imf.org/?sk=
F8032E80-B36C-43B1-AC26-493C5B1CD33B)

various countries in the period 1996–2018 shown in Figure 6.1. It
compares the financial development of China with those of other
countries. It can be seen that China's financial development as of
2017 was below those of the United States, Japan, and even
Thailand, although it was above those of India and Indonesia. This is
what we would expect, given what we discuss above about the history
of China. The index takes into account the development of financial
institutions and financial markets. Financial institutions include
banks, insurance companies, mutual funds, and pension funds.
Financial markets include the stock and bond markets. According to
the International Monetary Fund, which constructs the IMF Financial
Development Index, financial development is defined as "a combination of depth (size and liquidity of markets), access (ability of individuals and companies to access financial services), and efficiency
(ability of institutions to provide financial services at low cost and
with sustainable revenues, and the level of activity of capital
markets)" of the financial institutions and the financial markets.

Table 6.1 *Variables used to calculate the financial development index*

Category	Indicator
Financial Institutions	
Depth	Private sector credit to GDP
	Pension fund assets to GDP
	Mutual fund assets to GDP
	Insurance premiums, life and non-life to GDP
Access	Bank branches per 100,000 adults
	ATMs per 100,000 adults
Efficiency	Net interest margin
	Lending-deposit spread
	Non-interest income to total income
	Overhead costs to total assets
	Return on assets
	Return on equity
Financial Markets	
Depth	Stock market capitalization to GDP
	Stocks traded to GDP
	International debt securities of government to GDP
	Total debt securities of financial corporations to GDP
	Total debt securities of nonfinancial corporations to GDP
Access	Percent of market capitalization outside of top ten largest companies
	Total number of issuers of debt (domestic and external, nonfinancial and financial corporations)
Efficiency	Stock market turnover ratio (stocks traded to capitalization)

Source: Svirydzenka (2016).

This broad multidimensional approach to defining financial development follows the matrix of financial system characteristics developed by Čihák, Demirgüç-Kunt, Feyen, and Levine (2012). Thus, the index is rather comprehensive in its coverage.[1] Table 6.1 gives a more detailed description of the variables used to calculate the sub-indexes of the development of financial institutions and financial markets, which are then aggregated to form the financial development index.

6.1 WHY IS FINANCIAL DEVELOPMENT NECESSARY FOR RMB INTERNATIONALIZATION?

Financial development in China would lead to a broader, deeper, and more liquid financial market. Just like a more well-developed domestic financial market would increase the volume of domestic financial transactions intermediated through the financial institutions in the domestic economy, a more well-developed international financial market in China would increase the volume of financial flows into and out of China. Since these financial flows involve conversion from RMB into foreign currencies or from foreign currencies into RMB, the foreign exchange turnover share of the RMB would increase. As there is more buying and selling of RMB in the foreign exchange market, it becomes easier (cheaper, and faster) to find buyers or sellers of RMB. This in turn increases the liquidity of the RMB in the foreign exchange market, lowering the transaction costs and increasing the convenience of using RMB. The more people use the RMB, the easier it is to find buyers and sellers of it, which in turn leads to more people using the RMB, which makes it even easier to find buyers and sellers of it. Thus, there is a positive feedback (or snowballing) effect. This is called the "network externalities" effect in economics. It is also called thick market externalities in the literature on invoicing currency in international trade. It should be noted that in order for Chinese financial development to be effective in increasing the thick market externalities of the RMB, the capital account convertibility of the currency has to increase as well. Otherwise, Chinese financial assets cannot be easily bought and sold by foreigners, and money cannot be easily moved in and out of China, which means that the increase in volume of transactions of RMB and the ease of conversion into and out of the RMB in the foreign exchange market would be constrained by the lack of capital mobility. Thus, financial market development and capital account liberalization are complementary to each other in facilitating the internationalization of the RMB.

The financial market consists of many players. They include commercial banks, investment banks, insurance companies, mutual funds, pension funds, other asset management companies, and so on. Broadly speaking, the means through which economic units can borrow are loans and bonds. Loans are primarily intermediated through the banking system. Bonds are intermediated through the bond market. In developing countries, the bond market is usually not very well developed. Moreover, the stock market is often plagued with the problem of insider trading, poor corporate governance issues, and even government intervention. These countries primarily rely on the banking system for the allocation of capital in the economy. However, for further development of the financial market, a country must develop the bond market and a well-functioning stock market. Only when the bond market and stock market are well developed will they provide a large variety of financial products to both domestic and foreign investors. Only when these markets are free, efficient, and well-regulated and contracts are strongly enforced will large numbers of investors be willing to invest large amounts of money in the financial products. Only then will the financial markets be sufficiently broad, deep, and liquid to attract foreigners to own RMB-denominated assets in large amounts and support the RMB as a truly international currency.

In the rest of this chapter, I shall discuss the banking system of China, its financial repression, the risks of financial sector liberalization, the importance of financial regulations, the bond market, the stock market, and the opening of the financial markets to foreigners in recent years. I shall discuss what has been achieved and what still need to be done. I shall also explain why financial sector reform is so difficult in China.

6.2 THE BANKING SYSTEM OF CHINA AND FINANCIAL REPRESSION

The banking system, which was (and still is) largely controlled by the state, was an important financial institution in the development of China, especially in its initial stage of development. Under this system, deposit rates are kept artificially low so as to channel cheap

credit to state-owned enterprises for investment. In a country that was
short of capital in its early stage of development, this might have been
an economically beneficial policy. This is in fact a classic example of
financial repression (McKinnon 1973: 68–69). The rationale is that it
can deliver faster industrialization and thus faster economic growth,
on which the government puts a lot of weight. The phenomenon of
financial repression did not just take place in socialist countries like
China, but also in non-socialist countries like South Korea in its early
stage of development. In the case of China, financial repression is
intimately related to channeling cheap credit to state-owned
enterprises, which occupy a special status in the national economy.
The reason they are special is that besides serving economic functions, state-owned enterprises also serve social and even political
functions. Thus, it is harder for China to phase out financial
repression than it is for a non-socialist country.

However, at its later stage of development, financial repression
in China has become inefficient in allocating resources, both statically
and dynamically. It distorts the interest rate in the financial market.
Credit allocation favors state-owned enterprises at the expense of non-
state-owned enterprises. Thus, it leads to misallocation of capital.
There are no significant private financial firms or banks to challenge
the large state-owned banks and financial institutions. Because of the
lack of competition, the financial sector is quite inefficient. Without a
well-functioning and economically efficient financial system, a deep,
broad, and liquid financial market cannot be developed. This is
unfavorable to RMB internationalization. At the same time, because
credit is available at artificially low interest rates, many state-owned
enterprises lack the incentives to attain the best international standards. Thus, the banking sector and the state-owned sector need to be
reformed in tandem. However, the adverse social and political impacts
of phasing out the inefficient state-owned enterprises are serious obstacles to interest rate and banking sector reforms. Nonetheless, despite
the obstacles, financial sector reform continues to be carried out, as
the government realizes that there is no choice but to reform if high

growth is to be maintained. The measures include interest rate reform, continuing the development of an onshore bond market, and gradually allowing foreign financial institutions to operate onshore with majority ownership.

Financial repression in the banking sector includes interest rates controls, control of credit allocation, state ownership of major banks, and entry barriers. Interest rate control is the first and most important feature of financial repression. It is a legacy of the centrally planned economy before 1978. It continued after the reform and opening policy, which started in 1978. In the first stage of interest rate control after the establishment of the People's Republic, which stretched from 1949 to 1998, banks were required strictly to follow the benchmark deposit and lending rates set by the PBC. After 1998, in addition to setting a benchmark lending rate, a ceiling and a floor in the lending rate were set. They were gradually relaxed, until the ceiling was removed in 2004 and the floor was removed in 2013. After 1998, in addition to setting a benchmark deposit rate, a ceiling and a floor on the deposit rate were also set. They were gradually relaxed, until the floor was removed in 2004 and the ceiling removed in 2015. However, the benchmark lending and deposit rates have not been removed as of the time of writing (August 2020), although there was a reform in August 2019 to make the lending rates more market-driven, by requiring all loans to reference the more market-driven Loan Prime Rate (LPR) instead of the benchmark lending rate, which changes slowly with market condition. The market-based LPR reform will be discussed in more detail later in this chapter. However, today, self-discipline among the banks in the determination of deposit rates still dominates the market. In short, interest rates are still, to a large extent, not market-determined.

The dominance of state-ownership and existence of high entry barriers are the second feature of the financial repression. The largest four banks (the "Big Four") are all state-owned. They are Industrial and Commercial Bank of China (ICBC), Bank of China (BOC), China Construction Bank (CCB), and Agricultural Bank of China (ABC). By

December 2017, the "Big Four" alone owned about 35 percent of the total assets of the banking sector and held about 40 percent of the total deposits of the country.[2]

The control of credit allocation to favor SOEs is the third feature of the financial repression. For example, in 2012, although the share of SOEs (enterprises with the state holding controlling shares) in the value-added of the economy was only about 35 percent, they obtained 48 percent of bank credits. In fact, this percentage did not fall over time. In 2016, SOEs obtained 54 percent of bank credits.[3]

Generally, financial repression is a phenomenon that certain groups of people or firms in an economy are severely disadvantaged in borrowing in the national credit market. It is often caused by government intervention in the financial market to allocate capital so as to achieve certain economic or non-economic objectives. The policies can include interest rates restrictions, directed lending, high reserve requirements on bank deposits, and restrictions on capital movements. This is often seen along with a tight connection between government and banks, e.g., state-own banks. Financial repression widely exists in developing and transition economies (McKinnon 1973: 68–69). One consequence of financial repression is the creation of a privileged sector and an unprivileged sector with the former having access to cheap credits and the latter being rationed out (Lu and Yao 2009).

Financially repressive policies were used to facilitate the development of heavy industries under the centrally planned economy during 1949–1978, the first 30 years of the People's Republic. Basically, limited investment opportunities and strict restriction of capital outflows incentivized consumers to deposit savings at banks, which are state-owned. Deposits, paid at low interest rates, were then lent, at low interest rates, to state-owned entities. The official (benchmark) deposit rates and lending rates had been kept consistently lower than the market-determined levels. This led to credit rationing in the banking sector, in which SOEs are given priority and non-state enterprises were disadvantaged in the credit market. After the reform and opening policy was adopted in 1978, the policy continued, and it had been mainly used to channel easy credits to SOEs.

Policies that lead to financial repression are often regarded as inefficient because of the distortion of the financial market. However, some economists argue that government intervention in the financial system, such as credit rationing, may in fact be welfare-improving because there are significant market failures in the financial market due to imperfect information (Stiglitz and Weiss 1981; Stiglitz 1994). On the other hand, one can argue that this market failure due to information imperfection might diminish as the country develops so that the market distortion becomes a dominant factor instead. Thus, the effect of policies leading to financial repression on welfare or growth might be non-monotonic with respect to the stage of development in the sense that they might be beneficial when the country is relatively underdeveloped, but they turned into a stumbling block as the country became more developed. This is exactly what Huang and Wang (2011) have found. They studied the first three decades of China's economic development since its reform and opening policy started in 1978. They found that government intervention in the financial system had contributed to the fast growth of China in the first two decades due to the prudent and gradual approach to liberalization, but its net impact turned negative in the 2000s. Apparently, there are positive and negative impacts of government intervention in the financial market, and the positive effect can outweigh the negative one when the country is less developed, but then the reverse is true when the country becomes more developed. The positive effect arises from the government intervention to correct the market failure due to imperfect information in the financial market. The negative effect arises from the distortion of market prices (interest rates) and the erection of entry barriers in the banking sector that prevent competition. The net impact depends on which effect dominates.

When the People's Republic of China was founded in 1949, it was an extremely poor country. A combination of political, ideological, and economic factors led the country to adopt a heavy-industry-oriented development strategy. However, heavy industries were capital-intensive industries, which fundamentally conflicted with China's economic reality, as the country was richly endowed with labor but scarcely endowed with capital and therefore it had a comparative advantage in labor-intensive industries such as textiles. In an open and competitive market economy, the capital-intensive industries were not profitable in China and therefore not viable. The government was thus faced with the question of how to mobilize resources to develop such economically non-viable industries.

As a result of such an "import-substitution" strategy, measures were taken to allocate resources such that the development of heavy industries would be encouraged, which meant reducing the cost of capital for heavy industries as well as improving the government's ability in resource allocation. Thus, a macro-policy environment that suppressed the functioning of the market and artificially distorted the relative prices of factor inputs and goods and services was created. In the financial market, there were two main policies: low interest rates and an overvalued exchange rate.[4]

(1) A low interest rate policy

During the early days after the establishment of the People's Republic, the government adopted a low interest rate policy so as to channel funds into the heavy-industrial sector, which was almost totally state-owned. Historical figures have shown that the *monthly rate* of industrial credit was rapidly lowered within a very short period of time after 1950. At the end of July 1950, the monthly rate for loans to SOEs was first adjusted from 3 percent to 2 percent, and was further lowered to 1.5 percent–1.6 percent by April 1951, to 0.6 percent–0.9 percent by January 1953, and to 0.46 percent in 1954, after which the rate was maintained constant until 1960, when it was raised to 0.6 percent in June 1960. However, in August 1971, it was again reduced to around 0.42 percent.[5]

(2) An overvalued exchange rate policy.

In order to facilitate the development of capital-intensive heavy industries that required critical imported machinery and equipment, the Chinese government intervened in the foreign exchange market during the 1950s, artificially overvaluing the exchange rate. An overvalued exchange rate enabled domestic firms to purchase imported equipment at lower prices.

The exchange rate of the RMB against the dollar was RMB 4.2 per USD in March 1950, when the National Finance Conference opened, and was rapidly lowered 15 times during the following 14 months, until it became RMB 2.23 per USD in May 1951. From 1952 to 1972, however, the exchange rate of the RMB was no longer listed. Instead, it was maintained at an overvalued level by internal control of the government. From 1 March 1955 to December 1971, the exchange rate was maintained at RMB 2.46 per USD. In December 1978, the exchange rate of the RMB changed following the depreciation of the USD. In 1978, the exchange rate became around RMB 1.72 per USD.

After reform and opening started in 1978, financially repressive polices continued to be used. Their function was mainly to favor SOEs, which serve not only economic functions but also social and political ones. Under these policies, the Chinese people are forced to keep a high savings rate in the face of a weak social safety net and limited investment alternatives, both domestic and foreign. Their money is thus channeled to the banking system, which is dominated by state-owned banks (SOBs). Subject to political pressure, SOBs have to subsidize SOEs and local government. To protect SOBs' balance sheets from losses on uneconomic loans, the PBC continued to maintain low interest rates.[6]

6.2.1   Interest Rates Controls and Liberalization

As financial repression remained after China opened its door in 1978, it maintained a consistently lower official interest rate by as high as 50 percent–100 percent compared to the market-determined rate seen in informal credit markets. As a result of credit-rationing, the non-state sector received less than 20 percent of bank credit in the 1990s, despite accounting for a share of over 60 percent in the country's total value-added. Moreover, 94 percent of the loans issued by state-owned banks as of 1998 were rationed to SOEs, although one-third of them were in fact loss-making. Lu and Yao (2009) presented concrete data supporting the view that the official interest rates had been kept consistently lower than the market-determined rates in the late 2000s, which is an obvious sign of financial repression. This further led to substantial credit rationing in the banking sector, which means that non-state enterprises were usually sacrificed to keep the inefficient SOEs afloat. In the late 2000s, although banks were allowed to set their lending rates as high as 50 percent above the official benchmark rate, the market rate was still about 50 percent above this higher bound.[7]

Historically, the PBC set benchmark interest rates on both deposits and lending to be offered by commercial banks. From 1949 to 1998, banks were required to strictly follow these benchmark rates. After 1998, although the PBC still set the benchmark deposit and lending rates, they were not required to be strictly followed. Generally, the former was significantly lower than the latter, which means that the profits of the banks were protected. Figure 6.2 shows the benchmark lending and deposit rates from 1998 to 2019. It is interesting to note that the benchmark lending rate was almost always no less than 3 percentage points higher than the benchmark deposit rate over the period 1998–2019.

6.2.1.1 Liberalization of Lending Rate

As mentioned above, from 1949 to 1998, banks were required strictly to follow the benchmark lending rates. After 1998, in addition to setting a benchmark lending rate, a ceiling and a floor in the lending rate were set. The liberalization of interest rates started from 1993, with the issuance of a document by the State Council titled "Decisions of the State Council on Financial Reform." The first step took place in 1996, with the interbank offer rates first being liberalized. The relaxation of lending rates control began in 1998. The upper-bound restriction was fully removed in October 2004. The lower-bound restriction was abolished in July 2013.[8] However,

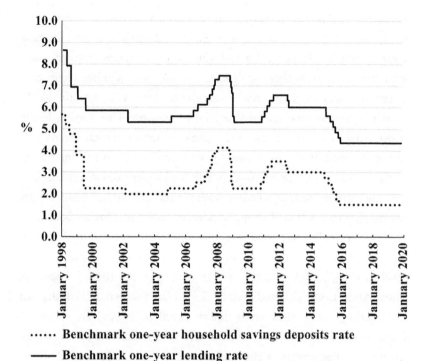

FIGURE 6.2 PBC benchmark one-year deposit and lending rates from 1998 to 2019.
Source: Bloomberg

the PBC continued to set the benchmark lending rate. The actual average lending rate was still not market-determined by 2013, due to the introduction of the so-called "Market Interest Rate Pricing Self-regulation Mechanism" (市场利率定价自律机制), set up in September 2013, whereby banks form "interest rates alliance" to avoid competition with each other in setting the lending rates. Figure 6.3 shows the timeline of lending rate liberalization up to July 2013.

6.2.1.2 *Market-Based Loan Prime Rate*

Further lending rate liberalization took place after the new governor of the PBC, Yi Gang, took office in March 2018. In August 2019, the PBC announced that the Loan Prime Rate (LPR, 贷款市场报价利率)

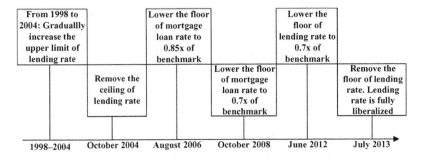

FIGURE 6.3 Lending rate liberalization timeline.
Source: Li and Liu (2019)

would become the new reference rate for lending in China and reformed how it is calculated. The main objectives of the new framework are to improve the transmission of monetary policy, increase competition among financial institutions and discipline banks to improve their pricing of risk. The LPR is the lowest rate banks offered to their best clients. Until August 2019, it had been calculated as the average of quotes submitted by a panel of ten banks, expressed as a multiple of the official benchmark lending rate, and it was not generally used as a reference rate for pricing the loans of banks' other customers. Changes to the official benchmark lending rate required approval by the State Council and it changed very slowly. (As of August 2019, no adjustments in the benchmark lending rate had been made since 2015. As a result, the LPR did not change much either since 2015.)

Under the new system, a group of 18 lenders (an enlarged set of banks) selected by the PBC would submit their one-year and five-year prime lending rate to the central bank on a monthly basis. The set of banks is expected to increase over time. Banks will submit their prime lending rate in the form of the number of basis points added to the interest rate on a type of funding they receive from the PBC called the medium-term lending facility (MLF). The MLF rate is determined by the open market operations (OMO) of the PBC. The spread between the prime lending rate and MLF for a bank is generally determined by a range of factors, including the bank's funding costs, the demand for loans and the pricing of credit risk associated with lending to the bank's best customers. Changes in the MLF rate do not need the approval of the State Council. Thus, it can be adjusted more quickly by the PBC in response to changes in economic conditions. The central bank will calculate the Loan Prime Rate as the average of those prime lending rates from the 18 banks (removing the highest and lowest ones) and publish it at 9:30 a.m. on the 20th of every month as the reference rate for the whole banking industry to follow. Banks have been told by the PBC that this more market-based LPR must be referenced in all new loan agreements – a major change from the past practice where all loan contracts referenced the official benchmark lending rate. In addition to making the loan market more market-based, the changes will eventually enable the PBC to have more power to influence the interest rates of the entire economy and financial markets via the MLF rate, as changes in the rate do not need the approval of the State Council. All loan contracts have to reference the LPR, and all prime lending rates (of the 18 banks) have to reference the MLF, the rate of which is controlled by the PBC. Thus, the new system can help to transition the monetary policy framework from one targeting the quantity of money supply and bank credit to one targeting interest rates as the main policy instrument, like those in most developed economies. It enables the central bank to influence the economy swiftly through the policy rate in response to rapidly changing economic conditions. If this reform is successful, it can bring the monetary policy framework of China one step closer to those of the developed countries.

In addition, the new system can increase competition, and therefore efficiency, in the banking sector. The PBC had been concerned that collusion among the large banks could lead to an implicit lending rate floor, which meant that lending rates would not fall in the face of lower funding costs and downward market pressure. The new arrangements may help to increase competition and break the implicit floor on lending rates. Furthermore, as banks are forced to become more efficient under the new system, it can discipline banks to improve their ability to independently price the risks of different borrowers. This can potentially increase their willingness to lend to higher-risk borrowers.

Figure 6.4 shows that the actual average lending rate showed its increasing independence from the benchmark lending rate during 2010–2020, indicating the effects of lending rate liberalization. More importantly, it also shows that, after August 2019, the LPR indeed fell immediately, which in turn brought down the actual average lending

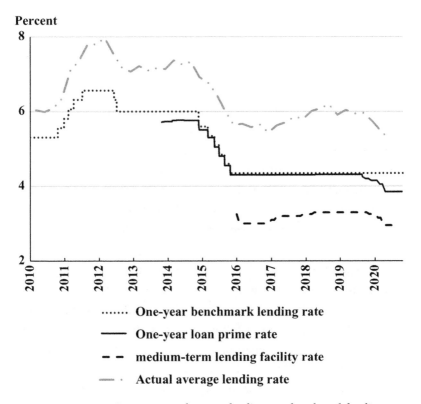

FIGURE 6.4 One-year actual average lending rate, benchmark lending rate, loan prime rate, and medium-term lending facility rate, 2010–2020.
Sources: CEIC; Wind (www.wind.com.cn)
Note: Actual average lending rate is "actual average lending rate to non-financial institutions."

rate immediately. This seems to confirm that the loan market had indeed become more competitive, achieving one of the goals of the reform. However, only time can tell whether this competitive effect will persist in the long run. Moreover, after August 2019, the MLF rate was quite closely correlated with the LPR, which in turn was correlated with the actual average lending rate. So, it seems that the new system did have the intended effect of influencing the actual average lending rate through the MLF rate, which is in turn controlled by the central bank through open market operations. However, the consistency of this new monetary policy transmission mechanism in the long run remains to be seen.

6.2.1.3   *Liberalization of Deposit Rate*

As mentioned above, from 1949 to 1998, banks were required to strictly follow the benchmark deposit rates. After 1998, in addition to setting a benchmark deposit rate, a ceiling and a floor on the deposit rate were also set. The relaxation of deposit rates control began in 2004, with the floor on deposit rates removed, while the benchmark rate set by the PBC served as the deposit rate ceiling from 2004 to 2012. The ceiling on deposit rates was gradually raised above the benchmark rates from 2012, until the ceiling was completely removed in October 2015.[9] However, the PBC continued to set the benchmark deposit rate. Again, due to the "Market Interest Rate Pricing Self-regulation Mechanism," even though there were no explicit ceilings on deposit rates, banks still practiced self-discipline in setting the deposit rates and to avoid competition with each other. Figure 6.5 shows that, even after October 2015, the time trend of the average of the deposit rates followed closely that of the benchmark rate set by the PBC. Comparing with Figure 6.4, we can see that the average deposit rate, which follows closely the trend of the benchmark deposit rate, is slower to liberalize than the average loan rate, which is more independent from the benchmark loan rate.

Although the relevance of the benchmark lending rate will probably diminish in the face of the LPR reform, the relevance of the benchmark deposit rates will probably remain for a relatively long

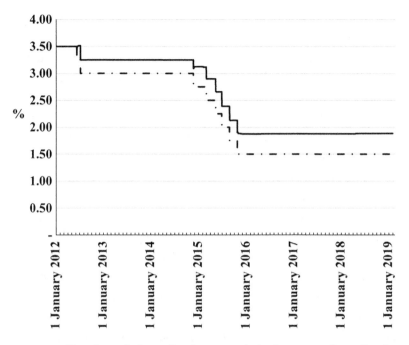

FIGURE 6.5 Actual average deposit rate and the benchmark deposit rate (1-year).
Sources: Wind (www.wind.com.cn); CEIC
The actual average deposit rate is calculated by the average of deposit rates offered by all the major banks in China (data provided by wind.com.cn), while the other indicators are provided by CEIC.

time, "to avoid banks setting high [deposit] rates in a fierce competition for deposits," according to Yi Gang, the governor of the PBC. This last caveat can be seen as a measure to cap the deposit rate, and, by extension, the lending rate, which is not unlike a continuation of some form of financial repression. In sum, the interest rate reform in the banking sector is still incomplete at the time of writing.

6.2.2 Dominance of State-Ownership of Banks

The Chinese financial system is dominated by the banking system. This is illustrated by the fact that the total amount of outstanding loans provided by banking and financial institutions to enterprises in 2016 was about RMB 62.58 trillion. (In addition, the total amount of outstanding loans provided to individuals was RMB 40.38 trillion in 2016.) By comparison, the total amount of corporate bonds outstanding in 2017 was about USD 3.35 trillion, which was equivalent to about RMB 21.8 trillion.[10] Therefore, for enterprises, bond financing was about 35 percent (=21.8/62.58) that of loan financing, and so firms overwhelming rely on bank loans for funding.

In 2015, only about 20 percent of the assets of the banking sector were controlled by non-state-owned or partially non-state-owned banks. The rest were controlled either directly or indirectly by the central government or local government. Banking and financial institutions can be categorized according to: policy banks, large commercial banks, joint-stock commercial banks, city commercial banks, city credit unions, rural small and medium-sized financial institutions, postal savings bank, foreign banks, and nonbank financial institutions. Only joint-stock commercial banks and foreign banks can be considered non-state-controlled or partially non-state-controlled. The dominance of the state-owned banks in the banking sector probably reflects high entry barriers for private firms to enter the sector. We shall refer to all state-controlled banks as state-owned banks.

The state-owned banks are categorized into wholly state-owned policy banks (which include the Agricultural Development Bank of China [ADBC], the China Development Bank [CDB], and the Export–Import Bank of China [Chexim]), large commercial banks (which include the Big Four and others), joint-stock commercial banks (with some private capital involved), and others.

Table 6.2 shows the assets and the asset shares of the different types of banks in December 2017, classified by ownership structure according to the People's Bank of China. Policy banks are fully owned by the state. The four major commercial banks are all publicly traded in the stock market, but still remain under majority-control by the state. Of the 12 major joint-stock commercial banks, eight are

Table 6.2 *The distribution of assets among China's banks as of December 2017*

	Number	Assets Amount (trillion RMB)	Assets Share (percentage)
Policy Banks (totally state-owned)	3	**25.53**	**10.11**
Large Commercial Banks (state-controlled)	5	**92.81**	**36.77**
Joint-stock Commercial Banks	12	44.96	17.81
Of which, the state-controlled ones	8	**32.84**	**13.01**
Of which, the non-state-controlled ones are:	4	12.12	4.80
Minsheng Bank		5.92	2.35
Pingan Bank		3.25	1.29
Zheshang Bank		1.54	0.61
Hengfeng Bank		1.42	0.56
Postal Savings Bank (state-owned)	1	**9.012**	**3.57**
Foreign Banks	134	3.24	1.29
City Commercial Banks	168	31.72	12.57
Urban Credit Cooperatives	–	–	0.00
Rural Commercial Banks	976	23.70	9.39
Rural Cooperative Banks	48	0.36	0.14
Rural Credit Cooperatives	940	7.35	2.91
New Rural Finance Institutions	1381	1.39	0.55
Nonbank Financial Institutions	–	11.94	4.73
TOTALS		252.40	100.00

Source: The author's own calculations. Primary data are from China Banking Regulatory Commission (CBRC); CEIC.

Note: State-owned banks are highlighted in bold type. The lower bound of the total assets of state-owned banks was about RMB 160 trillion (about 63.5 percent of total assets of all banks in China), which is the sum of all the numbers highlighted in bold type and underlined in this table.[12]

explicitly stated as being state-owned or state-controlled. All told, the state-controlled banks hold assets of no less than RMB 160 trillion, corresponding to no less than 63.5 per cent of total bank assets in 2017. If the state-controlled entities of the rest of the joint-stock commercial banks and those of the city commercial banks and rural commercial banks are included, the state-controlled banks might have held up to 70 percent of total bank assets.[11]

Table 6.2 shows the number and assets of each type of banking institution in China, based on the classification according to the China Banking Regulatory Commission (CBRC). It is worth noting that all the policy banks are state-owned, and although the large commercial banks (ICBC, BOC, CCB, ABC, and Bank of Communications) have gone public in the past two decades, they are still under state control. Of the 12 shareholding commercial banks, eight are state-owned or controlled by local governments. In sum, at least 63.5 percent (and maybe as large as 70 percent) of the total bank assets were still state-controlled as of the end of 2017. The GDP of China in 2017 was about RMB 80 trillion (USD 12.2 trillion). The assets of all banking institutions in China in that year was about RMB 252 trillion (USD 38.7 trillion), which was 3.2 times the GDP, while the total amount of deposits in all banks was about RMB 162 trillion (USD 24.9 trillion), which was 2.1 times the GDP.

In 2016, the total amount of loans outstanding to GDP ratio for China in 2016 was about 140 percent.[13] By contrast, in 2017, the outstanding loans from commercial banks to GDP ratio for Japan was 96.06 percent for Japan, 124.1 percent for the UK, and 46.6 percent for the United States. Thus, proportionally, the amount of loans created by the banking system in China is distinctly higher than those of more mature systems. It is widely believed that China's banking system is the largest in the world as of the time of writing. However, as will be discussed below, the bond and stock markets of China are less developed than the more mature systems both in size and sophistication. This means that the financial system of China is disproportionately reliant on the banking system. The banking sector needs to shrink and the bond and stock markets need to expand in order for the system to allocate capital more efficiently.

Historically, the largest four state-owned commercial banks, namely ICBC, BOC, CCB, and ABC, had been responsible for the majority of the formal bank lending in the country (over 90 percent in the early 1990s, 60 percent in 2005). However, these state-owned banks had not always performed well. For example, due to the huge non-performing loans (NPL) and inefficient operation, the whole banking system was virtually in a state of bankruptcy by the end of the 1990s as its net worth became negative.[14] The amount of outstanding NPL in the whole banking system was as large as 2.5 trillion yuan in the late 1990s. The NPL to gross loans ratio in the banking system reached almost 30 percent in 2001, an alarming rate. The efficiency of the state-owned banks has been improved since their public listing in the early 2000s. In addition, several asset management companies were established to take over the bad loans of the four largest state-owned commercial banks. The NPL to gross loans ratio in the banking system fell to 1.75 percent in 2016, which was quite manageable. Thus, the NPL situation has been greatly improved.[15]

6.2.3 Controls of Credit Allocation to Favor SOEs

The Chinese banking system is generally considered to be a tool for channeling funds to the industrial sectors, and economists often believe that SOEs are favored by the state-owned banks regardless of their profitability. It is also suspected that the situation became particularly bad during the global financial crisis in 2008, when directed lending surged due to the fiscal stimulus package introduced by the Chinese government. Although many measures have been taken to reform the financial system since then, it is still generally believed that the Chinese banking system is full of preferential treatments that biased towards certain groups of enterprises. In a report that lent support to the view that credits were controlled and directed by the government, the IMF pointed out in 2011 that the Chinese government's role in allocating credit was partly responsible for causing a build-up of contingent liabilities and making the much-needed reorientation of the financial system more difficult (IMF 2011).[16]

As mentioned above, in 2016, the total amount of bank loans outstanding provided by the banking system to all enterprises was RMB 62.58 trillion. Table 6.3 shows that loans provided to SOEs are significantly more than those to enterprises under other ownership types in that year. As noted earlier in this chapter, in 2012, although the share of SOEs in the value-added of the economy was only about 35 percent, they obtained 48 percent of bank credits. In fact, this percentage did not fall over time. As Table 6.3 shows, in 2016, SOEs obtained 54 percent of bank credits, while their share of the value-added of the economy was somewhere between 28 percent and 35 percent.[17]

6.2.4   *Financial Repression and Capital Misallocation*

Because the government uses policy intervention rather than predominantly relying on the market to allocate credits to enterprises, it distorts the financial market and leads to capital misallocation. For example, domestic private enterprises have to rely more on family and friends to obtain working capital and investment capital compared with SOEs, whereas SOEs are more likely to obtain them from the banks.[18] It is true that SOEs on average are more capital-intensive enterprises due to the sectors in which they operate being more capital-intensive. This can explain why they need more financial capital to produce each unit of their output. However, research has shown that on average the capital–labor ratio of a Chinese SOE tends to be higher than that of foreign firms in more advanced economies in the same sector. Given that China is a capital-scarce country, Chinese enterprises should adopt a lower, rather than higher, capital–labor ratio in their production than firms in the same sectors in more capital-abundant advanced countries. Thus, this indicates that there is probably a misallocation of capital in that SOEs use more than the efficient amount of capital for production as it is easy for them to get cheap credits from the banks.[19]

Table 6.3 *Distribution of loans to different types of enterprises according to size and ownership type in 2016*

	State	Collective	Domestic private	Hong Kong–Macao–Taiwan	Foreign	Total loans (trillion RMB)
Enterprises of all sizes	53.93%	7.04%	34.32%	3.02%	2.01%	62.58
Large enterprises	72.72%	5.97%	17.26%	2.82%	2.14%	22.06
Medium enterprises	49.58%	8.59%	35.94%	3.66%	2.23%	20.70
Small enterprises	37.79%	6.63%	51.35%	2.61%	1.62%	17.54
Micro enterprises	35.89%	6.60%	53.59%	2.25%	1.67%	2.28

Source: Wind (www.wind.com.cn).

6.3   THE RISKS OF FINANCIAL SECTOR LIBERALIZATION

The banking system is inherently fragile, as it depends on the confidence of the lenders. In addition, the financial market in general is full of information imperfection and financial products are full of risks. In sum, there is market failure in the financial market, in the sense that the free market is not economically efficient. Government interventions, in the form of regulations and safeguards, are in fact crucial in maintaining the stability and efficiency of the financial system. Thus, before engaging in any serious financial sector liberalization, it is very important that a well-functioning set of regulations and safeguards be put in place. This will minimize the risks that the liberalization brings to the banking and financial system while at the same time allow the market to allocate resources efficiently and innovate continually to meet the evolving needs of society. Below, we explain why the banking system requires regulation, what safeguards are required, and what China has done so far in banking and financial regulations.

6.3.1   The Fragility of the Banking System

A bank fails when it is unable to meet its obligations to its depositors and other creditors. Banks use borrowed funds to make loans and to purchase other assets, but some of a bank's borrowers may find themselves unable to repay their loans, or the bank's assets may decline in value for some other reasons. When this happens, the bank might be unable to repay its short-term liabilities, including demand deposits, which are largely repayable immediately without notice.

To understand the inherent fragility of the banking system, we should first look at a simplified balance sheet of the bank, as shown in Table 6.4.

On the assets side, loans are on average long-term contracts (e.g., mortgages). Thus, they are not very liquid. Marketable securities can fluctuate in their prices depending on the market and economic conditions. The bank may suffer losses if required to be sold in short order. Thus, they can be quite illiquid, especially under poor

Table 6.4 *Simplified balance sheet of a bank*

Assets	Liabilities
Loans	Demand deposits
Marketable securities	Short-term wholesale liabilities
Reserves at central bank	Time deposits and long-term debt
Cash in the vault	Capital

macroeconomic condition. Reserves at the central bank are deposits with the central bank, and they can be withdrawn relatively easily. Cash in the vault is the most liquid of all assets and can be mobilized immediately. On the liabilities side, demand deposits are allowed to be withdrawn anytime. Thus, the bank must have enough cash to meet the withdrawal demands of the holders of demand deposits. In case of a bank run, this part of the liabilities can dry up very quickly. Short-term wholesale liabilities can take various forms, including overnight loans from other banks (including the central bank) or a collateralized repurchase agreement (known as "repo"), in which the bank pledges an asset to the lender for cash, promising to buy the asset back later (often the next day) at a slightly higher price. In times of financial trouble for the bank or financial distress in the macro-economy, these kinds of liabilities can again dry up quickly. Time-deposits and long-term debts cannot be withdrawn immediately, and thus are paid higher interest rates. The capital is the difference between the liabilities and the assets of the bank. It provides a buffer to the bank to safeguard against sudden falls in the liabilities or defaults of the loans and debts. The larger is the capital, the safer is the bank against bankruptcy.

Thus, the balance sheet of the bank is characterized by term mismatch. Much of its assets, such as loans and marketable secur-ities, are either long-term contracts (e.g., loans such as mortgages) or illiquid in the short term (e.g., marketable securities, which when required to be sold in short order can fetch a much lower price). On the other hand, much of its liabilities (e.g., demand deposits and short-term wholesale liabilities) are short-term. For example, demand deposits can be withdrawn almost immediately; short-term wholesale liabilities may not be renewed if other banks do not want to lend. If all other banks refuse to lend, then the bank may have to sell its marketable securities in a hurry, possibly at a loss, in order to pay the holders of demand deposits.

Basically, a bank makes profits by exploiting the interest difference between its long-term assets and short-term liabilities. It makes profits by bearing the risk that the value of its assets can fluctuate due to default or illiquidity. Moreover, it also bears the risk that its viability is dependent on the confidence of the holders of deposits. Under normal times, when deposit holders are confident in a financially sound bank, they put most of their money in the bank in the form of deposits, and the bank is always able to meet the withdrawal demands of the holders of deposits. However, for whatever reason, if enough holders of deposits (especially demand deposits) lose their confidence in the bank, they demand to withdraw at the same time, and there will be a bank run. If the bank cannot liquidate enough of its assets, or borrow enough from other banks, or its owners cannot inject enough capital, then it cannot meet its obligations, and the bank goes bankrupt.

Even when an economy is fundamentally healthy, the banking system is fragile because it is built on confidence. First, a bank which is otherwise sound can fail just because deposit holders suspect that it is unable to pay. This is the information asymmetry between the bank and the depositors. Second, when one bank fails, it can lead to the failure of other banks, as banks are interconnected through mutual loans and derivative contracts, and deposit holders of other banks would suspect that the assets of their banks have suffered losses as well, thus losing confidence in their own banks. For this reason, we say that the failure of a bank confers negative externalities on the other banks. If this happens, there is a system-wide banking crisis.

Because of the information asymmetry and externalities problems, the banking market is characterized by market failure. Thus, some government interventions to provide safeguards to the banking system are crucial in maintaining the stability and efficiency of the system. In most of the relatively mature financial systems of the world, the safeguards include, among other things, deposit insurance, reserve requirements, capital requirements, bank examination, the central bank playing the role of the lender of last resort, and, if all fail, government bailouts.

In addition to the need for regulation of the traditional banking industry, in recent decades, a major regulatory issue emerged due to the increasing prominence of the "shadow banking system." Many financial or even non-financial entities play the role of financial intermediaries, as well as provide credit and payment services. However, unlike banks, they were not properly regulated. This poses systemic risks as the shadow banking system is closely connected with the traditional banking system through mutual borrowing and lending. For this reason, many countries have begun to regulate shadow banks.

6.4   FINANCIAL REGULATION IN CHINA

In the last decade, China has established a set of regulatory frameworks and safeguards in the financial system similar to those in countries with more mature financial systems. This paves the way for the liberalization of the financial sector, which includes the banking sector. The liberalization of the financial system would in turn facilitate the internationalization of the RMB.

The main regulatory body of the Chinese banking and insurance industry is the China Banking Insurance Regulatory Commission (CBIRC), which replaced the China Banking Regulatory Commission (CBRC) in April 2018. The CBIRC is charged with writing the rules and regulations, conducting examinations of banks and insurers, collecting and publishing statistics on the banking system, and resolving potential liquidity and solvency problems, among other supervisory activities.

China's Deposit Insurance Regulations went into effect in May 2015. For each bank, each depositor will be compensated for losses up to RMB 500,000 in case the bank becomes insolvent or goes bankrupt. As for capital requirements, the CBRC promulgated a regulation on 7 June 2012 with the intention to implement the Basel III capital requirements. This marked a milestone for the regulation of the banking sector in China.

To deal with the shadow banking system, the peer-to-peer (P2P) lending platform, received tighter regulations from August 2016. Under the new regulations, P2P platforms could only serve the function of information intermediaries instead of credit intermediaries. They became more closely monitored, for example, in terms of the amount of outstanding loans, sources of funding, etc. To deal further with the risks of the shadow banking system, in November 2017, the Chinese government drafted a set of regulations requiring financial institutions to keep a set amount of reserves for issuing asset-management products. It also prevented firms from providing implicit guarantees and packaging the investment products so that underlying assets are obscured. The asset-management products include banks' wealth-management products, mutual funds, private funds, trust plans, and insurance asset-management products. More generally, the central bank has been introducing regulations that tried to minimize risks that are "hidden, complex and potentially sudden, contagious and harmful," in the words of Zhou Xiaochuan, the former governor of PBC.

6.4.1   Regulatory Consolidation

Regulatory fragmentation was a key challenge to China's financial development. To address this issue, in November 2017, The Financial Stability and Development Committee, under State Council, was officially established. The committee was tasked with deliberating major reform and development programs for the financial sector, coordinating financial reform, development and regulation, coordinating issues concerning monetary policy, and coordinating the making of financial policies and related fiscal and industrial policies. The establishment of the committee was seen as a key step in the country's effort to safeguard financial security and prevent financial risk. Policymakers have put improving the financial regulatory system high on the agenda in an effort to contain risk.[20]

One important move of the Chinese government was the merger of China's banking and insurance regulators, the China Banking Regulatory Commission (CBRC), the China Insurance Regulatory Commission (CIRC) into one regulator, the China Banking Insurance Regulatory Commission (CBIRC) in April 2018. At the same time, the PBC took over the legislative and rules-making functions of the CBRC and CIRC, a significant increase in power. The new reorganization streamlined policymaking and implementation below the level of The Financial Stability and Development Committee. The overall push for reduction of financial risk became more credible because financial firms found it harder to shop for lighter-touch regulation by shuffling the same economic functions to a different type of company.[21] The merger plugged the loophole resulting from the difficulty of CBRC and CIRC to coordinate and launch an integrated crackdown on excessive risk-taking due to the collusion between banks and insurance companies. A consolidated banking and insurance regulator would adopt more effective measures to bring such activities under control.

6.5 WHY IS FINANCIAL SECTOR REFORM SO DIFFICULT IN CHINA?

In China, the financial sector is probably the one most difficult to reform. Although financial liberalization is risky, the risks can be mitigated by the introduction of a well-designed regulatory framework and a set of safeguards. These can be borrowed from other more developed countries. In fact, China has already introduced many of these measures, as explained above. So, the risks of financial sector reform cannot be the main reason for its slow pace. Rather, the main reason lies in China's system itself.

China's financial reform during 1978–2018 has been long in quantity but short in quality (Huang and Wang 2018), in the sense that there are a large number of financial institutions and huge amounts of financial assets in the system, but there are serious and extensive restrictions in the financial markets, resulting in financial repression. This gives rise to misallocation of resources, inefficiency, and lack of innovation. So, why is financial sector reform so difficult in China? It is because of the existence of SOEs and the vested interests that come with them.

Huang and Wang (2018) argue that China's financial reform during 1978–2018 is part of three dual-track strategies pursued by the Chinese government in its economic reforms: (1) state versus non-state sectors; (2) factor markets versus product markets; and (3) formal versus informal financial sectors. All these strategies are adopted so as to support a planned/state-controlled part of the economy, with SOEs playing a central role, even though many of these SOEs are unprofitable. In each of these dual-track strategies, one track is the planned part of the economy and the other is the market part of the economy. Naughton (1995) calls this growth model "growing out of the plan" – achieving fast growth while protecting the state sector. In the first strategy, the state sector, SOEs are protected while the non-state sector (private enterprises) is allowed to compete under a market system. In the second strategy, the labor, capital, and resources markets (factor markets) are controlled by SOEs or operate in favor of SOEs while the markets for goods and services (product markets) are liberalized. The credit subsidies to SOEs offered by the state-owned banks to SOEs is a good example of this. In the third strategy, the formal financial sector is dominated by state-owned banks, which offer services to large companies and wealthy households with heavily distorted pricing and allocation of financial resources, while the informal financial sector, such as the high-interest "curb market" that requires weak collateral and the shadow banking system, emerged to fill the needs of SMEs and low-income households. They are mainly market-driven and competitively priced.

Thus, the financial sector reform is so difficult mainly because without the state-owned banks channeling easy credits to SOEs, many of the SOEs would not be economically viable. Consequently, the root problem behind the failure to complete the interest rate reform and financial sector reform in general is the need to subsidize SOEs and keep them afloat, which requires keeping the lending rate below the market rate and rationing a disproportionally large share of capital to them. Why not allow unprofitable SOEs to go bankrupt? One reason is that SOEs do not just serve economic functions but also political and social functions. Politically, the dominant ideology among Chinese leaders is that the state should control the commanding heights of the economy, although well-functioning decentralized markets are allowed to exist and even thrive in certain sectors as long as they do not endanger the overall dominance of the state in the allocation of resources in the key areas of the economy. According to this ideology, the government must play a key role in some key sectors of the economy. SOEs today play this role. To understand the social role played by SOEs, consider why it is so hard to phase out the "zombie" firms. Most of these firms are in state-dominated heavy industries like coal, steel, cement, and glass. These are large employers. Letting them go bankrupt means that the local economy's GDP figures would be severely hit, and there would be mass layoffs and potential social stability. It is therefore no surprise that career-minded local officials are reluctant to let these zombie firms die. In 2016, the government said that there were 2000 state-owned zombies in operation, and it is believed that many of them still existed in 2019.[22]

6.6   THE BOND MARKET

For a currency to be an international currency, it must be widely used for invoicing and settling international trade in goods and services as well as trade in financial assets. From the investors' point of view, it is important to have a variety of financial instruments for store of value that differ in maturity, returns, liquidity, and risks. The bond market offers such a variety of relatively safe options for investors to park their money other than bank deposits. From the borrowers' point of view, the bond market offers an important alternative to raise funds other than loans from the banks. In fact, firms in general prefer bonds to other forms of leverage such as bank loans as the cost of funding is lower. For the above reasons, nowadays, bonds are the most widely used financial instrument in the world. Thus, in order to advance its financial development, it is important for China to develop a broad, deep, and liquid bond market. It can also make the RMB more attractive as a store of value for foreigners if they can freely invest in China's bond market. The development of the bond market is crucial for the healthy development of the capital market, which in turn is crucial for the RMB is to become a truly global currency.

China's bond market faces significant challenges, including regulatory fragmentation, moral hazard, a relatively narrow investor base, and low foreign ownership. By international standards, the scale of the Chinese bond market is disproportionately small. A far larger fixed-income sector will have to be established, accompanied by the gradual shrinking of the banking sector.

The bond market in China developed more slowly relative to the stock market. After Deng Xiaoping's reform and opening policy started in 1978, China relaunched treasury bonds in 1981. In 1982, a few enterprises began to take the initiative to raise interest-bearing funds, either internally or from the public. These became the early form of enterprise bonds. There was a long period of inactivity until 1997, when the PBC set up the inter-bank bond market, where mainly institutional investors trade through the China Government Securities Depository Trust & Clearing Co., Ltd. (CDC) platform. Most important developments in the Chinese bond market happened only since about 2015.

By 2016, a unified and multilayered market system has been formed in China's bond market, mainly inclusive of four sub-markets, namely the interbank bond market, the exchange bond market, the commercial bank over the counter (OTC) market, and the free trade zone (FTZ) market. The China interbank bond market (CIBM) is the largest of the four, consisting of 91 percent of the whole market in terms of the outstanding amount of bonds. The participants are various institutional investors such as commercial banks, securities

Table 6.5 *Depository amounts in bonds in different types of bond market, 2016*

	Type of Market			
	Interbank bond market	Exchange market	Commercial bank OTC market	FTZ bond market
Depository amount (trillion RMB)	51.86	4.45	0.69	0.003

Source: Refer to footnote 23.

companies, insurance companies, and so on. The exchange bond market and the commercial bank OTC market are retail markets. The FTZ bond market is defined as a domestic offshore market, attracting foreign investors to participate in domestic bond markets, but it is tiny compared with the other bond markets. Table 6.5 shows the depository amounts in bonds classified according to the type of market in which transactions take place.[23]

Figures 6.6–6.9 show a comparison between the Chinese bond market and those of other major countries. In 2017, China's outstanding amount of bonds was about USD 7.8 trillion, which was about 19 percent that of the United States (with an outstanding amount of USD 41.0 trillion), or 77 percent that of Japan (with an outstanding amount of USD 10.1 trillion). The turnover ratio of Chinese bonds was, however, substantially lower than those of the United States and Japan, being about 24 percent that of the United States and about 13 percent that of Japan in 2017. This indicates that the secondary market for bonds was not well-developed in China compared with the more developed markets. Of the total amount of bonds outstanding in China, 24 percent were issued by the central government, 33 percent by local (and other parts of) government, and 43 percent by corporations in 2017. By comparison, they were 35 percent, 36 percent, and 28 percent respectively in the United States and 82 percent, 7 percent, and 12 percent respectively in Japan.

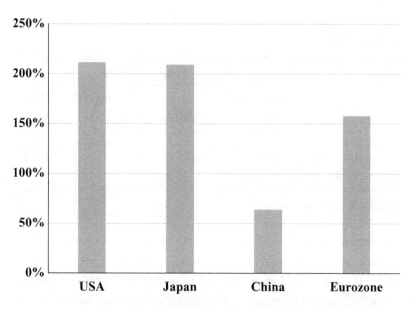

FIGURE 6.6 Total bond outstanding as percentage of GDP in 2017.
Sources: Japan: Japan Securities Dealers Association (www.jsda.or.jp/en/statistics/
bonds/); China: Chinabond (www.chinabond.com.cn/Channel/147253508?BBND=
2017&BBYF=12&sPageType=2#); US: Securities Industry and Financial Markets
Association (www.sifma.org/resources/research/us-bond-market-issuance-and-
outstanding/; www.sifma.org/resources/research/us-bond-market-trading-volume/);
euro Area: European Central Bank (www.ecb.europa.eu/stats/financial_markets_
and_interest_rates/securities_issues/debt_securities/html/index.en.html); UK:
United Kingdom Debt Management Office (Guilt and Treasury bill) (www.dmo.gov
.uk/data/gilt-market/turnover-data/; www.dmo.gov.uk/data/gilt-market/gross-and-
net-issuance-data/; www.dmo.gov.uk/data/gilt-market/); Bloomberg Terminal for
corporate bond

In 2017, the total value of bonds outstanding in China, United States, Japan, and the eurozone together was about USD 71.0 trillion, whereas the total stock market capitalization of the four economies (when only euronext is counted in the eurozone) was about USD 39.4 trillion, indicating that bond financing was more important than equity financing globally. However, the outstanding value of bonds to GDP ratio for China was much lower than those of the other three economies, as shown in Figure 6.6. It was 64 percent for China, compared to 211% for the United States, 209 percent for Japan, and

158 percent for the eurozone.[24] This indicates that China's bond market has much room for further development.

The central government bonds of the reserve currencies are considered the safest assets globally. Thus, they are a top asset class for global fund managers for parking their money and first choice for central bank reserve asset managers, who mostly hold safe assets for their liquidity. The development of a deep and liquid central government bond market, freely accessible by foreigners, is crucial for the currency to become a reserve currency for other countries, as foreign central banks need to know that they can do huge trades in the currency during periods of crisis without moving the value of the currency disadvantageously. The best example of a deep and liquid central-government bond market is the US Treasury bond market. It can accommodate trades of many tens of billions of dollars without excessive price changes. Thus, the development of a large, open, and liquid Chinese central government bond market is crucial for the RMB to become a truly global currency. In Figure 6.7, we see that even as recently as the end of 2017, the size of the market for the central government bond of China (Chinese government bonds [CGBs] issued by the Ministry of Finance) was only about the same as that of the UK, about 25 percent that of Japan, and about 14 percent that of the United States. In other words, there is a lot of room for the CGB market to expand before it reaches the proportion of the more mature markets. When the CGB market becomes sufficiently large, it can become more liquid, and it can also afford to have larger foreign holdings without leading to higher volatility of its prices. This will pave the way for the CGB to develop into a global asset class of its own, being regarded as a safe, sound, and liquid asset, freely accessible by foreigners.

The size of the central government bond market is important for providing liquidity, but size does not imply liquidity. Liquidity is measured by the turnover ratio of the asset. Figure 6.8 shows that the CGB market is much less liquid than the central government bond markets of the United States, Japan, and the UK. The lower liquidity

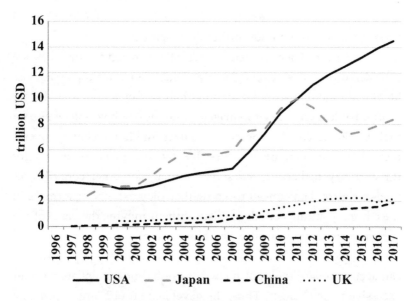

FIGURE 6.7 Central government bond outstanding in different countries, 1996–2017.

Sources: Refer to sources for Figure 6.6

Note: For the United States, only the marketable US Treasury securities are included.

of the CGB does not seem to be just due to the small size of the market, as the UK has the same size, but a much higher turnover ratio. The low turnover ratio could be due to many reasons, such as regulatory fragmentation, a relatively narrow investor base, and capital controls. Thus, in addition to the size, the low liquidity of the Chinese market is another area that has a lot of room for improvement.

One important factor underpinning the low capital account openness of China is that the percentage of foreign ownership of domestic bonds is still very small. For example, Figure 6.9 shows that foreign ownership of domestic central government bonds in China as of the end of 2017 was only 4.8 percent whereas it was 42.9 percent for the United States, 28 percent for the UK, and 11.2 percent for Japan. As explained earlier, in order for the RMB to be a truly global

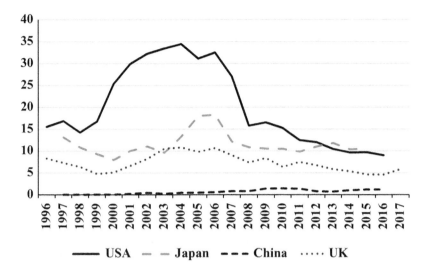

FIGURE 6.8 Central government bond turnover ratio, 1996–2017.
Sources: US Treasury; UK HM Treasury Debt Management Report 2018–19 (p.26); 中国债券信息网 (Chinabond.com.cn); FTSE Russell China Bond Research Report – April 2018; Ministry of Finance of Japan; Asia.nikkei.com. United States: http://ticdata.treasury.gov/Publish/mfh.txt; www.treasurydirect.gov/govt/reports/pd/mspd/2018/opds112018.pdf; UK: https://dmo.gov.uk/media/15381/drmr1819.pdf; China: www.chinabond.com.cn/jsp/include/CB_ENG/EJB_EN/document.jsp?sId=0300&sBbly=201712&sMimeType=4&sc=EN; www.ftserussell.com/sites/default/files/ftse_russell_china_bond_report_april_2018.pdf; Japan: www.mof.go.jp/english/jgbs/publication/newsletter/jgb2018_04e.pdf; https://asia.nikkei.com/Business/Markets/Capital-Markets/Foreign-investors-hold-more-JGBs-than-do-Japanese-banks
Note: for the United States, only the marketable US Treasury securities are included.

currency, the CGB market must be freely accessible by foreigners. So, China has to greatly increase the freedom of foreigners to trade in its CGB market. The good news is that the Chinese government has been taking measures to increase foreigners' access to the Chinese bond market, the latest measure being Bond Connect, which was introduced in 2017.

The success of the Bond Connect scheme signaled to the rest of the world that China intended to open its bond market to foreign investors. Since China's bond market is huge, it must not be ignored by international investors seeking to diversify their portfolio. As a

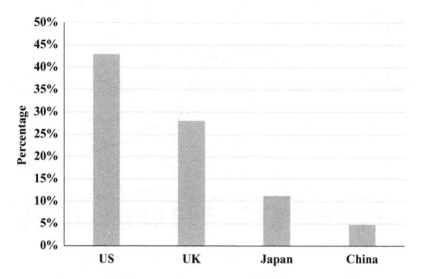

FIGURE 6.9 Foreign ownership of domestic central government bonds as of the end of 2017.
Sources: Refer to sources for Figure 6.6
Again, for the United States, only the marketable US Treasury securities are included.

result of the completion of several planned operational enhancements that were implemented by the PBC, Ministry of Finance, and State Taxation Administration, starting on 1 April 2019, 364 onshore Chinese bonds were added to the Bloomberg Barclays Global Aggregate Index over the following 20 months. The bonds would include 159 from the Chinese government, and the rest are from the policy banks: 102 from the China Development Bank, 58 from the Agricultural Development Bank of China, and 45 from the Export–Import Bank of China. As explained earlier in this chapter, the central government bonds and policy banks bonds are considered the safest of bonds in China. According to Bloomberg, when the bonds were fully added into the index, the weight of Chinese onshore bonds in the index would increase to around 6 percent and the RMB will become the fourth-largest currency component of the index, following the USD, euro, and Japanese yen. The inclusion would set to increase foreign ownership of Chinese safe assets, paving the way for the

RMB to become a reserve currency. Analysts estimate that the full inclusion would attract around USD 150 billion of foreign inflows into China's roughly USD 13 trillion bond market, which stood as the third largest in the world after the United States and Japan as of April 2019.[25]

The following timeline describes measures taken to increase foreign access to the Chinese onshore bond market in chronological order.

6.6.1 Government Policies Implemented to Encourage Foreign Access to China's Bond Market

2005   PBC approved the first foreign institutional investor in the Chinese Interbank Bond Market (CIBM), Pan Asia Fund.

2005   The International Finance Corporation and the Asian Development Bank issued RMB-denominated bonds of USD 138 million and USD 122 million respectively on the national inter-bank bond market. They were the first foreign institutions to issue panda bonds.

2010   PBC rolled out a pilot scheme allowing foreign institutional investors to trade on the CIBM up to the amount of monetary quota granted to them by PBC.

2011   PBC further expanded the scope of foreign institutional investors by allowing all qualified foreign institutional investors (QFIIs) and RMB-qualified foreign institutional investors (RQFIIs) to apply for approval and quota to invest in the CIBM through a Chinese settlement agent.

2015   PBC exempted foreign central banks, monetary authorities, international financial organizations, and sovereign wealth funds from the requirement for PBC approval and quota restriction on RMB investment in the CIBM. In May 2015, 32 QFIIs, many of them global players, were allowed to enter the interbank bond market.

2016   PBC permitted most types of foreign institutional investors to invest in the CIBM, including commercial banks, insurance companies, securities firms, fund management companies, and other asset management institutions, pension funds, charity funds, endowment funds, and other mid-term or long-term institutional investors recognized by PBC (the "Foreign Institutional Financial Investors"). The quota restriction was also removed.

2017   The Bond Connect, which is an arrangement that enables Mainland and overseas investors to trade bonds tradable in the Mainland and Hong Kong bond markets through the connection between the Mainland and Hong Kong Financial Infrastructure Institutions, was launched. Northbound Trading commenced first in the initial phase, i.e., overseas investors from Hong Kong and other countries and areas (overseas investors) began to invest in the CIBM through this scheme.

2019   The Bond Connect has become the major channel for foreigners to invest in the Mainland bond market. The policy is so liberal that it has more or less rendered the previous bond market opening policies reductant. Starting from 1 April 2019, 364 onshore Chinese bonds issued by the Chinese government and the policy banks would be added to the Bloomberg Barclays Global Aggregate Index over the following 20 months.

2020   On 28 February, J.P. Morgan Chase announced that it would add nine Chinese government bonds to its flagship Government Bond Index-Emerging Markets index series over the next ten months. The inclusion was expected to attract at least USD 20 billion of new capital to China's debt market over the period. On 24 September, FTSE Russell announced that the Chinese government bond (CGB) would be included in its World Government Bond Index (WGBI) as of October 2021. It is expected that the inclusion will bring an inflow of around USD 150 billion over a period of 12 months into the onshore government bond market.

6.7 THE STOCK MARKET

As explained earlier, the financial system is dominated by the commercial banks, with bonds and stocks playing a secondary role. This has to be changed in order to improve the efficiency of capital allocation. A large, deep, and efficient stock market is vital to China's ongoing economic transition. Market-based reform, the rule of law, enhanced regulation, and further opening will all help it develop into a global RMB asset class. A well-functioning, deep, broad, and liquid Chinese stock market that allows foreigners to invest in would attract foreigners to hold RMB as a store of value.

The capital-raising capacity of the Chinese stock market is low. China needs to have a stock market with much stronger fundraising capacity so as to reduce its reliance on bank loans. Fundraising is particularly important for new firms, emerging industries, and industrial upgrading. It helps to improve capital allocation and would facilitate the much-needed transformation of China's economy toward a more sustainable growth model.

The poor fundraising capacity arises from the conflicting roles of the government in the stock market. The stock market was initially mainly used to reform and fund the financially troubled SOEs. The government plays the roles of the controlling stakeholder, the rules maker, and the regulator. There is also the problem of lack of judicial independence. The Chinese government viewed IPO activities as part of its investment and capital formation targets set forth in its five-year plans. Therefore, IPOs were often driven by political considerations as much as by the economic goals of raising capital. This explains why many companies listed in the Hong Kong stock market instead, helping to boost the H-shares market (i.e., Mainland Chinese shares that are traded on Hong Kong's exchanges). Some even ventured to New York, London, and so on.[26]

Figure 6.10 compares the market capitalization of the Chinese stock market (including the Shanghai Stock Exchange and Shenzhen Stock Exchange) with those of other major markets in the world. As of

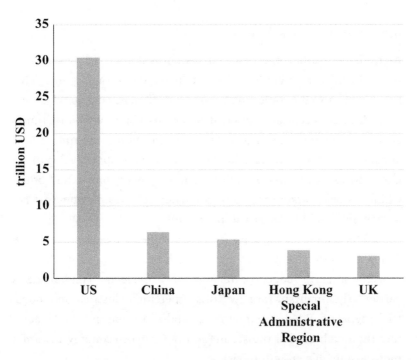

FIGURE 6.10 Market capitalization of the five largest stock markets by country/territory as of December 2018.
Source: The World Federation of Exchanges (www.world-exchanges.org/)

December 2018, the market capitalization of the largest stock markets by country are: USD 30.4 trillion for the United States, USD 6.3 trillion for Mainland of China, USD 5.3 trillion for Japan, USD 3.8 trillion for Hong Kong SAR, and USD 3.0 trillion for the UK.[27] Market capitalization of the stock market as a percentage of GDP in 2018 are 148 percent in the United States, 46 percent in Mainland China, 107 percent in Japan, and 105 percent in the UK. Thus, using the more mature markets as benchmarks, the Chinese stock market has a lot of room for expansion.

Although the Mainland Chinese stock market is already the second largest in the world in terms of market capitalization, it suffers from excessive government intervention that adversely affects investors' confidence about whether the stock prices truly reflect economic fundamentals. For example, in 2015, the government used administrative measures to prop up the stock prices in the face of a stock market sellout. A stock market bubble was formed in late 2014 and early 2015, and the bubble burst in June/July 2015, displaying both the immaturity of the stock market and the small extent to which the government could tolerate the adverse market outcome. As late as April 2015, financial leaders and Communist Party media still encouraged people to buy in, leading people to believe that the government backed the market. On 13 June 2015, the market regulator, the China Securities Regulatory Commission (CSRC), tightened the rules on margin lending. The subsequent crash was managed by a truly extraordinary set of interventions. The long list of measures include instructing big holders of stock not to sell, getting 21 big securities companies to promise to buy stocks of state enterprises, telling big companies not to sell their own shares, and allowing about one-third of the listed companies to suspend trading based on flimsy excuses. Foreign investors and regulators were taken aback both by the intensity of the government intervention and by a tendency to blame foreigners and alleged "malicious short sellers" for having manipulated the crash. One adverse consequence of heavy government intervention is that investors tend to focus on government policy instead of fundamental valuation. This defeats the purpose of the stock market as a mechanism of capital allocation by rewarding the economically well-performing firms and punishing the economically poor-performing firms.

Despite the setback in the Chinese stock market caused by excessive government intervention in 2015, the MSCI (Morgan Stanley Capital International) finally included Chinese A-share companies in its benchmark indexes for the first time in June 2018 after several rejections in the previous years. A-shares are yuan-denominated equities traded on the Shanghai and Shenzhen Stock Exchanges. The MSCI benchmarks were tracked by a total of USD 11 trillion of institutional funds globally. The index included 222 Chinese companies with a 0.73 percent weighting in the MSCI

Emerging Market Index. Analysts mostly believe the inclusion might not give Chinese equities any long-term boost, and that any significant inflows to A-shares will hinge more on the nation's economic growth and financial reform prospects. Yet, the inclusion by MSCI is another example to show that seeking external recognition creates pressure for domestic reforms in China. Many observers believe that improved accessibility of the A-share market allowed by the Chinese government (e.g., through the Stock Connects schemes) was the key reason that prompted the MSCI to grant the inclusion. In fact, MSCI vetoed A-share inclusion over the first three annual reviews, citing limited market access for global investors, capital controls, and the opaque regulatory framework. Indeed, China's stock market needs more transparency and less government intervention. It is expected that any further integration of the A-share stocks into the MSCI would require China to make further reforms along these dimensions.

6.7.1 *Major Events in the Development of the Equity Market of China*

1990   The Shanghai Stock Exchange and Shenzhen Stock Exchange were founded, offering companies the means to raise funds for investment.

1991   In November, the first B-share in China's securities market was listed on the Shanghai Stock Exchange. B shares are domestically listed shares, denominated in RMB, but subscribed to and traded in US or Hong Kong dollars by overseas investors.

1993   In June 1993, Tsingtao Brewery Company Limited was listed in Hong Kong, becoming the first Mainland Chinese company to issue H-shares.

2000   The China Futures Association, the national self-regulatory body for the futures industry, was established in Beijing.

2006   The China Financial Futures Exchange was set up in Shanghai.

2014   Introduction of the Shanghai–Hong Kong Stock Connect, which enabled Hong Kong and overseas investors to trade Shanghai Stock Exchange-listed securities in the Mainland market (SH Northbound Trading) and Mainland investors to trade Stock Exchange of Hong Kong-listed securities in the Hong Kong market (SH Southbound Trading).

2016   Introduction of the Shenzhen Stock Connect — the mutual stock market access between Shenzhen and Hong Kong. This was an extended version of the Mutual Market Access pilot program between Mainland China and Hong Kong on the foundation of the Shanghai Stock Connect which had been running successfully since its launch.

2018   Global index compiler MSCI included 226 China large market capitalization (large-cap) A-shares on its MSCI Emerging Markets Index and other global and regional composite indexes in June 2018.

6.8 OPENING OF THE FINANCIAL MARKETS TO THE ENTRY OF FOREIGN FIRMS IN RECENT YEARS

Despite the relatively low level of development of the financial markets, the pace of liberalization has been quite fast, not least in the last few years. In April 2018, Yi Gang, the new governor of the PBC, announced in the Boao Forum in Hainan Island of China that the government would allow foreign securities, fund management, futures, and life insurance companies to have 51 percent ownership in their Chinese subsidiaries within the year 2018, and that the cap would be removed entirely by 2021. It turned out that the promises have been honored. For example, UBS became the first foreign bank to hold a majority stake in its securities joint venture in late 2018. UBS's shareholder ratio in UBS Securities, a joint venture with Chinese companies, would increase to 51 percent. J.P. Morgan applied to set up a majority-controlled joint venture which would be launched in 2019 despite the trade spat between China and the United States. Nomura applied to set up a joint venture securities firm in May

2018. Citigroup was to end its existing joint venture and set up a majority-owned venture.

As for insurance business, it was promised that qualified foreign investors would be allowed to conduct insurance brokerage and assessment business in the country. Foreign-funded insurance brokers would have the same business scope as do their Chinese counterparts. In November 2018, China surprised the market, pleasantly, by giving the approval for Allianz, a German company, to set up the first wholly foreign-owned insurance holding company in Shanghai, three years earlier than what Yi Gang had promised.

Stock Connects: As promised, the daily quotas for the Stock Connects schemes between the Mainland and Hong Kong was quadrupled starting from 1 May 2018. The northbound daily quota increased from RMB 13 billion for each of the Shanghai Connect and the Shenzhen Connect, to RMB 52 billion, while the southbound daily quota increased from RMB 10.5 billion for each of the Shanghai Connect and the Shenzhen Connect, to RMB 42 billion. The Shanghai–London Stock Connect program was launched on 17 June 2019.

Yi Gang also made other promises in 2018, such as canceling foreign equity restrictions on banks and financial asset management firms, with equal treatment for domestic and foreign-funded institutions. Moreover, foreign banks would be allowed to set up branches and subsidiaries at the same time in the country. Interestingly, there were no major moves by foreign banks on this front. Apparently, foreign banks did not find it profitable to operate banking business in China. Banks like HSBC and Standard Chartered Bank did not indicate any plan to increase their shares in their respective joint ventures. Citigroup and other global banks have in fact sold their stakes in their respective joint ventures in China in recent years.

Despite the "decoupling" effort by the Trump administration, American financial companies gained increasing autonomy and access in the Chinese financial markets as a result of the recent wave of liberalization concerning foreign ownership. In 2019, PayPal acquired a 70 percent stake in the Chinese firm GoPay, making PayPal the first foreign company to provide online payment services in China. In March 2020, Goldman Sachs received approval to step up its 33 percent minority stake in its joint venture securities firm to a 51 percent majority ownership. Morgan Stanley was able to increase its ownership stake in its joint venture securities firm from 49 percent to 51 percent. In June 2020, American Express received approval to be the first foreign credit card company to launch onshore operations in China through its joint venture with a Chinese fintech firm, allowing it to conduct network clearing operations. Visa and Mastercard have applied to form network clearing licenses. American credit rating companies have also gained in increased access. In 2019, S&P Global set up a wholly owned firm that is the first licensed to conduct credit rating services in China's domestic debt market. In May 2020, Fitch's wholly owned subsidiary was approved to rate China's onshore issuers, including banks, nonbank financial institutions and insurers, and their bonds. (Lardy and Huang 2020).

6.9   CONCLUSION

The Chinese financial system is still characterized by financial repression, and this is not favorable to RMB internationalization.

The biggest problem with the financial system is the banking sector and the existence of a large number of unprofitable SOEs. The banking sector is still characterized by interest rates controls, dominance of state-owned banks, entry barriers, and control of credit allocation to favor SOEs. The main obstacles to banking sector reform is that the state-owned banks have the responsibility to channel easy credits to SOEs, either because they are in the "key" sectors, or they provide employment to workers in certain unprofitable firms so as to keep social stability, or simply because they have good connections with the political establishment. Thus, the subsidization of unprofitable or economically unsound SOEs through cheap credits allocated by the state-owned banks is a key obstacle to the banking sector reform and by extension the financial market reform.

If the pricing mechanism (interest rate determination mechanism) in the banking system is distorted, interest rates in other financial markets of the country are distorted as well, since the different financial markets are interrelated through the interest rate mechanism. The distortion of the interest rates in the financial markets would adversely affect the pace of development of the financial system, such as the bond market, insurance market, mutual funds market, and even the stock market. It would hinder the development of a deep, broad, and liquid financial market and slow down the pace of RMB internationalization.

If the deposit rate is kept below the market-determined level, it would be more risky to open the capital account, as it would cause capital outflows as households move their deposits in the domestic banks to invest in foreign assets, which yield higher returns. The delay in the opening of the capital account would slow down the pace of RMB internationalization.

Like any government intervention in allocation of resources, credit rationing can breed corruption. This, again, would hinder the development of a well-functioning financial market, as the rule of law is the pillar of financial development.

To move financial reform forward, the Chinese government should (1) let the market determine interest rates and allocate resources in the financial markets; (2) phase out the protection of SOEs through intervention in the financial markets; (3) when designing the regulatory framework, strike the right balance between ensuring financial stability and allowing financial innovation to take place; (4) open the financial markets both to investments from foreign investors and to entry of foreign firms.

The structure of the financial sector of China is lopsided. The banking sector is disproportionally large compared with the bond market and the stock market. This is because of the underdevelopment of the bond and stock markets. The relative importance of the banking sector in the allocation of capital should shrink while that of the bond market and the stock market should rise in order to keep

China in line with countries with more advanced financial systems. Besides, the banking system is still not sufficiently market-oriented. The bond market is too small, illiquid, and there is a lack of foreign participation. The stock market is still hampered by past government intervention, a lack of transparency, limited foreign access, and capital controls, to name a few shortcomings. The further development of the bond and stock markets is essential for RMB internationalization. An underdeveloped financial market cannot be broad, deep, and liquid. It also cannot be open, as it is too risky to open the financial market to foreigners when banks are not market-oriented, competitive, well-managed, and well-regulated.

The development of the bond market, especially the central government bond market, is crucial to making the RMB a truly global currency. However, there are many obstacles that prevent the bond market from becoming an effective instrument to facilitate capital market opening and by extension RMB internationalization, such as its small size, lack of liquidity, and the small share of foreign ownership.

Regarding the stock market, despite the inclusion of some Chinese A-shares in the global MSCI index, it is not clear to what extent foreigners are interested in investing in the A-shares given the track record of government intervention in the Chinese stock market, the lack of transparency, capital controls, and other issues. If foreigners lack confidence in the fairness of the stock market, they will not be interested in investing in it, and so capital account opening will suffer. It would again be unfavorable to RMB internationalization.

Nonetheless, progress has been made in reforming the financial system of China. For example, interest rate ceilings have been removed, foreign banks majority ownership is allowed (but foreign banks seem not to be too interested; in fact, many of them have sold their minority share), there was rapid development of the bond market, regulations were improved to reduce systemic risks (e.g., consolidation of regulatory agencies, regulation of the shadow banking system). However, there are still many problems to address.

The good news is that China has not slowed down its pace of financial market liberalization. If anything, market opening and integration with the rest of the world has sped up in recent years. This seems to be a conscious policy direction of the central government. If so, it is a favorable sign for the growth and development of China and for RMB internationalization.

NOTES TO CHAPTER 6

1 See also Svirydzenka 2016.
2 Sources: ICBC, BOC, CCB, ABC (http://v.icbc.com.cn/userfiles/ Resources/ICBCLTD/download/2018/720180423.pdf; http://pic .bankofchina.com/bocappd/report/201803/P020180329593657417394.pdf; www.ccb.com/en/newinvestor/upload/20180817_1534487897/ 20180817143224827527.pdf; www.abchina.com/en/investor-relations/ performance-reports/annual-reports/201803/P020180428379127252057 .pdf).
3 Source: Pei, Yang, and Yang 2015. According to the authors, as of the end of 2012, the total productive asset in the economy was RMB 487.53 trillion, out of which RMB 258.39 trillion (53 percent) was under the public sector (公有制经济). In the primary sector, the total asset in the economy was RMB 37.27 trillion, out of which 32.26 trillion (86.6 percent) was under the public sector. In the secondary and tertiary sectors, the asset shares of public and non-public sectors were 50.44 percent and 49.56 percent respectively. In 2012, in the secondary and tertiary sectors, the estimated proportions of value-added of non-public sector and public sector were 67.59 percent and 32.41 percent respectively, and the employment provided were 75.2 percent and 24.8 percent respectively. It is estimated that the primary sector contributed to about 10 percent of the value-added of the country in 2012. See also Wang 2016 (in Chinese).
4 See Lin, Cai, and Zhou 2003.
5 See Lin, Cai, and Zhou 2003.
6 See, for example, Johansson 2012.
7 See Lu and Yao 2009
8 According to Li and Liu 2019, "Liberalization of the lending rates first started in 1998. The goal was to give commercial banks more authority in

pricing their deposits and loans. The gap between the interest rate ceiling and floor was gradually widened over time before being finally removed. Initially, banks could set lending rates between 90 percent and 110 percent of the benchmark rate for large enterprises, and between 90 percent and 130 percent of the benchmark rate for small or medium-sized enterprises. Five years later [in October 2004], the retail lending rate ceiling was removed, but the lending rate floor was maintained for about eight more years. In 2012, the lending rate floor was further lowered to 70 percent of the benchmark rate and 1 year later [in July 2013], the lending rate floor was totally removed, suggesting that the PBC fully liberalized the retail lending rate."

9 According to Li and Liu 2019, "The benchmark rate set by the PBC served as the deposit rate ceiling for about 8 years. Since June 2012, banks could offer deposit rates as high as 110 percent of the benchmark rate to their customers. Two years later, the deposit rate ceiling was raised to 120 percent of the benchmark rate. In 2015, the PBC quickened the pace of deposit rate liberalization. The deposit rate ceiling was raised to 130 percent of the benchmark rate in March and further to 150 percent in May. On October 23 [2015], the PBC removed the ceiling of the deposit rate, signifying that China has completed liberalization of both the retail deposit and lending rates. At the same time, China introduced a deposit insurance scheme which covers RMB 500,000 for each account, thus paving the way for more competition among banks in China."

10 Sources: 1. CEIC for loans outstanding in 2016; 2. www.chinabond.com .cn/Channel/147253508?BBND=2017&BBYF=12&sPageType=2# for corporate bonds outstanding in 2017.

11 See Johansson 2012 and Walter and Howie 2011.

12 This is a lower bound because, first, eight out of the 12 joint-stock commercial banks are explicitly said to be state-owned or state-controlled. But since we do not know the amount of state-owned assets in the other four shareholding commercial banks, we do not include them as state-owned. Second, many of the city commercial banks and rural commercial banks are controlled by private capital, although many of them are controlled by local government. They are very hard to distinguish from each other. Since we do not know the exact assets in city commercial banks and rural commercial banks that are controlled by the government, we do not include them as state-owned.

13 The total amount of outstanding loans provided by banking and financial institutions was RMB 102.96 trillion [RMB 62.58 trillion (to enterprises) + RMB 40.38 trillion (to individuals)] in 2016, which was equivalent to about USD 15.84 trillion. The GDP of China in 2016 was USD 11.23 trillion, which was equivalent to about RMB 73 trillion. Thus, the total amount of loans outstanding to GDP ratio for China in 2016 was about 140 percent.

14 See Lardy 1998: 109–111.

15 Economic Research at Federal Reserve Bank of St. Louis (https://fred.stlouisfed.org/tags/series?t=banks%3Bchina).

16 See Johansson 2012 and Walter and Howie 2011.

17 Zhang 2017 estimated that the contribution of SOEs to the GDP of China was about 23 percent to 28 percent and their share in employment was about 5 percent to 16 percent in 2017.

18 For example, Dollar and Wei 2007 report that SOEs are 50 percent more likely to rely on local banks in obtaining working capital (36 percent to 38 percent of their total working capital), compared to domestic private firms (22 percent), which would regard family and friends as an important source. When it comes to financing for investment, SOEs are still more likely to rely on banks than private firms, although with a moderately smaller magnitude of difference than for working capital. About 8.7 percent of the private firms rely on family and friends for financing for investment.

19 For example, Song, Storesletten, and Zilibotti 2011 point out that the fact that domestic private enterprises have substantially lower capital–output and capital–labor ratios than SOEs is a sign for financial repression on domestic private enterprises. They observe that, according to *Chinese Statistical Yearbook, 2007* (National Bureau of Statistics of China 2007), the average capital–output ratio was 1.75 in SOEs and 0.67 in domestic private enterprises. After taking capital-intensive and labor-intensive industries into consideration, the average capital–output and capital–labor ratio in SOEs was still significantly higher than that in domestic private enterprises. Like Dollar and Wei 2007, they observe that SOEs finance a substantially higher percentage of their investments through bank loans than domestic private enterprises (more than 30 percent for the former compared to less than 10 percent for the latter). See also Boyreau-Debray and Wei 2005.

20 "China establishes financial stability and development committee." See State Council of the People's Republic of China 2017.

21 "See Chorzempa 2018.
22 See, for example, Yang and Ke 2019.
23 See "Overview of China's Bond Market (2016 version)" published by China Central Depository and Clearing Company Limited (www.scribd.com/document/423679426/China-s-Bond-Market-Overview-2016-2-pdf).
24 The bonds in the eurozone are issued by individual member countries. Thus, the eurozone bond market is in fact a collection of sovereign bonds issued by different member countries. They carry different interest rates and risks. The total amount of bonds outstanding as a percentage of GDP stated should be regarded as the average percentage for the eurozone members.
25 Refer, for example, to www.cnbc.com/2019/04/01/china-bonds-debut-on-bloomberg-barclays-global-aggregate-index.html and Bloomberg: www.bloomberg.com/company/press/bloomberg-confirms-china-inclusion-bloomberg-barclays-global-aggregate-indices/.
26 See, for example, Wang, Yen, and Lai 2014: 66–67 and Overholt, Ma, and Law 2016.
27 Source: The World Federation of Exchanges (www.world-exchanges.org/).

7 The Importance of the Offshore RMB Market

Historically, when a country wants to internationalize its currency, it would allow the currency to be more fully convertible, in particular convertible in the capital account, meaning that discretionary capital controls are largely removed. Examples are post-war United States, Britain, Germany, and Japan. As RMB is not fully convertible in the capital account, and China wants to open its capital account in a controlled manner, establishing offshore RMB markets (where RMB is allowed to be fully convertible) with the help of government policy is crucial in encouraging the international use of the RMB. The fact that China uses the "one currency, two markets" approach to implement RMB internationalization may be viewed as a sign that it does not want to remove onshore capital controls any time soon. Instead, China wants to set up a firewall between the onshore and offshore markets for a prolonged period of time. In short, it appears that they want to have an internationalized RMB while at the same time retain the option of imposing discretionary onshore capital controls when there is a need. If viewed in this light, Hong Kong's status as the primary offshore RMB center could last for a long time.

What is an offshore currency market? Roughly speaking, it is a financial market in which financial products denominated in a certain currency are bought and sold, but the market is located outside the currency-issuing country. The financial products can be bank deposits or bonds or other financial products. An offshore currency market is usually located in a reputable international financial center that has a long tradition of rule of law, sound financial infrastructure, mature regulatory framework, strong enforcement of contracts, and favorable tax policies for the financial industry.

Historically, offshore currency markets emerged due to three main reasons. First, depositors desired to separate the country risks (such as expropriation or limitation on movement of capital) from the non-country risks (such as currency risks). For example, during the Cold War, some citizens of the Soviet Union desired to hold USD deposits but did not want to put the money in the United States. Thus, offshore USD bank accounts satisfied this demand, fueling the growth of offshore USD banking. As a result of the growth of the offshore USD market, there was a wide circulation of dollars overseas, and the development of a separate, less-regulated market for the deposit of those funds. Second, there was regulatory asymmetry between onshore and offshore banks, which could give rise to an advantage of offshore banking over onshore banking. For example, there could be yield differential between the offshore USD deposits and onshore USD deposits due to the different legal/tax treatments of onshore and offshore deposits. Historically, before 3 October 2008, the required reserve of onshore US banks paid zero interest, while offshore banks did not have any reserve requirement. This meant that offshore banks had a cost advantage and were thus more profitable. Third, there is the convenience factor: To some investors and fund-raisers, the regulatory environment, accounting standards, language, and time zone of the location of the offshore markets made them more convenient than the onshore markets. In the case of the USD, by the 1950s, there was already a strong desire for foreigners to hold the USD, so there was a strong demand for offshore USD banking and offshore USD trading when the onshore market became less attractive for depositors or less profitable for banks. In the case of the RMB today, however, there was no strong desire for foreigners to hold RMB, so the demand for offshore RMB banking and offshore RMB trading had to be created.

The use of an offshore currency market is crucial for launching the internationalization of the RMB, for a number of reasons. First, the success in internationalization of RMB requires a high degree of capital account convertibility of the currency, and China may not want to allow this to happen in the onshore market any time soon.

Nonetheless, the RMB in the offshore market can be allowed to be fully convertible in the capital account. This can be done so long as the offshore RMB is not totally free to move onshore and the onshore RMB is not totally free to move offshore. This is the rationale for the concept of "one currency, two markets." Such a policy would allow the Mainland to liberalize its capital account at its own pace while at the same time start building up the RMB as an international currency to be used for trade invoicing, trade settlement, and funding of enterprises outside of China.

Second, having a transaction taking place in an offshore center helps to separate the "currency risks" of a financial asset from the "country risks" of the country in which the institution selling the asset, such as a bank, is domiciled. By contrast, when a transaction takes place onshore, the currency risks and country risks are bundled together. Currency risks are primarily associated with the variability of the exchange rate. Country risks are associated with the legal, political, economic, social, and other risks of the country, e.g., risks that the contract is governed by the laws of the country of domicile of the institution selling the asset, such as how strongly contracts are enforced and depositors' rights are protected, the risk of expropriation by the government of the country, and capital controls. For example, when foreigners keep RMB deposits in a bank in Hong Kong, the contract is governed by Hong Kong laws. The currency risks are those of the RMB. But the country risks are those of Hong Kong, the offshore market, not China, the issuing country of the currency. Because Hong Kong is a reputable international financial center with a long tradition of rule of law, an independent judiciary, the absence of capital controls, and strong enforcement of contracts, the confidence in the safety of the deposit is enhanced when the deposit is kept in a bank in Hong Kong. The reliability and efficiency of the banks in Hong Kong also gives confidence to foreigners in using the RMB to denominate and settle trade and financial transactions through the banking system in Hong Kong. Thus, the offshore RMB market in Hong Kong increases the attractiveness of the international use of the RMB as a store of value and a medium of exchange. As we shall see below, the

Stock Connects and Bond Connect schemes, which enable foreigners to invest in Mainland stocks and bonds through Hong Kong, are examples of the separation of currency risks (of the RMB) from country risks (of Hong Kong). For trading and settlement activities, Hong Kong investors participating in the "Connects" schemes through the Stock Exchange of Hong Kong (SEHK) participating entities (some of which are domiciled in the Mainland) will be protected by the Securities and Futures Ordinance of Hong Kong.

Third, the offshore RMB centers have international credibility and a well-developed financial infrastructure. These offshore centers, together with the new international payment system (CIPS), facilitate efficient flows of funds between the onshore and offshore markets and enhance the impacts of onshore financial development and capital account opening on RMB internationalization. They also facilitate the efficient operation of the offshore financial markets and the offshore use of the RMB by third parties.

Is it possible to create a market of fully convertible RMB in an onshore location (this is called an onshore–offshore RMB market)? In the foreseeable future, it seems that it will be hard to find any such viable location. At present, there is simply no onshore location that has the institutional environment and credibility to the international community that can allow a sizable market of fully convertible RMB to operate. In addition, given the underdeveloped financial and legal infrastructure as well as immature regulatory regime of Mainland China, it is hard to find any onshore location that can effectively segregate the offshore and onshore financial transactions in an onshore–offshore RMB market. Furthermore, the onshore–offshore RMB market still carries the country risk of China; thus, it cannot separate the currency risks from the country risks of the RMB assets. There have been some attempts to create onshore–offshore RMB markets in the Shanghai FTZ and the Shenzhen Qianhai FTZ, but the attempts did not yield any result. The United States did set up an onshore–offshore USD market called International Banking Facilities (IBF) in December 1981. It required banks to keep separate accounts and follow different regulations in dealing with offshore and onshore transactions. But that would be hard for China to mimic. This leaves the use of an offshore–offshore fully convertible RMB market as the only option for RMB internationalization.

To understand the international economic environment in which internationalization of the RMB is being carried out and why places like Hong Kong, Singapore, and London are chosen as the first batch of major offshore RMB centers, we need to have some basic knowledge about the international capital market, offshore banking, offshore currency trading, and international financial centers.

7.1 THE INTERNATIONAL CAPITAL MARKET AND OFFSHORE BANKING

The main actors in the international capital market include commercial banks, nonbank financial institutions, multinational corporations, and central banks. Commercial banks are the most important actors in the international capital market, as they run the international payment system and provide a broad range of financial services. Banks are at the core of the international financial intermediation. Bank liabilities consist chiefly of deposits of various maturities, as well as debt and short-term borrowing from other financial institutions, while their assets consist largely of loans (to corporations and governments), deposits at other banks (interbank deposits), and various securities including bonds. Nonbank institutions such as insurance companies, pension funds, mutual funds, and hedge funds are net lenders in the international capital market. They have become important players in the international capital market as they increasingly hold foreign assets to diversify their portfolios. Multinational corporations (MNCs) are the net borrowers in the international capital market. They often finance their investments by drawing on foreign funds. These funds may come from loans from foreign banks or institutional lenders, or foreign investors buying the company's stocks or bonds. Corporations frequently denominate their bonds in the currency of the financial center in which the bonds are being offered for sale, and even offer bonds denominated in different currencies in the same financial center. Central banks are net lenders in the international financial markets as they hold foreign government bonds as foreign reserves. They participate in the international financial market whenever they carry out foreign exchange intervention through the buying and selling of foreign government bonds.

The scale of transactions in the international capital market has grown much more quickly than world GDP since the early 1970s. One major factor in this development is that countries have gradually reduced barriers to private capital flows across their borders. An important reason for that development is related to the exchange rate systems. Most developed countries had come to adopt a flexible exchange rate regime since the early 1970s, when the Bretton Woods system ceased to operate. This has allowed countries to reconcile open capital markets with domestic monetary autonomy, according to the open-economy trilemma.

One notable feature of commercial banking industry today, compared with the Bretton Woods era, when the fixed exchange rate regime prevailed, is that banking activities have become globalized as banks have branched out from their home countries into foreign financial centers. The term "offshore banking" is used to describe the business that banks' foreign offices conduct outside of their home countries. Banks may conduct foreign business through an agency office located abroad, a subsidiary bank located abroad, or a foreign branch. Offshore banking and offshore currency trading have grown in tandem. An offshore deposit is simply a bank deposit denominated in a currency other than that of the country in which the bank resides. Many of the deposits traded in the foreign exchange market are offshore deposits.

There are a few reasons for the rapid growth of offshore banking and offshore currency trading in the last three to four decades. First is the rapid growth of international trade and international corporate activities. For example, domestic firms engaged in international trade and direct investment require overseas financial services, and domestic banks have naturally expanded their domestic business with these firms into foreign areas. By offering more rapid clearing of payments and the flexibility and trust that have been established in past dealings, domestic banks located in the foreign country compete with the foreign banks that could also serve domestic customers. Offshore currency trading is another natural outgrowth of expanding world trade in goods and services. Foreign importers of domestic goods frequently need to hold domestic-currency deposits, and it is natural for banks based in the foreign country to offer services to these importers.

A second reason for the rapid growth of offshore banking in the last few decades is regulatory asymmetry between the home country and the offshore banking centers. Domestic banks tried to avoid domestic government regulations on financial activities (and sometimes taxes) by shifting some of their operations abroad and into foreign currencies. The regulatory asymmetry is further fueled by the fact that the governments in the offshore banking centers impose less-stringent regulations on foreign-currency banking activities than domestic banking activities. Domestic currency deposits, for example, often were more heavily regulated as a way of maintaining control over the domestic money supply, while banks were given more freedom in their dealings in foreign currencies.

A third reason for the growth of offshore banking is the desire by some depositors to separate the currency risks of their deposits from the country risks of having their account held inside the issuing country of the currency. The country risks can include the risk of expropriation or freezing of the bank accounts, due to political reasons, for example.[1]

7.2   HONG KONG, SINGAPORE, AND LONDON

International financial centers like Hong Kong, Singapore, and London are offshore banking and offshore currency trading centers. Regulatory asymmetries explain why those financial centers whose governments historically imposed the fewest restrictions on foreign currency banking became the main offshore currency centers. London is the leader in this respect, but it has been followed by Hong Kong, Singapore, Luxembourg, and other countries that have competed for international banking business by lowering restrictions and taxes on foreign bank operations within their borders. Hong Kong, being part of China and a well-developed international financial center, is an obvious choice to be the primary RMB offshore center. Singapore, being a close economic partner of China and located in Southeast Asia, a region of great political and economic importance to China, is an obvious choice for an offshore RMB center outside of the Greater China Area. The UK is one of China's closest economic partners in Europe. Thus, London can provide a foothold for RMB banking and RMB business in a strategic region of the world economy. In the rest of this book, when we discuss offshore RMB centers, we mostly use Hong Kong as an example, as it is the most important offshore RMB center, and much of the experience there is shared by other offshore RMB centers.

7.3   CHINESE GOVERNMENT POLICIES TO FACILITATE THE FORMATION OF THE OFFSHORE RMB MARKET

The first policy measure is the designation of BOCHK as the sole clearing bank for offshore RMB business in Hong Kong in February 2004. The clearing services include those related to deposits, exchange, remittance, and bank cards to some participating banks in Hong Kong. In 2007, the first dim sum bond, a bond issued outside of the Mainland of China but denominated in RMB, was issued in Hong Kong by China Development Bank, worth RMB 5 billion, making it the first publicly listed bond to be traded and settled in RMB in Hong Kong. The total amount of dim sum bonds issuance by Mainland banks was RMB 20 billion by the end of 2007. In 2009, China entered into bilateral currency swap agreements with monetary authorities in Hong Kong and other regions or countries. However, what really enabled the RMB business in Hong Kong to take off and made

Hong Kong the first offshore RMB center was the pilot scheme for RMB cross-border trade settlement launched on 6 July 2009. Under the scheme, the Mainland designated enterprises in Shanghai, Guangzhou, Shenzhen, Dongguan, and Zhuhai to be allowed to use RMB as the settlement currency when trading with designated non-Mainland enterprises in Hong Kong, Macau, and ASEAN member countries. In 2010, the RMB trade settlement scheme was expanded to 20 provinces and municipalities, and overseas trade settlement was extended to the rest of the world. Since mid-2010, the pilot RMB trade settlement scheme was expanded to include all trade between China and the rest of world. The launch of RMB trade settlement to all countries in the rest of the world was an important milestone in RMB internationalization as it was the first time a large amount of onshore RMB was allowed to flow out of the Mainland to the rest of the world for payment purposes, i.e., as an international medium of exchange, one important function of an international currency. Considering the huge amount of international trade that China engages in with the rest of the world, the amount of RMB outflow could be enormous. Thus, starting from 2010, the offshore RMB business took off in Hong Kong and it became the most important offshore RMB center in the world until today. In January 2011, the government allowed certain approved Mainland companies to conduct outward direct investment (ODI) in RMB (called the RODI scheme). Moreover, a pilot scheme for RMB-settled inward foreign direct investment (RFDI) was launched in the same year. In addition, China launched the RMB Qualified Foreign Institutional Investor (RQFII) Scheme in 2011, Shanghai–Hong Kong Stock Connect in 2014, Shenzhen–Hong Kong Stock Connect in 2016, and Bond Connect in 2017. All these policies provided channels for RMB to flow from the Mainland to the outside world to become offshore RMB and for the offshore RMB to flow back to the Mainland to become onshore RMB again. In other words, RMB was truly used outside of China in large quantities as medium of exchange (e.g., to settle trade) and as store of value (e.g., as bank deposits and bonds).

Next, we shall explain how "one currency, two markets" works. Afterwards, we shall discuss the operation of the offshore market in Hong Kong and the problems and issues of the offshore market.

7.4   ONE CURRENCY, TWO MARKETS

The two markets refer to the onshore RMB market and the offshore RMB market. Each of them has its own foreign exchange market and financial market. The foreign exchange market consists of the spot market and the markets for derivatives such as futures, options, forwards, and swaps. The operation of the offshore foreign exchange market is different from that of the onshore foreign exchange market, as the onshore RMB is convertible only in the current account but not in the capital account, whereas the offshore RMB is convertible in both the current account and the capital account. Moreover, there are capital controls in the movement of onshore RMB to offshore and the movement of offshore RMB to onshore. However, the capital controls are imperfect as there are legal and not-so-legal channels by which people can move RMB in both directions. Such imperfect capital controls imply that the exchange rate of the onshore RMB and offshore RMB cannot deviate too much, otherwise there would be arbitrage that would narrow the gap between the two exchange rates. On average, the two exchange rates differ by less than 0.5 percent.

The financial market supplies financial products and services intermediated by the banks and other financial institutions such as asset management companies. The RMB-denominated financial products and services available in the onshore market include bonds, bank deposits, banking services, asset management products, A-share stocks (mainly open to domestic investors), offshore bonds that can be purchased using onshore RMB through Bond Connect, and Hong Kong stocks that can be purchased using onshore RMB through Stock Connect. The RMB-denominated financial products and services available in the offshore market include offshore RMB deposits, offshore RMB bonds (dim sum bonds), onshore bonds that can be

204 7 THE IMPORTANCE OF THE OFFSHORE RMB MARKET

purchased using offshore RMB through Bond Connect, stocks in the Mainland A-share market that can be purchased using offshore RMB through Stock Connect, onshore financial products purchased through the RQFII scheme, and an array of banking services such as RMB trade settlement and RMB direct investment settlement.

7.4.1 The Onshore RMB Foreign Exchange Market

The onshore RMB FX market is divided into two layers. The first layer is the retail market whose participants are the banks and their customers. This is a decentralized market where firms and individuals carry out FX transactions with their banks. The second layer is the wholesale market among banks, where banks trade FX with each other through the platform of the China Foreign Exchange Trade System (CFETS). This is a centralized market. The interbank FX market is much larger than the retail market. In 2018, the onshore interbank FX market turnover reached USD 24.8 trillion, about six times the retail FX market turnover (USD 4.2 trillion).

The main participants in the interbank FX market are banks and nonbank financial institutions, including commercial banks, policy banks, foreign banks, rural credit unions, and finance companies. Some conglomerates engaged in foreign operations also have access to the interbank FX market. Institutions involved in spot FX transactions significantly outnumber those involved in FX derivatives transactions. By 26 October 2020, there were 708 members eligible for spot FX transactions in the interbank FX market, 249 members eligible for forward transactions, 245 members eligible for swap transactions, 200 members eligible for currency swap transactions, and 153 members eligible for options transactions.[2] The PBC also actively participates in the FX market. Changes in the PBC's foreign reserves in a period basically reflect the PBC's net purchases/sales of foreign assets during that period.

Since 30 September 2015, the interbank FX market has been opened to foreign central banks and other official reserve management agencies, international financial institutions, and sovereign wealth funds. These types of institutions can access the interbank FX market through the PBC as an agent, or through a member of the interbank FX market as an agent, or by becoming a foreign member of the interbank FX market. There is no quota imposed on the amount of their transactions.

By 2018, the onshore interbank FX market covered 27 foreign currencies. RMB/USD transactions accounted for 96.8 percent of spot transactions, followed by much smaller percentages for transactions of renminbi/Japanese yen, renminbi/euro, and renminbi/other foreign currencies. In addition, 11 pairs of foreign currencies were facilitated in the spot, forward, and swap transactions in the interbank FX market, including the USD against nine foreign currencies and the euro against two foreign currencies. The interbank FX market opens at 9:30 a.m. and closes at 11:30 p.m. each trading day. Compared with the FX markets of other major international currencies, there are fewer cross-border transactions and fewer forwards and options trans- actions in China's onshore RMB FX market.

The key spot exchange rates for onshore renminbi FX market include the central parity rate and the market rate. The renminbi central parity rate is released by the CFETS at 9:15 a.m. each trading day. The renminbi market rate is the actual trading rate of renminbi in the interbank FX market. On 11 August 2015, the PBC reformed the formation mechanism for the central parity rate, narrowing its deviation from the market rate. Every morning on a trading day, the market makers would quote their rates to the China Foreign Exchange Trade System (CFETS), which then input these quotes into a formula (a weighted average of the quotes excluding the highest and lowest ones) to calculate the central parity rate. Compared with the previous mechanism, the biggest difference is that market makers are required to refer to the closing rate of the previous trading day. For this reason, after 11 August 2015, the central parity rate has been very close to the closing rate of the interbank FX market on the previous trading day.

The renminbi trading rate in the interbank market is con- strained by the central parity rate and the trading band. The

1994 exchange rate regime reform required that the renminbi trading rate in the interbank market shall not exceed the range set by the PBC. As of July 2005, the trading band was ±0.3 percent around the central parity rate. Since then, the PBC has widened the trading band several times, to ±0.5 percent on 21 May 2007, ±1 percent on 16 April 2012, and ±2 percent on 17 March 2014.[3] Since 11 August 2015, the RMB has moved to a managed floating exchange rate based on market supply and demand with reference to a basket of foreign currencies. China has stated that the basket is dominated by the US dollar, euro, Japanese yen, and South Korean won, with a smaller proportion made up of the British pound, Thai baht, Russian ruble, Australian dollar, Canadian dollar, and Singapore dollar.[4]

After 1994, the exchange rate of the RMB has been determined by the market, reflecting the supply and demand of FX. This, however, did not mean that the exchange rate was determined by the free market. Between 1994 and 2005, the market was still heavily influenced by the PBC through its buying or selling of RMB in exchange for foreign currencies in the onshore interbank market. From 1995 to 2005, the RMB/USD exchange rate was maintained at the level of 8.28 (subject to a narrow trading band) through the intervention of the PBC. After 2005, the RMB was under "managed float," and so the exchange rate was allowed to fluctuate more freely. The supply and demand of FX is influenced by many factors, such as the imports and exports of China, appreciation or depreciation expectations of the RMB, and the interest rates of China and those of other countries. Nonetheless, the PBC has been, and still is, the most important force that influences the exchange rate of renminbi. The PBC influences the market exchange rate in two ways: (1) constraining the market rate through the central parity rate and the trading band; (2) buying/selling FX in the market. After the reform of the central parity rate formation mechanism on 11 August 2015, the central parity rate began to be dominated by the closing rate of the previous trading day, but the PBC can still influence the market rate by the buying and selling of FX in the market.

7.4.2 *The Offshore RMB Foreign Exchange Market*

After the pilot RMB trade settlement scheme was expanded to include all trade between China and the rest of world in mid-2010, the offshore RMB FX market expanded rapidly. In 2014, the total daily turnover of the offshore RMB FX market in Hong Kong, Singapore, and London together reached more than USD 230 billion, four times that of the onshore market. Most of the offshore renminbi FX transactions take place in Hong Kong, the UK, Singapore, the United States, and Taiwan. Hong Kong's renminbi turnover has exceeded that of Mainland China.

The offshore renminbi FX forward transactions can be divided into two types: deliverable forward (DF) and non-deliverable forward (NDF). NDF transactions usually take place at offshore financial centers, which are not subject to currency issuing countries' restrictions on FX transactions. The RMB NDF market was first started in Singapore, but its volume was gradually surpassed by Hong Kong, a latecomer. Compared with DF contracts, NDF contracts involve no physical delivery and only require the participants in the contracts to settle the difference between the settlement price and the contracted price in foreign currency, usually in USDs.

However, the offshore RMB NDF market has been gradually overtaken by the deliverable offshore CNH market. NDF trades are mostly adopted on currencies whose issuing countries have been involved in the global economy but have limited capital account openness. As the CNH market further develops, the RMB NDF market is further substituted by the deliverable CNH market.

The formation of the offshore RMB FX market was closely related to the development of the offshore renminbi business. In late 2003, Hong Kong launched the personal renminbi business, marking the beginning of offshore renminbi business. In July 2009, companies began to settle cross-border trade in renminbi. In July 2010, the scope of renminbi business in Hong Kong expanded as all types of firms and institutions were allowed to open renminbi accounts, and banks were allowed to trade renminbi with each other. The offshore renminbi market began to take shape.

In the offshore market, the renminbi are mainly traded against the USD. In Hong Kong, renminbi/USD transactions accounted for 95 percent of renminbi FX turnover in 2018, followed by RMB/HKD and RMB/other currencies. The offshore renminbi FX market trades more derivatives than the onshore market.

The offshore renminbi spot exchange rate started to exist in July 2010. Before July 2010, offshore banks could only exchange and borrow renminbi through clearing banks when their renminbi operations generated a supply of renminbi funds or demand for RMB funds, and therefore the Hong Kong market did not have its own renminbi exchange rate. After July 2010, the new clearing agreement allowed offshore banks to trade renminbi with each other, and the offshore RMB interbank FX market and the offshore renminbi exchange rate began to form.

On 27 June 2011, the Hong Kong Treasury Markets Association (TMA) introduced the Hong Kong renminbi spot exchange rate (CNH) fixing, which is the average of quotes provided by banks excluding the two highest and two lowest quotes. Unlike the onshore renminbi central parity rate, however, the CNH fixing has no constraint on offshore market rate.

Because of a lack of free capital mobility between the offshore and onshore RMB markets, there is a difference between exchange rates of the CNH and CNY. However, because the capital controls between the onshore and offshore markets are imperfect, whenever the difference in CNH and CNY exchange rates becomes too large, companies engaged in cross-border trade would arbitrage through cross-border trade settlement in renminbi, which would narrow the difference.

The CNH is more volatile than the CNY. This is because, unlike CNY, CNH is not subject to the limits created by the central parity rate and the trading band, or direct intervention by the PBC. When changes in economic conditions at home or abroad lead to renminbi exchange rate fluctuations, CNH tends to change more than CNY. In general, renminbi appreciation is usually accompanied by a premium on CNH, while depreciation is usually accompanied by a discount on CNH.

7.5 SETTLEMENT AND CLEARING OF RENMINBI PAYMENTS

RMB transactions in Hong Kong are settled through the Real Time Gross Settlement (RTGS) system, called CHATS (Clearing House Automated Transfer System), which is operated by the Hong Kong Interbank Clearing Limited (HKICL).[5] The Hong Kong RTGS system settles payments in HKD, USD, RMB, and EUR. Thus, RMB is only one of the currencies settled through the RTGS. The Bank of China (Hong Kong) Limited, being the clearing bank in Hong Kong, maintains a settlement account with the People's Bank of China and is a member of China's National Advanced Payment System (CNAPS). The renminbi RTGS system in Hong Kong can be regarded as a technical extension of CNAPS in Mainland China, but governed by Hong Kong laws. As of September 2019, the daily amount of RMB settlement through the Hong Kong RTGS (over RMB 1 trillion per day) had exceeded that of the HKD settlement (about HKD 0.94 trillion per day, which was equivalent to about RMB 0.84 trillion per day) to become the most settled currency in the Hong Kong RTGS.[6]

As for cross-border payments of RMB in the onshore market, China has, since 2015, set up a payment system that would potentially greatly enhance the efficiency of the interbank payments of RMB across the globe. It is called the Cross-Border Interbank Payment System (CIPS). Phases I and II of CIPS started operation in 2015 and 2018 respectively.

As mentioned before, China has established a number of offshore renminbi clearing banks around the world that participate in clearing and settlement of RMB payments. Before CIPS started to function, an offshore foreign entity could carry out cross-border clearing and settlement of RMB payments with China in the following two ways.

– The first way is through an offshore official RMB clearing bank, with which the offshore company has an account. This channel makes use of the High Value Payment System (HVPS) of the CNAPS.[7]
– The second way is through an onshore commercial bank acting as correspondent of an offshore commercial bank, with which the offshore company has an account. This channel makes use of the Society for World Interbank Financial Telecommunication (SWIFT) system for transmission of the payment messages.

After CIPS becomes fully functioning, all cross-border payments are expected to use either CIPS or CNAPS, with a preference for CIPS by the PBC.

7.6   THE CROSS-BORDER INTERBANK PAYMENT SYSTEM

The Cross-Border Interbank Payment System (CIPS) is a modern large-value payment system (LVPS) backed by the PBC. Phase 1 of the system was launched on 8 October 2015, and the latest phase (Phase 2) was launched on 2 May 2018. Its main purpose is to facilitate the use of the renminbi globally by cutting costs and processing times and allowing participation by more global institutions.[8] CIPS provides new channels for clients wanting to make RMB payments more efficient. Aside from lower direct cost and higher speed, clients have benefited from higher straight-through processing (STP) rates.[9] The PBC describes it as a "highway" for RMB internationalization.

There are two types of designated participants. Various international and domestic banks are direct participants in the system. Direct participants (such as the China branch of a foreign bank) must open nostro accounts with CIPS Shanghai Ltd.[10] Indirect participants (such as an offshore branch of a foreign bank) can use CIPS through one of the direct participants. As of the end of March 2018, a total of 31 domestic and foreign direct participants, as well as 695 domestic and foreign indirect participants have joined CIPS, expanding its actual business scope to 148 countries and jurisdictions. The number of participants using the system is widely expected to increase over time.

The SWIFT messaging system that is universally used for global payments does not support Chinese characters, causing a connection issue with CNAPS. By contrast, CIPS supports transmission in both Chinese and English, making it compatible with the existing SWIFT MT messaging system. As mentioned above, before the full functioning of CIPS, cross-border renminbi clearing and settlement of the payments of foreign entities to and from China were often conducted through clearing banks in the offshore hubs. The clearing banks were allocated buying and selling quotas of RMB in the FX market to provide sufficient RMB liquidity to the offshore market. In addition, they were allocated quotas in the onshore interbank lending market so as to provide extra RMB liquidity to the offshore market. When the capital account becomes more open, and CIPS becomes freely accessible by foreign banks without going through the clearing banks, these measures will no longer be needed, and the clearing banks will no longer be the main channel for cross-border RMB clearing and settlement.

Competition between the CNAPS and CIPS is expected to increase efficiency in the Chinese international payment system. Right now, CIPS adopts a non-state-owned shareholding governance structure so that its corporate governance and market-oriented nature would be more conducive to efficiency and innovation. It is run by an entity that is not a part of the government but rather under the supervision and administration of the PBC, with its members being the major commercial banks in the world.[11] This, it is hoped, will help CIPS to quickly become a world-class, professional system with the help of its member banks, which are global banks full of experience in international transactions. The PBC highly recommends that banks use CIPS for all renminbi cross-border transactions. For now, banks can still choose between the two options – CIPS or CNAPS. The Chinese regulatory authority is working on a series of access mechanisms to promote and monitor CIPS performance.

The operating hours of CIPS have been extended to $5 \times 24 + 4$ hours, basically covering the working hours of all financial markets in every time zone around the globe. Deferred net settlement (DNS) has been introduced as a supplement to real-time gross settlement (RTGS) so as to meet diversified demands of CIPS participants and to facilitate cross-border e-commerce.[12] Thus, it is a hybrid system. There will be more discussion on the differences between DNS and RTGS later in this chapter. Compared with the old system, CIPS has been capable of supporting more foreign direct participants and is ready to incorporate more eligible foreign institutions.

According to the PBC, the launch of CIPS is a milestone in financial market infrastructure development in China, signaling a remarkable progress in building a modern payment system that supports both domestic and cross-border RMB payments. It is expected that CIPS will continue to upgrade its services and functions based on the demands of the market and the requirements of RMB internationalization.[13] The operator of CIPS said that it processed 135.7 billion yuan (USD 19.4 billion) a day in 2019, with participation from 96 countries and regions. By comparison, SWIFT processes around USD 5 to 6 trillion per day. Thus, CIPS is still a small player in the game.

In order to understand the relationship between CIPS and CNAPS, it is useful to understand CHIPS and Fedwire of the United States. By and large, CIPS is modelled after CHIPS, while CNAPS is like the Fedwire. The High Value Payment System (HVPS) of CNAPS is a RTGS system. It has been in operation nationwide since June 2005. HVPS mainly handles inter-city and local credit transfers above a given value as well as urgent low-value transfers electronically. Payment instructions are sent in real time and cleared transaction by transaction. CNAPS is mainly a payment system for onshore transactions. The CIPS, in contrast, is a hybrid system. It handles both DNS and RTGS. It is set up mainly to deal with cross-border RMB payments. CIPS is operated by Cross-Border Interbank Payment & Clearing (Shanghai) Co., Ltd., which is supervised by the PBC.

Fedwire is a large-value payment system owned and operated by the Federal Reserve System of the US government. It is a real time gross settlement (RTGS) system, meaning that it settles payments in real time, and requires settlement of gross payments from any party rather than the payment of the net balance between any two parties at the end of a trading day. Fedwire is mainly used for domestic USD payments within the United States but is also partially used for cross-border USD payments.

The Clearing House Interbank Payments System (CHIPS) is also a large-value payment system, but it is privately owned.[14] It is a hybrid system, meaning that it combines components of both net (DNS) and real-time gross settlement (RTGS). Some payments may be settled individually, as in RTGS, while others, usually less urgent payments, may be pooled together and netted (using DNS). As of 2012, about 95 percent of cross-border USD payments between the United States and other countries are processed by CHIPS.[15]

What are the pros and cons of Fedwire and CHIPS? First, because settlement is based on real time, Fedwire is faster than the DNS of CHIPS on that account. However, since most cross-border transactions do not require immediate settlement – settlement at the end of the day is usually good enough – DNS in CHIPS is not that much worse than Fedwire in terms of the speed of settlement. Second, 97 percent of settlement commands of CHIPS is automated (compared with about 50 percent for Fedwire), using straight-through processing (STP), so the processing time is mostly within 20 minutes.[16] Thus, the time efficiency of CHIPS is comparable to that of Fedwire. Third, and most important, as Fedwire is a RTGS, it requires higher intraday liquidity to complete the settlements. Thus, it is more expensive in terms of liquidity cost compared with a hybrid system such as CHIPS. By contrast, DNS in CHIPS clears bilateral payments on a net basis, which means that the bilateral payments between two parties will be netted and settled at the end of the day. Thus, the liquidity requirements are much lower, and so the system is cheaper. For example, under Fedwire, if Bank A has to transfer USD 100,000 to Bank B, and

Bank B has to transfer USD 40,000 to Bank A, each transaction will be executed separately and in real time. So, there will be two transactions. The intraday liquidity required of Bank A is USD 100,000, and that of Bank B is USD 40,000. The total intraday liquidity required for both banks together is USD 140,000. Under DNS in CHIPS, if Bank A has to transfer USD 100,000 to Bank B and Bank B has to transfer USD 40,000 to Bank A, based on netting, only a net amount of USD 60,000 needs to be transferred from Bank A to Bank B at the end of the day. So, there will be only one transaction at the end of the day. Thus, it is slower than real time settlement. However, the liquidity requirements are much lower. The intraday liquidity required of Bank A is USD 60,000, and that of Bank B is zero. The total amount of intraday liquidity required is only USD 60,000. One expects that a similar comparison in terms of liquidity costs applies to CNAPS and CIPS.

7.7   WOULD CIPS MAKE CHINESE INTERNATIONAL PAYMENTS FREE FROM THE LEGAL REACH OF FOREIGN COUNTRIES?

Structurally, there are two components in funds transfers: "the instructions," which contain information on the sender and receiver of the funds, and the actual movement or "transfer of funds." The instructions may be sent in a variety of ways, including by electronic access to networks operated by payment systems such as the Fedwire or CHIPS or CIPS; by access to financial telecommunications systems, such as SWIFT; or email, facsimile, telephone, or telex. Fedwire and CHIPS are used to facilitate USD transfers between two domestic endpoints or the USD segment of international transactions. SWIFT is an international messaging service that is used to transmit payment instructions for the vast majority of international interbank transactions, which can be denominated in numerous currencies.

The SWIFT network is a messaging infrastructure, not a payment system, which provides users with a private international communications link among themselves. For transfers of USD, the actual funds movements (payments) are completed through correspondent bank relationships, Fedwire, or CHIPS. More generally, movement of payments denominated in different currencies occurs through correspondent bank relationships or over funds transfer systems in the relevant country (i.e., the counterparts of Fedwire and CHIPS in other countries, such as CIPS of China, TARGET2 of the EU, CHAPS of the UK, and BOJNET of Japan). In contrast to Fedwire and CHIPS, a SWIFT message may travel directly from a US financial institution to a foreign institution or vice versa, in the case of international USD payment.

Currently, SWIFT is the most widely used messaging system for international funds transfer. Funds transfers between the domestic country and a foreign country often involve a combination of a SWIFT message and messages in a national payment system such as Fedwire or CHIPS or other domestic institutions in the same transaction. For example, a US institution may receive a SWIFT message from a foreign institution and map the message into a Fedwire or CHIPS message before passing it along to the additional US financial institutions serving as correspondents. When a funds transfer requires multiple correspondents' participation and involves more than one message system, one or more of the institutions translates or "maps over" the data from one message format to another. An estimated 70 percent of the traffic on the CHIPS system, for example, originates from SWIFT message traffic.

The competitive advantage of SWIFT is that it provides automation of the transmission process through standardization of the messages as well as providing security of the messages being transmitted. Standardization and automation make the payment process more efficient. Its success is probably related to network externalities – it has established a standard of messaging within a vast network of banks, and it is hard for an alternative standard to challenge SWIFT when most of the existing banks are already communicating with each other using the established standard.

SWIFT is a cooperative society under Belgian law owned by its member financial institutions with offices around the world.

However, there have been many reports about how the United States has used its influence or technology to try to prevent foreign countries from using the SWIFT payment messaging system for the purpose of sanctioning other countries or to collect international interbank payment information of other countries for the sake of its own national interest.[17] For example, Iranian banks were disconnected from SWIFT in March 2012 as international sanctions tightened against Tehran over its disputed nuclear program. However, in 2016, Iranian banks which were no longer on international sanctions lists were reconnected to SWIFT as part of the Iran nuclear agreement called JCPOA.[18] Even though this enables movement of money from and to these Iranian banks, foreign banks remain wary of doing business with the country. Due to primary sanctions, transactions of US banks with Iran or transactions in USD with Iran both remain prohibited. Elsewhere, the German newspaper *Der Spiegel* reported in September 2013 that the National Security Agency (NSA) of the United States widely monitors banking transactions via SWIFT, as well as credit card transactions.[19] According to the report, the NSA intercepted and retained data from the SWIFT network used by thousands of banks to send transaction information, presumably securely. SWIFT was named as a "target," according to documents leaked by Edward Snowden. The documents revealed that the NSA spied on SWIFT using a variety of methods, including reading "SWIFT printer traffic from numerous banks."

As mentioned in a previous chapter, one of the objectives of RMB internationalization is to be independent from foreign countries, foreign currencies, and the payment systems controlled by foreign countries, such as the United States, the USD and the payment system controlled or strongly influenced by the United States. In order to be independent from the foreign-controlled payment system, not only does China have to encourage the use of RMB for international payments but it also has to establish its own international payment system for RMB payments and its own international payments messaging system. Presumably, CIPS can play such an important role. However, it will probably take a long time for such independence to be realized, given that the vast majority of China's international payments are denominated in USD and that the situation is unlikely to change in the foreseeable future.

The relationship between CIPS and SWIFT is an interesting issue. SWIFT, as a funds transfer messaging system, is an important component of the infrastructure for global payments. SWIFT, being the largest global interbank payment messaging system, remains at the center of the global infrastructure for financial payments. CIPS seems likely to serve as a complementary offering as it operates using the same standard messaging syntax to enable easy adoption. It will use SWIFT for interbank messaging and SWIFT BIC code as its routing code. But in the future, it is believed that it will operate independently and have its own direct communication line between financial organizations. Thus, in the long run, the CIPS can potentially make Chinese international payments free from the legal reach and sanctions of foreign countries.

7.8 THE OPERATION OF THE HONG KONG OFFSHORE MARKET

7.8.1 Supply of Offshore Renminbi

The main sources of supply of offshore RMB are as follows.

The supply of offshore RMB mainly comes from the settlement of China's imports of goods and services in RMB – Chinese firms pay for their imports in RMB so that RMB flows out of China.

The second source of supply of offshore RMB is through the remittance of the RMB-denominated wage income of foreigners working in Mainland China to foreign countries or regions such as Hong Kong. This is equivalent to China paying for the imported labor services in RMB. The above two sources are based on RMB settlement of current account transactions in the balance of payments accounts of China.

The third source of supply is RMB outward direct investment (RODI). For example, when Chinese firms set up manufacturing facilities in foreign countries, they may pay for the costs of the buildings, machines, and equipment using RMB. Or, when they acquire foreign companies abroad, they may pay for the amount in RMB.

The fourth source of supply of offshore RMB is when Chinese financial institutions invest abroad using RMB through the RMB Qualified Domestic Institutional Investors (RQDII) scheme. The above two sources are based on RMB settlement of capital account transactions in the balance of payments accounts.

A fifth source of liquidity, in the case of Hong Kong, is the RMB Liquidity Facility from the HKMA. This facility is intended for securing the confidence of financial institutions in the Hong Kong offshore market. The sources of RMB in HKMA for providing the liquidity are the HKMA's own source of RMB funds as well as the bilateral currency swap arrangement between the HKMA and the PBC (the value of the swap line is RMB 400 billion, although it is rarely used). Through the RMB Liquidity Facility, financial institutions (called authorized institutions) can borrow from the HKMA using certain approved types of assets as collaterals. As of December 2018, the quota from the RMB Liquidity Facility is: intra-day 10 billion yuan, overnight 10 billion yuan, and 2 billion per bank for nine banks (total 18 billion per day), totaling 38 billion yuan per day.

In the case of other offshore centers, the fifth source of RMB liquidity is from the PBC under the bilateral currency swap agreement between the PBC and the central bank of the offshore center.

7.8.2   The Back-Flow Channels of Offshore Renminbi

The main back-flow channels of the offshore RMB are described below.

The first back-flow channel of offshore RMB to the onshore market is the settlement of China's exports of goods and services in RMB. Foreign firms pay for their imports of Chinese goods and services using offshore RMB, and so the RMB flows back to the Mainland.

The second channel is the issuance of dim sum bonds (i.e., RMB-denominated bonds issued offshore) by entities such as domestic or foreign firms or Chinese government agencies, and the proceeds then flow back to the Mainland for investment or governmental uses. There are many types of issuers of dim sum bonds. They include Chinese companies and banks, foreign companies that do business in China, the Ministry of Finance of China, and even the PBC. By issuing dim sum bonds in Hong Kong, they borrow RMB from the offshore market and use the funds in the onshore market. The third channel is through cross-border RMB loans from offshore banks to onshore entities.

The fourth channel is the use of offshore RMB for inward direct investment in Mainland China through the RMB foreign direct investment (RFDI) scheme. The fifth channel is the use of offshore RMB to invest in the onshore financial market such as the stock market or bond market by qualified foreign institutional investors through the RMB Qualified Foreign Institutional Investors (RQFII) scheme.

Finally, offshore RMB can flow back to Mainland China through the Shanghai–Hong Kong Stock Connect, Shenzhen–Hong Kong Stock Connect, and Bond Connect schemes. Whereas offshore RMB must be used to invest in Mainland China through the Stock Connect schemes, both offshore RMB and foreign currencies can be used to invest in Mainland China through the Bond Connect scheme. Investment principal and returns through Bond Connect can return to Hong Kong as offshore RMB because the investment originates from the offshore market. However, if one invests in bond funds through a bank in Mainland China (not through Bond Connect), the principal and returns both cannot return as offshore yuan, as the investment originates from the onshore market.

7.8.3 The Offshore Financial Market

One of the most common measures of the size of a financial market is the amount of bank deposits. At the end of April 2020, the total amount of RMB deposits in Hong Kong (excluding certificates of deposit) was 654 billion yuan. By comparison, the size of the same deposit pool fell from more than 1 trillion yuan in December 2014 to

547 billion yuan in December 2016. This is the consequence of the setback to the offshore market triggered by the reform of the formation mechanism of the central parity of the exchange rate in August 2015.

However, the deposit pool cannot fully capture the scale of activities of the RMB offshore market. It is arguable that the Hong Kong RGTS captures the scale of activities of the offshore market better, as it shows the amount of RMB payments settled by the banking system in Hong Kong. In 2019, the Hong Kong RGTS recorded more than 1 trillion yuan of payments per day on average.

Another important financial product in the Hong Kong offshore RMB market is the dim sum bond. The value of issuance of dim sum bonds has fallen in the last few years, however. In 2017, the amount of dim sum bonds issued totaled 56.2 billion yuan (USD 8.74 billion), down from its peak of 288.5 billion yuan in 2014. According to the *South China Morning Post*, the 80.5 per cent decline from 2014 to 2017 "coincides with cheaper funding costs in China's onshore bond market, as well as competing market access avenues that have made it easier for foreign investors to gain direct access into the 52.3 trillion yuan onshore interbank bond market."[20] The outstanding amount of dim sum bonds peaked at 380.5 billion yuan at the end of 2014, and it has gradually fallen since then.

In the past, many issuers of dim sum bonds were Mainland companies or the central government, but there has been an increase in the issuance of dim sum bonds by foreigners. On 7 November 2018, the PBC began to sell PBC bills, a kind of dim sum bond, in Hong Kong. It is noteworthy that by absorbing RMB in Hong Kong, the issuance of PBC bills can raise interest rates in the offshore market in Hong Kong and the cost of shorting the currency. Instead of mentioning this effect, however, the PBC and HKMA emphasized the fact that the issuance of PBC bills could facilitate the construction of the yield curve of the offshore RMB-denominated government bond market. Indeed, PBC bills are short-term bonds, with 10 billion yuan of 1-year maturity and 10 billion yuan of 3-month maturity. On the other hand, the bonds issued by the Ministry of Finance in Hong Kong are all of 2-year to 30-year maturity.

Other financial products and services offered by banks and nonbank financial institutions in the offshore RMB market are: RMB FX spot and FX derivatives transactions, RMB-based funds (including listed, unlisted, and exchange-traded funds), RMB offshore loans and cross-border loans, cross-border RMB investment in stocks and bonds (through the Stock Connect and Bond Connect schemes), RMB cross-border trade and direct investment settlement, and other RMB payment services. The details of these activities have been discussed in the previous chapters.

BOX 7.1 **The economics behind the operation of the Hong Kong offshore market**

Determination of the Interest Rates and Exchange Rate in the Offshore Market

Given the small size of the offshore market relative to that of the onshore one, it is quite unlikely that the activities in the offshore market can exert any substantial effects on the onshore variables such as the money supply, interest rates, and exchange rates. Thus, it is reasonable to assume that the onshore exchange rate and interest rates are determined by the onshore foreign exchange market, monetary policy, and financial market. The offshore exchange rate is basically determined by the onshore exchange rate through cross-border arbitrage, as the onshore capital controls are imperfect. The offshore interest rate is then determined by the uncovered interest parity condition, as there is free capital mobility for CNH in the offshore market.

The following model can help us to understand how the offshore exchange rate and interest rates are determined by the onshore variables. We then use the model to carry out a thought experiment in which there is an expectation of depreciation of the RMB in the onshore market to see how it affects the interest rate in the offshore

BOX 7.1　**(cont.)**

market. The model and the thought experiment can help us better understand the relationship between onshore and offshore interest rates, and how the extent of capital controls affects such a relationship.

Let us consider the following three assets: a 1-year interbank loan in the offshore RMB market, a 1-year interbank loan in the onshore market, and a 1-year interbank loan in the offshore USD market. The rates of return to these assets are 1-year CNH HIBOR in the offshore RMB market, 1-year CNY SHIBOR in the onshore RMB market, and 1-year USD LIBOR in the offshore USD market. HIBOR is Hong Kong Interbank Offered Rate; SHIBOR is Shanghai Interbank Offered Rate; LIBOR is London Interbank Offered Rate. Let us define the following variables:

R_{CNH} = 1-year CNH HIBOR
R_{CNY} = 1-year CNY SHIBOR
R_{USD} = 1-year USD LIBOR

E_{CNH} and E_{CNY} are exchange rates of CNH and CNY respectively, in terms of the amount of RMB per USD. Thus, a higher exchange rate means that the RMB depreciates against the USD. $(E_{CNH})^e$ and $(E_{CNY})^e$ are the expected values of E_{CNH} and E_{CNY} respectively.

The conditions to consider in determining the interest rate and exchange rate of CNH are given below.

(7.1) $R_{CNH} = R_{USD} + [(E_{CNH})^e - E_{CNH}] / E_{CNH}$ (**uncovered interest parity in the offshore market**, which holds because there is free capital mobility)

(7.2) $E_{CNH} \approx E_{CNY}$, as the **capital controls are imperfect**, and so when the difference in the two exchange rates gets too large, companies engaged in cross-border trade would arbitrage through cross-border trade settlement in renminbi.

(7.3) $(E_{CNY})^e \approx (E_{CNH})^e$ as implied from (7.2)

(7.4) $R_{CNY} = R_{USD} + [(E_{CNY})^e - E_{CNY}] / E_{CNY} - \delta$ (**modified uncovered interest parity condition in the onshore market**, taking into account capital controls)

where the magnitude of δ reflects transaction cost, which is positively related to the strength of control on capital flow; δ is positive (negative) if there is control on capital outflow (inflow);

BOX 7.1   **(cont.)**

$[(E_{CNH})^e - E_{CNH}] / E_{CNH}$ = expected rate of depreciation of CNH;
$[(E_{CNY})^e - E_{CNY}] / E_{CNY}$ = expected rate of depreciation of CNY.

Assume that R_{CNY}, R_{USD}, $(E_{CNY})^e$ and δ are exogenous, while R_{CNH}, E_{CNY}, E_{CNH} and $(E_{CNH})^e$ are endogenous.

There are four equations (7.1), (7.2), (7.3), and (7.4) and four unknowns (i.e., the endogenous variables).

When some exogenous variables change, the endogenous variables will change as well. For example, when there are some shocks that cause people to expect that the CNY would depreciate, it can lead the interest rate in the offshore CNH to increase, even though the onshore CNY interest rate remains unchanged. The reason is as follows. There is capital control in the onshore market while there is no capital control in the offshore market. So, the expected rate of return to foreign currency interbank loans (when converted back to yuan) can be different from the rate of return to onshore interbank CNY loans as there is capital control in the onshore market. By contrast, the expected rate of return to foreign currency interbank loans (when converted back to yuan) must be equal to the rate of return to offshore interbank CNH loans as there is no capital control in the offshore market and any difference between the two rates of return would lead to buying or selling of CNH in the offshore market, leading to a change in R_{CNH} until the two rates of return are equalized.

Initially, we assume that there is no capital inflow or outflow. As the government sees no need to control capital inflow or outflow, it sets $\delta = 0$ initially. So, it must be the case that $E_{CNH} = E_{CNY}$, otherwise arbitrageurs would move RMB from onshore to offshore or vice versa, as capital controls are imperfect. When the shock arrives, it causes the market to expect the future exchange value of CNY to decrease, so $(E_{CNY})^e$ increases. According to the modified uncovered interest parity condition equation (7.4), this causes E_{CNY} to increase as investors (banks) sell CNY and buy USD in the onshore market and lend out USD to other banks in the USD interbank lending/borrowing market. The increase in E_{CNY} means that $E_{CNY} > E_{CNH}$ initially. This creates

BOX 7.1   (cont.)

incentives for people with onshore RMB to arbitrage by moving the RMB from onshore to offshore. Thus, there is capital outflow from the onshore market to the offshore market. Oftentimes, in order to curb the capital outflow, the PBC would strengthen the capital controls. This would lead to an increase in δ to a positive number. If δ increases by a sufficiently large amount, E_{CNY} falls back to its original level, according to equation (7.4). Thus, $E_{CNH} = E_{CNY}$ is restored, and there is no capital outflow anymore. In the meantime, the increase in $(E_{CNY})^e$ leads to an increase in $(E_{CNH})^e$ as well, according to equation (7.3). Thus, R_{CNH} increases according to equation (7.1). This explains why when there are some shocks that cause people to expect that the CNY would depreciate we often see that the offshore CNH interest rate rises while the onshore CNY interest rate can remain unchanged. This can explain why the interest rate in the offshore market, e.g., CNH HIBOR, is more volatile than the onshore market – the onshore interest rate is kept more stable by the PBC, while the offshore interest rate is allowed to fluctuate according to the market condition.

Figure Box 7.1A shows that the exchange rate of the onshore RMB (CNY) is slightly different from that of the offshore RMB (CNH), but the difference is usually not very large. On average, the two exchange rates differ by less than 0.5 percent. This is because the capital controls are imperfect, and so there is arbitrage when the two variables differ too much. This justifies the assumption that $E_{CNH} \approx E_{CNY}$. However, when the market expects there to be a large depreciation (appreciation) of the onshore RMB, the exchange value of the CNH would be distinctly smaller (larger) than that of the CNY, i.e., the CNH has a negative (positive) premium over the CNY. This happened on 12 August 2015, when the CNH has a premium of −1.66 percent over the CNY. An even larger offshore–onshore differential occurred on 6 January 2016, when the CNH premium reached −2.23 percent. This means that the offshore exchange rate is more volatile, as it is more market-determined.

Figure Box 7.1B shows that the CNH interest rate (HIBOR interbank offer rate) is distinctly more volatile than the CNY interest rate

BOX 7.1   (cont.)

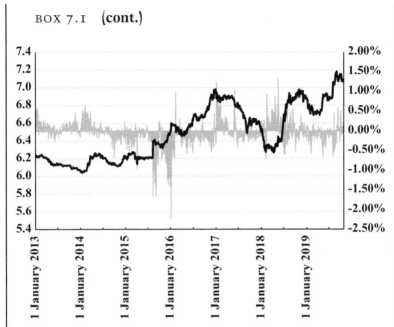

Percentage premium of CNH over CNY (right-hand scale)

— CNY/USD (left-hand scale)

FIGURE BOX 7.1A CNY/USD exchange rate and percentage premium of CNH over CNY, 2013–2019.
Note that the CNH exchange rate is more volatile than the CNY exchange rate, as the former is subject to less government intervention. Large RMB appreciation is usually accompanied by a premium on CNH, while large depreciation is usually accompanied by a discount on CNH. On average, the percentage difference is not large due to arbitrage (as a result of the imperfect capital controls).

(SHIBOR interbank offer rate), providing evidence to support the prediction of the model presented above. The SHIBOR was rather stable as there was usually government intervention in the determination of that rate. By contrast, the CNH HIBOR is largely market-determined, and it is very sensitive to changes in the depreciation/appreciation expectation of the onshore RMB, as explained in our model above. Unlike the difference between the onshore and offshore exchange rates, which is quite small (in percentage terms) on average, the difference

BOX 7.1   **(cont.)**

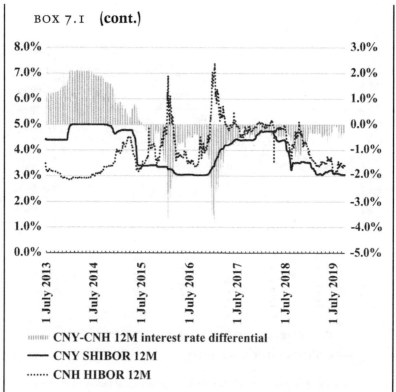

┉┉ **CNY-CNH 12M interest rate differential**
— **CNY SHIBOR 12M**
⋯⋯ **CNH HIBOR 12M**

FIGURE BOX 7.1B CNY SHIBOR 12-month rate vs. CNH HIBOR 12-month rate, 2013–2019.
Refer to the right-hand scale for the CNY–CNH interest rate differential. Note that the CNH interest rate is more volatile than the CNY interest rate, as the former is subject to less government intervention and more sensitive to depreciation/appreciation expectations of the onshore RMB. Capital controls lead to a non-trivial CNY–CNH interest rate differential.

between the onshore and offshore interest rates is quite large (in percentage terms) on average. This shows that capital controls can in fact sustain a large difference between the interest rates in the onshore and offshore markets as it imposes a non-trivial transaction cost on conversion between the onshore and offshore RMB. Thus, we can see more clearly "one currency, two markets" in action here. It is also interesting to note that before mid-2015, the CNH HIBOR rate was generally below the CNY

BOX 7.1 (cont.)

SHIBOR, whereas after mid-2015, the reverse was true. Indeed, there is evidence to indicate that the government tried to curb capital inflows before mid-2015, whereas it tried to curb capital outflows after mid-2015. This support our view, expressed through the model above, that when the Chinese government tries to control capital inflow (outflow), CNY SHIBOR is larger (smaller) than CNH HIBOR.

In contrast to the large onshore–offshore interest rate differential for the RMB, the onshore–offshore interest rate differential for the USD is much smaller under normal circumstances, as shown in Figure Box 7.1C.

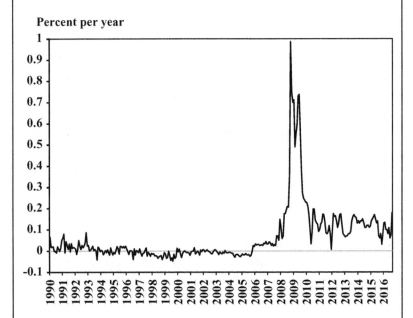

FIGURE BOX 7.1C London three-month Eurodollar rate less US three-month money market rate, 1990–2016.

Note that the average onshore–offshore interest rate differential for the USD is much lower than that of the RMB, as shown in Figure Box 7.1B. The difference between the London and US interest rates on dollar deposits is usually very close to zero, but it spiked up sharply in the fall of 2008 as the investment bank Lehman Brothers collapsed.

Source: Krugman, Obstfeld, and Melitz (2018): Fig. 9.4; original source: Board of Governors of the Federal Reserve System and OECD, monthly data.

BOX 7.1   **(cont.)**

Before mid-2007, the onshore–offshore interest rate differential was trivial, being always less than 0.1 percentage point. Starting from August 2007, as the global financial crisis was brewing, the differential began to creep up. In October 2008, the month after the collapse of Lehman Brothers, during the global financial crisis, the offshore USD interest rate reached a peak of about 1 percentage point higher than that of the onshore interest rate. Apparently, investors believed that the onshore USD deposits would be backstopped by the US authorities, while the offshore USD deposits would not receive much protection. The difference between the offshore and onshore deposit rates is a risk premium. After mid-2010, the offshore market more or less got back to normal, and the magnitude of the offshore–onshore interest rate differential subsided to less than 0.2 percentage point. From January 1990 to January 2017, excluding the abnormal time of the years 2008 and 2009, the magnitude of the differential is less than 0.1 percentage point on average. This is much smaller than the magnitude of the average offshore–onshore interest rate differential of the RMB, which is about 0.94 percentage point from 1 July 2013 to 1 July 2019. The difference between the two offshore–onshore interest rate differentials is clearly due to the fact that there is free capital mobility in the United States, but much less free capital mobility in China.

Covered Interest Parity (CIP)
The covered interest parity condition is a market equilibrium condition which states that the rates of return to deposits in any two currencies at a given future date should be equal when the proceeds from investing in the two deposits are converted into the same currency at that future date at the forward exchange rate. Theoretically, the condition should hold when two currencies are both fully convertible and the deposits are located in the same country. If the two deposits are located in two different countries, there may be deviation from CIP if one of the governments imposes regulations that impede the free movement of foreign funds across national borders. This is what we expect can happen in the case of the

BOX 7.1 **(cont.)**

conversion between onshore RMB (CNY) deposits and USD deposits, as there are capital controls onshore.

The covered interest parity condition states that the following equation should hold when investors are indifferent between holding home currency deposits and foreign currency deposits.

$$1 + R = \frac{F}{E}(1 + R^*) \tag{7.5}$$

where R and R^* are the interest rates of home and foreign currency deposits respectively and E and F are the spot exchange rate and forward exchange rate (in number of domestic currency units per foreign currency unit) respectively. In equation (7.5), the left-hand side is the gross return of investing in domestic time deposits, while the right-hand side is the gross return of investing in foreign time deposits (of the same maturity) when converted back to the domestic currency upon maturity. If the left-hand side is larger than the right-hand side, then an investor would have no incentive to hold any foreign currency deposit, as the return to holding home currency deposit is higher than that to holding foreign currency deposit. Thus, people would sell foreign currency and buy home currency, leading to a depreciation of the foreign currency until the CIP holds. Figure 7.1D shows how well the CIP fits reality.

Treating USD as the home currency, and RMB as the foreign currency, Figure Box 7.1D shows the expected 1-year gross return of investing in USD time deposits (black curve), CNH time deposits (dotted curve), and CNY time deposits (gray curve) when converted back to USD after one year. Following conventional practice (e.g., Du, Tepper, and Verdelhan 2018), we use the inter-bank offer rates as proxies for time-deposit rates, i.e., USD LIBOR to stand for R, and CNH HIBOR or CNY SHIBOR to stand for R^*.[1]

In the case that the home currency is USD and the foreign currency is CNY, one can expect there to be deviation from CIP, as there are capital controls in China. When China tries to curb capital inflow, one can expect the left-hand side of equation (7.5) to be less than the

BOX 7.1   **(cont.)**

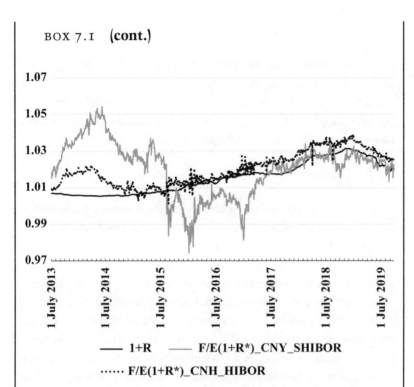

FIGURE BOX 7.1D Deviation from covered interest parity, 1990–2016
Note that the deviation of the grey curve from the solid black curve
indicates deviation from covered interest parity (CIP) of the CNY
(onshore RMB). The deviation of the dotted black curve from the solid
black curve indicates deviation from CIP of the CNH (offshore RMB).
The larger deviation of the CNY from the CIP reflects the onshore
capital controls.
R= 1-year LIBOR USD interest rate; R*= 1-year HIBOR CNH or
SHIBOR CNY interest rate; F= 1-year deliverable forward exchange
rate of CNH/USD or non-deliverable forward exchange rate of CNY/
USD; E= spot exchange rate of CNH/USD or CNY/USD.

right hand side, for without capital controls, capital would flow from
offshore to onshore to take advantage of the higher return to CNY
deposits. Conversely, when China tries to curb capital outflow, one can
expect the left-hand side of equation (7.5) to be greater than the right-
hand side. A comparison between the gray curve (right-hand side of
the equation (7.5)) and the black solid curve (left-hand side of the

BOX 7.1   **(cont.)**

equation (7.5)) in Figure 7.1D shows that the left-hand side of equation (7.5) is less than the right-hand side before mid-2015, indicating that China had to control capital inflows. After mid-2015, until mid-2017, Figure 7.1D indicates that China had to control capital outflows. After mid-2017, the left-hand side of equation (7.5) and the right-hand side are about equal, indicating that there was no major control of capital inflows or outflows. The dotted curve shows that the deviations from CIP are much smaller for the CNH and USD, indicating the free convertibility of CNH and the free capital mobility in the Hong Kong offshore market. From mid-2013 till late 2014, there seems to be a risk premium placed on CNH compared with the USD, as the return to CNH deposit is a bit higher than that to USD deposit.

1 SHIBOR (Shanghai Interbank Offered Rates) is set daily based on the average interbank offered rates of 18 banks, with tenors ranging from overnight to one year. The National Interbank Funding Center is authorized to calculate and release SHIBOR rates.

7.9   PROBLEMS AND ISSUES WITH THE HONG KONG OFFSHORE MARKET

The growth of the offshore market depends on (1) onshore financial development and (2) the integration between the onshore and offshore markets through capital account liberalization. The Hong Kong offshore market will be able to grow faster and function better, offering a growing variety of financial services, only when it is more deeply integrated with the onshore market, i.e., when there are much freer northbound and southbound capital flows across the border. This is because foreigners must be able to invest in a deep and liquid onshore financial market and be free to move their capital out of the country whenever they want in order for them to be willing to hold large amounts of assets denominated in the currency outside of China. Most of these cross-border investment and international payment activities take place in the offshore market. Thus, the scale of the offshore market depends on the depth, breadth, and liquidity of the onshore financial market as well as the openness of the capital account of the onshore market. Unfortunately, there are many impediments to the further development of the onshore financial market, as we have discussed in Chapter 6.

One impediment to Chinese financial development that we did not discuss in detail in Chapter 6 is the weak institutional framework. One example is that the bankruptcy laws are inadequate, so they do not provide sufficient protection to bond holders. This deters potential buyers of corporate bonds and creates uncertainties for the bond issuers, and so hinders the development of the onshore bond market. For example, when a firm goes bankrupt, the claim procedure is either non-existent, unclear, or unfair. Oftentimes, those who move fast would get more compensation. In addition, the laws, if they exist, are not always enforced. In sum, there is inadequate legal and judicial infrastructure, such as legal protection for investors and enforcement of contract laws, to support the development of the financial markets.

The Hong Kong offshore RMB market can be quite volatile due to its sensitivity to policy changes in the Mainland. For example, in the aftermath of 11 August 2015, the RMB depreciated by 5 percent to 7 percent within a week. The Chinese government soon tightened capital controls. The market quickly switched from expecting the RMB to appreciate to expecting it to depreciate. As a result, RMB bank deposits in Hong Kong fell sharply, and cross-border capital flows into Hong Kong rapidly dried up. The offshore market quickly lost steam due to one single incident, demonstrating how volatile the offshore market could be.

The open-economy trilemma might have constrained the degree of capital account opening – given that monetary autonomy is to be maintained, in order to stabilize the exchange rate, there cannot be a high degree of capital mobility. Soon after 11 August 2015, the Hong Kong subsidiaries of the state-owned banks of China intervened in the Hong Kong offshore market to keep the CNH and CNY exchange rates aligned. That meant reducing RMB liquidity so as to raise the interbank borrowing rate (i.e., CNH HIBOR) to check the rapid depreciation of the RMB in the offshore FX market. The liquidity shortage greatly hurt the offshore market. In the onshore market, the expected depreciation of the RMB caused large capital outflows. The government dealt with it by imposing tighter capital controls. Even the open-minded governor of the PBC at that time, Mr. Zhou Xiaochuan, might have been scared by the amount of capital outflows following the steep depreciation and decided that opening the capital account too fast was not advisable, and so using administrative measures to curb the outflows of capital to prevent further slide of the RMB was considered justifiable. In short, China was not yet ready for further capital account liberalization, as it led to too much exchange rate fluctuations, which could cause too much financial market instability. This explains why almost every measure of capital account opening was accompanied by some quotas, or some conditions. In other words, China is still tiptoeing forward with regard to capital account opening.

The growth of the offshore market is also determined by the political and economic systems of the onshore market. This point can be illustrated by the comparison between the offshore RMB market and the offshore USD market. The Chinese government tends to use administrative measures rather than legislation to govern capital account openness. In addition, in the onshore financial market, the laws are not always adequate and not always enforced. This creates uncertainties for investors and firms that invest in the onshore market through the offshore market and hurt the Hong Kong offshore market. By contrast, the US government basically uses legislation rather than administrative measures to govern capital flows and the financial market, and allows the market to work as long as the market actors obey the laws. The laws are passed by a proper legislative procedure and enforced by law enforcement agencies. There is a credible constitution that lays down the fundamental rights of every individual, which cannot be easily changed by the executive and legislative branches of the government. This gives certainty and confidence to investors and firms and helps the development of the offshore USD market.

7.10   COMPARISON BETWEEN THE RMB OFFSHORE MARKET AND THE USD OFFSHORE MARKET

The use of the Eurodollar (offshore USD) dates back to the period after World War II, when much of Europe was devastated by the war and the United States provided funds via the Marshall Plan to rebuild the continent. As a result, there was wide circulation of dollars overseas, and the development of a separate, less-regulated market for the deposit of those funds. Unlike domestic US deposits, offshore deposits were not subject to the Federal Reserve System's reserve requirement, and eliminating that cost allowed banks to pay higher interest.

When the USD offshore market (Eurodollar market) began to grow in the 1950s, the USD was already a widely accepted global reserve currency. There was already a very large demand for the USD internationally. The US government in fact tried to control the growth of the USD offshore market. For example, the Interest Equalization Tax (1963) narrowed the USD funding costs of domestic and offshore bond issuers; the Voluntary Foreign Credit Restraint Program (1964) limited the onshore banks' lending to nonresidents; and Regulation D (1969) imposed marginal reserve requirements on US bank borrowings from the offshore USD market.

The RMB offshore market, however, emerged under very different circumstances from those under which the USD offshore market emerged. The RMB faces different domestic and overseas conditions than the USD did then. China is experimenting with financial liberalization and currency internationalization, and its purpose is to expand the offshore market. By contrast, the United States tried to limit the offshore market's influences on its domestic economy. The differences in the global status of the two currencies and in the scope and scale of the offshore dollar and RMB markets explain the dissimilar actions taken by the two governments.

China has made some concerted effort to push the RMB onto the global stage and to convince the rest of the world to adopt its currency for international transactions. However, RMB internationalization is being constrained by the underdeveloped financial market and China's capital controls. Thus, despite its rapid growth, the offshore RMB market is still quite small compared with the onshore market. This large size difference constrains the ability of the offshore market to affect the development of the onshore market. One can see this clearly by comparing the relative size of the offshore USD market with that of the offshore RMB market. According to He and McCauley (2012), as of June 2010, the amount of USD deposits in banks inside the United States was USD 8.27 trillion (i.e., total amount of onshore USD deposits), whereas the amount of USD deposits in banks outside of the United States was USD 2.59 trillion (i.e., total amount of offshore USD deposits). In other words, the offshore USD deposits are about 31 percent of the onshore USD deposits. By contrast, the total amount of onshore RMB deposits was about 151 trillion yuan (USD 21.8 trillion) by the end of 2016, whereas the total amount of offshore RMB deposits in Hong Kong, Taiwan, Singapore, UK, and South Korea totaled about 1.05 trillion yuan at that time. In other words, the offshore RMB deposits are 0.7 percent of onshore RMB deposits.[21] This also means that the size of the offshore USD market relative to that of the onshore USD market is 44 times the size of the offshore RMB market relative to that of the onshore RMB market.

Besides the quantitative difference between the USD offshore market and the RMB offshore market, there is a qualitative difference as well. In principle, an offshore currency center should intermediate between lenders and borrowers who may be located in different countries. There are four possible patterns defined by the direction of the flow of funds from the location of the lender (where the fund originates) to the location of the borrower (where the fund is finally used): 1. onshore → onshore; 2. onshore → offshore; 3. offshore → onshore; and 4. offshore → offshore. As pointed out by He and McCauley (2012), all four patterns exist for the USD market. However, they also observe that, historically, USD offshore centers, such as London, mainly played the role of financial intermediation among entities who are not residents of the United States, whereby offshore USD deposits are channeled to offshore borrowers through London (i.e., offshore ➔ offshore). This is quite different from the RMB off-shore centers, such as Hong Kong, whose intermediation activities are overwhelmingly characterized by "offshore ➔ onshore." That is, the banks in Hong Kong overwhelmingly serve as a conduit for renminbi lending from the rest of the world to the Mainland. Yet, one would expect that the more internationalized is a currency the more preva-lent will be the "offshore ➔ offshore" type of intermediation by the offshore centers, as this signifies that the currency is a vehicle currency used by residents outside of the issuing country for funding purposes. This is another indication that the offshore RMB market has a lot of room to further develop.

7.11   CONCLUSION

The offshore RMB market allows China to internationalize its cur-rency without having a fully convertible currency as there is a firewall that separates the capital flows between the onshore and offshore markets. The offshore market can also promote the holding of RMB-denominated assets outside of China by separating the currency risks from the country risks. The credibility and the well-developed finan-cial infrastructure of the offshore centers facilitate international pay-ments flows and the development of the offshore financial markets, thus enhancing the impacts of onshore financial development and capital account liberalization on the international use of RMB. A network of offshore RMB centers in different time zones and geo-graphic locations around the globe ensures that the currency can be traded 24 hours a day and that global RMB liquidity and RMB finan-cial services are available uninterrupted around the clock. All these facilitate the acceptance of the RMB in the global market. The off-shore market also facilitates the use of RMB as a vehicle currency for transactions by parties other than China.

To appreciate the impact of the offshore market on the inter-national use of the RMB, one can compare the turnovers in the onshore and offshore RMB FX markets. It can be seen that, without the offshore RMB market, the FX turnover of the RMB would have been much smaller. The offshore RMB market started to exist only in July 2010. Yet, in 2013, the offshore RMB FX turnover in Hong Kong (about USD 49 billion per day) was already larger than that in Mainland China (about USD 34 billion per day). In 2014, the combined daily RMB FX turnovers in all the offshore markets (more than USD 230 billion, including Hong Kong, Taiwan, Singapore, UK, and so on) was four times that in the onshore market. In other words, the offshore market accounted for 80 percent of the global total FX turnover share of the RMB in 2014. Although that share fell to 73 percent in April 2016 (out of a global total turnover of USD 205 billion per day, with Hong Kong accounting for USD 77.1 billion per day) and 64 percent in April 2019 (out of a global total turnover of about USD 285 billion per day, with Hong Kong accounting for USD 107.6 billion per day), the offshore FX market is still considerably larger than the onshore one by 2019.[22]

However, one has to bear in mind that the existence of the offshore market alone cannot be the main driver of RMB internationalization. The main drivers are still onshore financial development and capital account openness. In this regard, one should note one important difference between the offshore RMB market and other developed offshore currency markets, such as the offshore USD market. The difference is that the development of the offshore USD market, for example, was largely market-driven and fueled by a high degree of capital mobility, a well-developed domestic financial market, and full convertibility of the currency. By contrast, the development of the offshore RMB market has been largely driven by government policy, and its development has been constrained by such factors as capital controls in China, its immature financial market and the lack of full convertibility of the currency. As a result of these factors, the size of the offshore RMB market relative to that of the onshore RMB market is very small when compared with that of the offshore USD market. In other words, the development of the offshore RMB market still has a long way to go. This constraint on the growth of the offshore market will in turn limit the progress of RMB internationalization.

Offshore currency trading and offshore banking facilitate the international trade, foreign direct investment, and multinational corporate activities of the domestic companies. Thus, the expansion of the offshore currency markets in the last few decades is an outcome of trade globalization. It is also an outcome of financial globalization – as the barriers to capital flows are reduced, the demand for financial intermediation between international lenders and borrowers from different countries increases, fueling the growth of offshore banking businesses. However, such financial globalization is not without costs. International banks are increasingly interconnected as they hold offshore currency deposits with each other. They are the counter-parties of each other. When a major bank in one country goes bankrupt, it jeopardizes the balance sheets and the health of banks all over the world. The global financial crisis in 2007–2009 demonstrates this danger clearly. The crisis shows that financial globalization might have gone too far. The 1998–1999 Asian Financial Crisis and the 2007–2009 global financial crisis make China skeptical of financial globalization and hesitant to fully open its capital account. For this reason, China wants to adopt the strategy of retaining discretionary onshore capital controls for a significant period of time while allowing the offshore, fully convertible RMB market to be fully integrated with the international capital market. This allows China to participate in financial globalization in a controlled manner. This is the rationale for the "one currency, two markets" approach to RMB internationalization.

It is often said that when the capital account of China becomes sufficiently open, the importance of the offshore RMB centers, such as Hong Kong, in the internationalization of RMB will fade, and the onshore centers such as Shanghai will take over. For how long can the Hong Kong RMB offshore market play the key role in RMB internationalization before being replaced by Shanghai? Based on the above argument, we conjecture that the Hong Kong offshore RMB center will continue to play an important role in RMB internationalization for quite a long time while Shanghai will continue to be the primary onshore financial center of China.

NOTES TO CHAPTER 7

1 Historians have pointed to the Soviet Union's placement of dollar deposits in London as one of the origins of the Eurodollar market. See, for example, Einzig and Scott-Quinn 1977.

2 Source: http://116.236.198.44/english/mdtmmbfmm/.

3 The trading band provides a signal to the market concerning how large the exchange rate volatility is tolerated by the authority. In practice, the bounds of the band are rarely exceeded.

4 See, for example, Cheung, Chow, and Qin 2017: chap. 3.

5 Hong Kong Interbank Clearing Limited is a private company jointly owned by the Hong Kong Monetary Authority (HKMA) and the Hong Kong Association of Banks (HKAB).

6 See Hong Kong Interbank Clearing Limited (www.hkicl.com.hk/eng/information_centre/statistics_of_clearing_transaction_volume_and_value.php).

7 The offshore company can also open an account with a "participating bank," which is an offshore commercial bank that has signed a clearing agreement with the offshore clearing bank. The offshore company can then effect the cross-border RMB payment indirectly via the clearing bank through the participating bank.

8 See, for example, https://securities.bnpparibas.com/insights/what-is-it-cips.html.

9 Straight-through processing is an automated electronic payment process that is used by corporations and banks. STP allows for the entire payment process, from initiation to final settlement, to be free of human intervention.

10 Nostro is a banking term to describe a current account that a domestic bank holds with a foreign bank.

11 According to the webpage of CIPS Co. Ltd., "the CIPS is operated by CIPS Co., Ltd., which conducts business under the supervision and administration of the People's Bank of China (PBC), in accordance with rules and regulations including *Business Rules on Cross-Border Interbank Payment System (CIPS), Guidlines on Business Operation of CIPS, CIPS Participants Agreement*, etc. . . . The PBC approved the Company's plan of capital increase and introduction of overseas investors in March, 2018. A total of 36 domestic and overseas financial institutions jointly signed a capital increase agreement in July, 2018. On December 3rd, 2019, the first

meeting of the Company's shareholders was held in Shanghai, with delegates from all 36 shareholders attending, followed by the first meeting of its Board of Directors."

12 A deferred net settlement (DNS) system effects the settlement of obligations or transfers between or among counterparties on a net basis at some deferred time (e.g., at the end of the day) instead of immediately. See Bank for International Settlements 2003.

13 Source: PBC site (www.pbc.gov.cn/english/130721/3533376/index.html),

14 CHIPS is operated by The Clearing House Payments Company, LLC, which is the United States' main electronic funds-transfer system for processing international USD funds transfers made among international banks.

15 See Federal Financial Institutions Examination Council: http://www.ffiec .gov/bsa_aml_infobase/pages_manual/olm_057.htm and US Department of the Treasury: www.fincen.gov/sites/default/files/shared/Appendix_D.pdf.

16 See footnote 9.

17 See, for example, "Society for Worldwide Interbank Financial Telecommunication": Wikipedia 2021e.

18 See "Update: Iran Sanctions Agreement," SWIFT website, 17 January 2016 (www.swift.com/insights/press-releases/update_iran-sanctions-agreement) and "Iranian Banks Reconnected to SWIFT Network after Four-Year Hiatus," Reuters report, dated 17 February 2016 (www.reuters .com/article/us-iran-banks-swift/iranian-banks-reconnected-to-swift-network-after-four-year-hiatus-idUSKCN0VQ1FD).

19 See "NSA 'Follow the Money' Program Spies on International Bank Activity," *Der Spiegel* report, dated 15 September 2013 (www.spiegel.de/ international/world/spiegel-exclusive-nsa-spies-on-international-bank-transactions-a-922276.html).

20 See *South China Morning Post*, 18 June 2018.

21 The amount of onshore RMB bank deposits is from CEIC (www.ceicdata .com/en/indicator/china/total-deposits). The amount of offshore RMB deposits is from HKMA.

22 Source: Bank for International Settlements Triennial Central Bank Survey 2013, 2016, and 2019 (www.bis.org/publ/rpfx16.htm). "Net-net" basis, percentage shares of average daily turnover in April of the year.

8 The Potential of the RMB as a Payment Currency

One important function of an international currency is to serve as an international medium of exchange, i.e., to serve as a payment currency. How does the RMB fare so far in this regard, and what is its potential in the future? In this chapter, I will explore this topic. In addition, in the later part of the chapter, I will devote some space to discuss how the Belt and Road Initiative can affect the potential of the RMB as a payment currency and a currency to denominate international debt securities.

8.1 THE PAYMENT SHARES OF CURRENCIES

Table 8.1 indicates the payment shares of six currencies in 2016 for comparison purposes. (Transactions through global market infrastructures and intra-Eurozone payments are excluded. Global market infrastructures are payment intermediaries that facilitate certain kinds of payments. It includes institutions such as CLS and TARGET2, which are explained in the footnote in Box 8.1.) They are the USD, euro, Japanese yen, British pound, Canadian dollar, and the RMB. From Table 8.1, it can be seen that, in 2016, the RMB had a payment share of 1.62 percent, which was disproportionately small compared with the GDP share of China in 2016, which was 14.74 percent. On the other hand, the GDP share of the United States in 2016 was 24.53 percent but the USD had a payment share of 55.31 percent, which was disproportionally large compared with the GDP share of the issuing country.

In Chapter 5, I describe a theory that suggests that the use of a currency for international payment depends crucially on four factors: the GDP of the issuing country, the stability of its exchange rate, the financial development, and capital account openness of the issuing

Table 8.1 *Payment shares and GDP shares in 2016, excluding transactions through global market infrastructure and intra-eurozone payments*

Currency	Payment share in 2016 (percentage)	GDP share of issuing country in 2016 (percentage)	Issuing country
USD	55.31	24.53	United States
EUR	20.52	15.72	Eurozone
JPY	5.86	6.52	Japan
GBP	5.28	3.49	UK
CAD	3.23	2.02	Canada
RMB	1.62	14.74	China

Source: SWIFT and the author's own calculations.
Note: Customer-initiated and institutional payments. Excluding transactions through global market infrastructure and intra-eurozone payments. Messages exchanged on SWIFT. Based on value.

country. Given that China's GDP was already the second largest in the world in 2016, and its exchange rate was quite stable, the low payment share of the RMB is mainly due to the low level of financial development and low degree of capital account openness of China, according to the theory. In this chapter, I present a more rigorous empirical analysis to support the view that financial development and capital account openness are the two crucial factors determining the payment share of the RMB. I first estimate an empirical model, called "gravity model," that is shown to be quite successful in explaining inter-country bilateral payments flows by currency. Then I use the estimated model to carry out "in-sample" predictions of the payment shares of different currencies, including the RMB. I then go on to use the estimated model to make some "out-of-sample" predictions concerning the future prospects of the RMB as a significant international payment currency.

8.1.1   Thought Experiments Based on the Gravity Model

Based on Equation (8.3) in Box 8.1, we can carry out a number of thought experiments, which can throw light on a few questions. For

BOX 8.1   **The gravity model for explaining inter-country bilateral payments flows by currency**

To explain the pattern of inter-country bilateral payments flows by currency, I use a mathematical model called the "gravity model," as shown below. According to the model, the total bilateral payment flow from country i to country j denominated in currency "cur" is given by equation (8.1).

$$M_{ijt}^{cur} = \mu_0 + \mu_1 Y_{it} + \mu_2 Y_{jt} + \mu_3 \delta_i + \mu_4 \delta'_j + \mu_5 \overline{d_{ij}} + \mu_6 \theta_{cur,t}^{shareratio} + \mu_7 \theta_{it}^{tradeshare}$$
$$+ \mu_8 \theta_{jt}^{tradeshare} + \mu_9 \theta_{it}^{co-m} + \mu_{10} \theta_{jt}^{co-m} + \mu_{11} cur_{cur} + \mu_{12} time_t + \varepsilon_{ijt}$$

$$(8.1)$$

where

"ln" stands for natural logarithm;

M_{ijt}^{cur} is ln of total payment flow from i to j denominated in currency cur in trillion USD in year t;

Y_{it} is ln of the GDP of i in trillion USD in year t (time-varying);

Y_{jt} is ln of the GDP of j in trillion USD in year t (time-varying);

δ_i is the fixed effect for i as an origin country (i.e., country dummy of the origin) (constant over time);

δ'_j is the fixed effect for j as a destination country (i.e., country dummy of the destination) (constant over time);

$\overline{d_{ij}}$ is the origin-destination fixed effect capturing all payment frictions between i and j;

$\theta_{cur,t}^{shareratio}$ is ln of ratio of the currency's FX turnover share to GDP share of the issuing country in year t (time-varying);

$\theta_{it}^{tradeshare}$ is ln of trade share of issuing country in i's trade in year t (time-varying);

$\theta_{jt}^{tradeshare}$ is ln of trade share of issuing country in j's trade in year t (time-varying);

θ_{it}^{co-m} is co-movement between i's currency and the currency in question in year t (time-varying);

θ_{jt}^{co-m} is co-movement between j's currency and the currency in question in year t (time-varying);

cur_{cur} is the currency fixed effect capturing all attributes of the currency and the issuing country (constant over time);

BOX 8.1   **(cont.)**

time$_t$ is a year dummy (or time fixed effect) to capture business cycle effect
ε_{ijt} is an error term that is specific to i, j and t.

This model draws from the work of Lai and Yan (2020). The rationale for this equation is that flows of bilateral payments that we use for our analysis should be mainly driven by settlement of trade or investment, broadly defined. Theoretically, these activities are positively related to the economic sizes of the origin and destination countries and negatively related to "payment friction" between the two countries. This is why the model gets its name "gravity" – according to Newton's law of gravity, the attractive force between two masses is positively related to the magnitudes of the masses and negatively related to the distance between them. In this model, payment friction stands for "distance" in Newton's law of gravity. Regarding trade settlement flows, the payment friction is affected by bilateral trade costs such as distance, common language, common border, common colonial heritage, and common legal systems. Some of these effects are positive and some of them are negative. Regarding investment flows, the payment friction is affected by a similar set of factors. The choice of currency for trade payment (i.e., trade settlement) is affected by a set of currency-specific factors, such as the trade share of the issuing country in the origin (destination) country, thick market externalities of the currency (captured by the capital account openness and the level of financial development of the issuing country), and co-movement between the currency and the origin (destination) currency. The choice of currency for investment flow payment (i.e., settlement) is affected by a similar set of currency-specific factors.

All the amounts used for the regression are in terms of nominal USD. The theory predicts that the nominal bilateral payments flows in USD between countries i and j in a certain year are determined, among other things, by the nominal GDPs of i and j in USD terms in that year. This is because a country that has more purchasing power denominated in USD would be able to pay more in terms of USD to other countries to

BOX 8.1   (cont.)

buy goods, services, and assets. Similarly, a country that can produce goods and services that are worth more in terms of USD would be able to sell goods, services, and assets that are worth more in terms of USD to other countries.

The share ratio (expressed as the ratio of the share of FX turnover of the currency divided by the share of nominal GDP of the issuing country), trade share, and exchange rate co-movement have no units. Although the origin fixed effect, destination fixed effect, origin–destination fixed effect, and currency fixed effects are constant over time, there is also a time fixed effect that varies from year to year.

Here, following Lai and Yu (2015), I argue that thick market externalities of a currency, controlling for its GDP, can be captured by the share ratio of the country. The FX turnover share of a currency is reported by the Bank for International Settlement (BIS) once every three years based on a triennial survey it conducts. In the top panel of Table Box 8.1A, we list the FX turnover shares of some currencies as reported by the BIS once every three years from 1995 to 2019. The FX turnover share of a currency reported by the BIS measures the percentage of payments that involved the currency in question. Since two currencies are involved in each FX transaction, the shares add up to 200 percent. The values we list below are "normalized" by dividing each value reported by BIS by 2 so that the shares add up to 100 percent. The middle panel lists the GDP share of the issuing countries in the BIS reporting years. The bottom panel lists the share ratio. It can be seen that the share ratios of the major established currencies such as USD, GBP, and EUR rise more slowly over time. On the other hand, the share ratios of the currencies of theemerging economies such as RMB, MXN, and SGD tend to rise more rapidly. This observation is consistent with our hunch that developed economies already established mature and open financial markets a long time ago and so the share ratios increased only due to financial globalization. On the other hand, the emerging economies were catching up in financial development and capital account

Table Box 8.1A *Global FX turnover share, GDP share, and the share ratio, 1995–2019*

FX market turnover share (in percentage)

Currency name	1995	1998	2001	2004	2007	2010	2013	2016	2019
USD	41.51	43.40	44.93	44.00	42.80	42.43	43.52	43.79	44.15
EUR	–	–	18.96	18.70	18.52	19.52	16.70	15.70	16.14
RMB	–	0.007	0.004	0.048	0.23	0.43	1.12	1.99	2.16
JPY	12.30	10.86	11.77	10.42	8.62	9.49	11.52	10.81	8.40
GBP	4.63	5.51	6.52	8.25	7.43	6.44	5.91	6.40	6.40
CAD	1.71	1.76	2.24	2.10	2.14	2.64	2.28	2.57	2.52
THB	–	0.07	0.08	0.10	0.10	0.10	0.16	0.18	0.24
MXN (Mexican peso)	–	0.23	0.41	0.55	0.66	0.63	1.26	0.96	0.86
SGD	0.23	0.55	0.53	0.45	0.58	0.71	0.70	0.90	0.90

Source: Bank for International Settlements Triennial Central Bank Survey 1989–2019: www.bis.org/statistics/rpfx19.htm. Net-net basis, percentage shares of average daily turnover in April of the year. The shares are "normalized" so that the total is equal to 100%.

GDP share (in percentage)

Country Name	1995	1998	2001	2004	2007	2010	2013	2016	2019
United States	24.84	29.00	31.83	28.03	25.03	22.69	21.66	24.53	24.40
Euro area	24.35	22.79	19.74	23.17	22.26	19.17	17.12	15.72	15.21

	1995	1998	2001	2004	2007	2010	2013	2016	2019
China	2.38	3.28	4.01	4.47	6.14	9.25	12.47	14.74	16.31
Japan	17.66	12.86	12.90	11.00	7.81	8.64	6.69	6.52	5.79
United Kingdom	4.33	5.23	4.86	5.48	5.32	3.70	3.56	3.49	3.23
Canada	1.96	2.02	2.21	2.34	2.53	2.45	2.39	2.02	1.98
Thailand	0.55	0.36	0.36	0.39	0.45	0.52	0.55	0.54	0.62
Mexico	1.17	1.68	2.27	1.79	1.82	1.60	1.65	1.42	1.44
Singapore	0.28	0.27	0.27	0.26	0.31	0.36	0.40	0.41	0.42

Source: World Bank

FX turnover share/GDP share

Currency Name	1995	1998	2001	2004	2007	2010	2013	2016	2019
USD	1.67	1.50	1.41	1.57	1.71	1.87	2.01	1.79	1.81
EUR	–	–	0.96	0.81	0.83	1.02	0.98	1.00	1.06
RMB	–	0.002	0.001	0.011	0.037	0.047	0.090	0.135	0.132
JPY	0.70	0.84	0.91	0.95	1.10	1.10	1.72	1.66	1.45
GBP	1.07	1.05	1.34	1.51	1.40	1.74	1.66	1.83	1.98
CAD	0.87	0.87	1.02	0.90	0.85	1.08	0.95	1.27	1.27
THB	–	0.20	0.21	0.25	0.21	0.19	0.29	0.33	0.39
MXN (Mexican peso)	–	0.14	0.18	0.31	0.36	0.39	0.77	0.68	0.60
SGD	0.80	2.02	1.97	1.74	1.88	1.98	1.77	2.21	2.14

Source: author's calculation.

BOX 8.1   **(cont.)**

openness, in addition to being influenced by financial globalization, and so the share ratios increased rapidly over time.

Data

To test our theory, we make use of the SWIFT FIN message data which is a proprietary data set owned by SWIFT. The use of it requires special permission. The data we use include the values of MT 103 and MT 202 messages ("MT" stands for "message type") on the monthly bilateral flows of payments between all country pairs broken down into different currencies during the period 2011–2016, where MT 103 covers "Single Customer Credit Transfer" and MT 202 covers "General Financial Institution Transfer." For each country pair, all payments denominated in the same currency are grouped together with no distinction in terms of underlying reason/ transaction type related to the payments. During this period, about 10 percent of the value of all payments are MT 103 and about 90 percent are MT 202.

As stated above, MT 103 is described as the "Single Customer Credit Transfer." Its message type is Category 1, which is "Customer Payments and Cheques." An MT 103 message is sent by a financial institution on behalf of itself or its ordering customer directly or via intermediary banks, to the final beneficiary's financial institution. The ordering customer or beneficiary customer, or both, are non-financial institutions from the perspective of the Ordering Institution. Examples are international wire transfers and telegraphic transfers.

MT 202 is described as a "General Financial Institution Transfer." Its message type is Category 2, which is "Financial Institution Transfers." An MT 202 message is sent by a financial institution directly or via intermediary banks to the final beneficiary institution.

For our analysis, we exclude payments flows that involve all traffic sent/received to/from global market infrastructures such as CLS and TARGET2.[1] The main reason is that payments sent/received to/from global market infrastructures by a country do not reflect bilateral

BOX 8.1 **(cont.)**

inter-country payments. Incidentally, by excluding all payments to/ from CLS, we also exclude a vast majority of payments for FX transactions, which is what we want to exclude, as we are only interested in bilateral inter-country payments flows resulting mainly from trade settlement and investment settlement, and not settlement of FX transaction.

For tractability, we include in our analysis only the top 13 currencies and top 13 countries/territories in the dataset. Eurozone is treated as a single country. Only international payments are included in our analysis. The total amount of payments to and from these 13 countries accounts for about 85 percent of the total amount of payments to and from all countries/territories in the population (which consists of 233 countries/territories) in the period 2011–2016. Thus, the analysis is considered quite representative of the entire population of countries. The thirteen countries/territories and their corresponding currencies in our sample of study are given in Table Box 8.1B.

Table Box 8.1B *Countries/territories and their currencies*

Country/Territory	Currency
AUS= Australia	AUD=Australian dollar
CAN= Canada	CAD = Canadian dollar
CHE=Switzerland	CHF=Swiss Franc
CHN=China	RMB=Chinese yuan
DNK=Denmark	DKK=Danish kroner
EMU=euro Area	EUR=euro
GBR=Great Britain	GBP=British pound
HKG=Hong Kong	HKD= Hong Kong dollar
JPN= Japan	JPY=Japanese yen
NOR=Norway	NOK=Norwegian kroner
SGP=Singapore	SGD=Singapore dollar
SWE=Sweden	SEK=Swedish kroner
USA = United States of America	USD = US dollar

BOX 8.1   (cont.)

Empirical Estimation of the Gravity Model

Before we empirically estimate the gravity model, we want to justify rigorously that the share ratio is strongly affected by both financial development and capital account openness. To do that, we run the following regression.

$$\theta_{cur,t}^{shareratio} = 50.87 * RFD_i + 6.46 * RKAO_i \text{-} 2.85 \tag{8.2}$$

where $\theta_{cur,t}^{shareratio}$ = share ratio of country i = ratio of the foreign exchange turnover share of i's currency to i's GDP; RFD_i = "relative financial development index of i," where the financial development index is taken from the International Monetary Fund; $RKAO_i$ = "relative capital account openness of i," where capital account openness is defined as the gross international investment position of i divided by GDP of i.[2] Yearly data are used for 2011–2016, for 13 currencies and their respective issuing countries. There is no time fixed effect. All the coefficients are significant to 1 percent level, and the goodness of fit is high (adjusted R^2 = 0.739). Thus, we can now say with confidence that the share ratio is a good proxy for financial development and openness.

Using data from SWIFT to run the regression equation (8.1), we find that the payment flow from country i to country j denominated in currency cur in trillion USD can be approximated by the following equation.

$$M_{ijt}^{cur} = 4.051 + 0.906 Y_{it} + 1.606 Y_{jt} + \mu_3 \delta_i + \mu_{13} \delta_j' + \mu_4 \overline{d_{ij}} + 1.066 \theta_{cur,t}^{shareratio}$$
$$+ 0.911 \theta_{it}^{tradeshare} + 1.545 \theta_{jt}^{tradeshare} + 0.210 \theta_{jt}^{co-m} + \mu_{10} cur_{cur} + \mu_{11} time_t + \varepsilon_{ijt} \tag{8.3}$$

We find that Equation (8.3) fits the actual payments flows by currency quite well. (In econometric terminology, all the coefficients are significant at 1 percent level, and the goodness of fit as measured by the adjusted R^2 is equal to 0.965 out of a maximum of 1.) Another way to appreciate how well the model predicts the data is to compare the

BOX 8.1 **(cont.)**

Table Box 8.1C *Actual and predicted payment shares in 2016, excluding transactions through global market infrastructure and intra-eurozone payments*

(1)	(2)	(3)	(4)	(5)
Actual rank	Currency	Actual share (percentage)	Predicted share (percentage)	Predicted rank
1	USD	55.31	54.17	1
2	EUR	20.52	20.57	2
3	JPY	5.86	4.98	4
4	GBP	5.28	5.58	3
5	CAD	3.23	4.34	5
6	CHF	2.12	2.02	7
7	AUD	2.11	2.17	6
8	RMB	1.62	1.70	8
9	HKD	1.14	1.31	9
10	SEK	0.98	1.04	10
11	NOK	0.71	0.67	13
12	DKK	0.63	0.75	11
13	SGD	0.50	0.69	12

actual payment shares of different major currencies with the predicted payment shares in 2016. This is shown in Table Box 8.1C. Column (3) shows the actual payment shares while column (4) shows the predicted payment shares. The two sets of numbers are quite close, indicating that the model is quite successful in predicting the data. In econometric jargon, we say that the model is quite successful in "in-sample" predictions.

1 CLS (originally, Continuous Linked Settlement) is a specialist US financial institution that provides settlement services to its members in the foreign exchange market. TARGET2 is a payment system owned and operated by the Eurosystem. It is the leading European platform for

BOX 8.1   **(cont.)**

processing large-value payments and is used by both central banks and commercial banks to process payments in euro in real time.

2 The "relative financial development index of i" is defined as the financial development index of i divided by the sum of the financial development indexes of all countries. Similarly, the "relative capital account openness of i" is defined as the measure of capital account openness of i divided by the sum of the measures of capital account openness of all countries.

example, we can assess the relative importance of the economic size of a country and its financial development and openness (proxied by the ratio of the currency's FX turnover share to GDP share of the issuing country, defined as the "share ratio" of the issuing country) on the payment share of its currency. We can also predict the future payment shares of various currencies based on assumptions about the hypothetical values of the GDP growth rates of various countries in the world and hypothetical values of their future levels of financial development and openness. When we carry out these thought experiments using the model, we carry out "out-of-sample" predictions. We have some confidence in these out-of-sample predictions since the model's in-sample predictions are quite accurate.

In the first thought experiment, we compare the impacts of the following two hypothetical changes in 2016: (1) increasing China's GDP to that of the United States but letting its financial development and openness remain unchanged; (2) increasing its financial development and openness but letting its GDP remain unchanged. The result is shown in Table 8.2. To summarize, we find that if China's GDP in 2016 was equal to that of the United States in the same year, while its level of financial development and openness remained the same, and everything else being equal, then the payment share of the RMB in 2016 would have increased from 1.62 percent to 2.4 percent (ranked 6th, much lower than Canadian dollar). However, if China's GDP in

Table 8.2 *Thought experiment 1*

Predicted payment shares in 2016, excluding transactions through global market infrastructure and intra-eurozone payments.

	In 2016, China's GDP becomes that of the United States, but its level of financial development and openness remains the same.		In 2016, RMB's level of financial development and openness becomes that of Thailand, but China's GDP remains the same.	
Predicted rank	Currency	Predicted share (percentage)	Predicted rank	Currency	Predicted share (percentage)
1	USD	54.58	1	USD	51.66
2	EUR	19.92	2	EUR	20.54
3	GBP	5.38	3	GBP	5.61
4	JPY	5.04	4	JPY	4.96
5	CAD	4.23	5	CAD	4.35
6	RMB	2.40	6	RMB	4.23
7	AUD	2.14	7	AUD	2.17
8	CHF	1.95	8	CHF	2.03
9	HKD	1.33	9	HKD	1.28
10	SEK	1.00	10	SEK	1.05
11	DKK	0.72	11	DKK	0.76
12	SGD	0.67	12	SGD	0.69
13	NOK	0.65	13	NOK	0.68

2016 was unchanged but its level of financial development and openness became that of Thailand in 2016 (i.e., RMB's share ratio becomes 2.45 times its actual level in 2016), which seems possible for China to achieve, then the payment share of the RMB would have increased from 1.62 percent to 4.2 percent (6th highest, just below the Canadian dollar).[1] On the other hand, if China's financial openness and development reaches those of Mexico in 2016 (i.e., RMB's share ratio becomes about 5 times its actual level in 2016) while its GDP remains unchanged, RMB's share in international payments would increase from 1.6 percent to about 9.2 percent. Thus, the effect of increasing China's financial development and openness to that of Mexico in 2016 is about 3.8 times the effect of increasing China's GDP to that of the United States in 2016. So, it is clear that the increase in the level of financial development and openness is distinctly more important than the increase in the economic size of China for the RMB to become a significant global payment currency.

In the second thought experiment, we try to predict the payment shares of the RMB and other currencies in 2030 based on some assumptions about economic growth and financial development. We assume that from 2016 till 2030, China's GDP grows at 5.5 percent per year, United States at 2.5 percent, eurozone at 1.5 percent, UK at 1.5 percent, Australia at 3 percent, Japan at 1 percent, Canada at 2.5 percent, the rest of the world at 4 percent, and everything else being equal. Here, we assume that the share ratios (and hence the levels of financial development and openness) of other countries remain unchanged. The result is shown in Table 8.3. Specifically, we find that if the share ratio of China is going to be unchanged, then the payment share of the RMB would become 2.6 percent (6th, below the Japanese yen). Suppose instead that China's share ratio in 2030 is 2.45 times what it was in 2016, it would attain the same level of financial development and openness as that of Thailand in 2016, which is not impossible to achieve given that the financial development and openness of Thailand in 2016 was not considered particularly high even by developing-country standards (see Figures 5.2 and 6.1). In that case, China's payment share in 2030 would be approximately 6.6 percent. That would make the RMB

Table 8.3 *Thought experiment 2*

Starting from 2016 till 2030, China's GDP grows at 5.5 percent per year, United States at 2.5 percent, eurozone at 1.5 percent, UK at 1.5 percent, Australia at 3 percent, Japan at 1 percent, Canada at 2.5 percent, and the rest of the world at 4 percent.

Predicted payment shares in 2030, excluding transactions through global market infrastructure and intra-eurozone payments.

In 2030, China's level of financial development and openness remains the same as in 2016.			In 2030, China's level of financial development and openness becomes that of Thailand in 2016.		
Predicted rank	Currency	Predicted share (%)	Predicted rank	Currency	Predicted share (%)
1	USD	57.20	1	USD	54.84
2	EUR	17.07	2	EUR	16.37
3	GBP	4.41	3	RMB	6.63
4	CAD	4.27	4	GBP	4.23
5	JPY	4.02	5	CAD	4.10
6	RMB	2.61	6	JPY	3.86
7	CHF	2.47	7	CHF	2.37
8	AUD	2.34	8	AUD	2.24
9	HKD	1.80	9	HKD	1.73
10	SEK	1.26	10	SEK	1.21
11	DKK	0.89	11	DKK	0.85
12	SGD	0.86	12	SGD	0.83
13	NOK	0.78	13	NOK	0.75

the third largest payment currency after the euro by 2030. We think this scenario is not too far-fetched if China is willing to open its capital account and liberalize its financial sector at a fast pace in the next decade or so. This thought experiment shows once again that China's financial development and openness has a distinctly stronger impact than its GDP on the extent to which the RMB is used for international payments.

8.2   THE BELT AND ROAD INITIATIVE

There has been some discussion that the Belt and Road Initiative (BRI) could have a large impact on the internationalization of the RMB.[2] However, as far as I know, there has not been any quantitative analysis of the impacts. Here I try to carry out quantitative estimates of the effects of the BRI on RMB internationalization.

According to an official document issued by the Chinese government in March 2015:

> The Belt and Road Initiative aims to promote the connectivity of
> Asian, European and African continents and their adjacent seas ...
> The Initiative will enable China to further expand and deepen its
> opening-up, and to strengthen its mutually beneficial cooperation
> with countries in Asia, Europe and Africa and the rest of the
> world. ... To be specific, they need to improve the region's
> infrastructure, and put in place a secure and efficient network of
> land, sea and air passages, lifting their connectivity to a higher
> level; further enhance trade and investment facilitation, establish a
> network of free trade areas that meet high standards, maintain
> closer economic ties, and deepen political trust.[3]

The Belt and Road Initiative is structured around two main components: (i) the Silk Road Economic Belt (SREB) and (ii) the 21st-Century Maritime Silk Road (MSR). More specifically, the "Belt" links China to Central and South Asia and onward to Europe, while the "Road" links China to the nations of South East Asia, the Gulf

Countries, East and North Africa, and on to Europe. Those parts are themselves organized around six economic corridors: (1) the China–Mongolia–Russia Economic Corridor; (2) the New Eurasian Land Bridge; (3) the China–Central Asia–West Asia Economic Corridor; (4) the China–Indochina Peninsula Economic Corridor; (5) the China–Pakistan Economic Corridor; and (6) the Bangladesh–China–India–Myanmar Economic Corridor.

There is no official list of countries in the Belt and Road Initiative. Following de Soyres, Mulabdic, Murray, et al. (2018), we focus on a list of 71 economies identified by them. Countries in the list should be interpreted as economies that are geographically located along the Belt and Road as proposed by China.

In Chapter 4, we mention that, by and large, there can be five indicators of the degree of internationalization of a currency, namely the use of the currency in the following dimensions: (i) denomination of international debts; (ii) denomination of international loans; (iii) foreign exchange turnover; (iv) the use in global payments; and (v) the use as foreign exchange reserves. Here, we focus on (i) and (iv), which are the most relevant impacts of the BRI on the internationalization of the RMB. Accordingly, there should be two major effects of the BRI on RMB internationalization. First, it would increase the use of the RMB in international payments as a result of increased trade flows between China and the Belt and Road (B&R) countries and among the B&R countries themselves. Second, the BRI should lead to RMB-denominated financing of the BRI projects, which, among other things, prompts the issuing of RMB-denominated bonds. This would increase the RMB's share in international debt securities. We elaborate these points below.

8.2.1 *The Increase in the Use of the RMB in International Payments*

To estimate this effect, we first use a gravity model to estimate the determinants of inter-country bilateral RMB-denominated payments flows using data from SWIFT in the years 2011–2016. The set of

258 8 THE POTENTIAL OF THE RMB AS A PAYMENT CURRENCY

countries we use is the union of the top 30 outbound RMB-payment
countries and top 30 inbound RMB-payment countries.

BOX 8.2   Estimation of the gravity model for inter-country bilateral RMB payments flows

Using data from SWIFT for 2011–2016, we estimate the gravity model
and we find that the RMB-denominated payments flow from country i
(the origin country) to country j (the destination country) can be
approximated by the following equation.

$$M_{ijt}^{RMB} = 0.119 + 0.676Y_{it} + 0.411Y_{jt} + \vec{\mu_1}\vec{\delta_i} + \vec{\mu_2}\vec{\delta_j} - 0.251d_{ij} \\ + 0.54\theta_{jt}^{tradeshare} + \mu_3 time_t + \varepsilon_{ijt} \tag{8.4}$$

where

M_{ijt}^{RMB} is ln of total RMB-denominated payments flow from i to j in
billion USD;

Y_{it} is ln of the GDP of i in trillion USD (time-varying);

Y_{jt} is ln of the GDP of j in trillion USD (time-varying);

$\vec{\delta_i}$ is a set of fixed effects for offshore RMB centers (i.e., Hong Kong,
Singapore, and London) when they are origin countries (constant
over time);

$\vec{\delta_j}$ is a set of fixed effects for offshore RMB centers (i.e., Hong Kong,
Singapore, and London) when they are destination countries (constant
over time);

d_{ij} is ln of distance between i and j (constant over time);

$\theta_{jt}^{tradeshare}$ is ln of trade share of issuing country in j's trade (time-
varying);

$time_t$ is a year dummy (or time fixed effect) to capture business cycle
effect;

ε_{ijt} is an error term that is specific to i, j and t.

In contrast to the analysis in the other parts of this chapter,
payments between countries within the eurozone are considered
international payments in the above regression. This is because it is
important to capture RMB payments flows within the
eurozone countries.

8.2.1.1 Thought Experiments Based on the Gravity Model

There are two possible channels through which the BRI can increase RMB-denominated payments flows, as explained below.

(a) The first channel through which RMB-denominated payments flows increase is that the BRI increases China's outward direct investments to the B&R countries. Because overseas Chinese-owned companies tend to use more China-produced goods and services, this would lead to more trade flows between China and the B&R countries, which in turn increases the use of the RMB for trade settlement and investment settlement between China and the B&R countries. This would increase global RMB payments flows and enhance RMB internationalization.

Based on the estimated gravity model equation (8.4), we carry out a counterfactual thought experiment of increasing the share of trade with China of each B&R country in 2016 by 50 percent and calculate the resulting increases in bilateral inter-country RMB-denominated payments flows for all country pairs in the sample. This is supposed to capture the effect that the BRI increases outward direct investment from China to the B&R countries, which in turn is expected to increase trade flow between China and each of these B&R countries.

Our estimate is that, to the extent that the BRI increases the trade shares of all B&R countries with China by 50 percent due to the increase in outward direct investments of China into these countries, the BRI will increase total global RMB-denominated payments in 2016 by about 16 percent. This is a non-trivial amount.

(b) The second channel through which the BRI can increase RMB-denominated payments flows around the world is that it reduces the trade costs of the B&R corridors, which increases trade and investment flows between China and the B&R countries along the corridors, which in turn increases RMB-denominated payments flows between China and these countries.

According to de Soyres, Mulabdic, Murray, et al. (2018), trade costs would fall by 5.6 percent for the China–Indochina Peninsula

Economic Corridor (CICPEC) and by 21.6 percent for the China–Central Asia–West Asia Economic Corridor (CCWAEC) if the infrastructure projects of BRI are enhanced by trade facilitation measures such as shorter border delays. There is no mentioning of the enhanced effect on the China–Mongolia–Russia Economic Corridor (CMREC), but I assume that it is about the same as CICPEC.[4]

Apparently, the greatest impacts on trade costs would be on these three corridors, and, for our purpose, given the countries that we are considering, only two of the corridors, viz. China–Indochina Peninsula Economic Corridor and China–Mongolia–Russia Economic Corridor, seem to matter. So, we choose to focus on these two corridors. Based on the regression result of equation (8.4), we carry out the following counterfactual thought experiment. We assume that bilateral trade costs, proxied by d_{ij}, reduce by 10 percent among any pair of the following countries (on CICPEC): China, Hong Kong, Singapore, Thailand, Malaysia, Philippines, Indonesia. We also assume that bilateral trade costs also reduce by 10 percent among any pair of the following countries (on CMREC): China, Mongolia, Russia. We give these trade costs a reduction of 10 percent, a somewhat larger percentage than estimated by de Soyres, Mulabdic, Murray, et al. (2018), so as to see the upper bounds of the effects. Our result indicates that such reduction in trade costs will increase total global RMB-denominated payments by about 0.8 percent in 2016, a very modest amount. That means that the reduction of trade costs per se would have very little impact on RMB payments flows.

As of 2016, the estimated RMB payment share in the world in 2016 was 1.62 percent, by my own estimate (which excludes intra-Eurozone international flows and flows due to international FX market transactions), and the RMB was ranked 8th in payment share in that year (see Table 8.4). Summarizing the findings above, our thought experiments indicate that the total impact of the BRI on RMB payments flows in 2016 is equal to: +16 percent (increased RMB payments flows resulting from increased trade between B&R

Table 8.4 *Payment shares of countries without BRI, and estimated payment shares with BRI, in 2016*

Actual payment shares in 2016 – without BRI			Counterfactual payment shares in 2016 – with BRI		
Rank	Currency	Share (percentage)	Rank	Currency	Share (percentage)
1	USD	55.31	1	USD	55.31
2	EUR	20.52	2	EUR	20.52
3	JPY	5.86	3	JPY	5.86
4	GBP	5.28	4	GBP	5.28
5	CAD	3.23	5	CAD	3.23
6	CHF	2.12	6	CHF	2.12
7	AUD	2.11	7	AUD	2.11
8	**RMB**	**1.62**	8	**RMB**	**1.90**

countries and China) + 0.8 percent (increased RMB payments flows resulting from reduced trade costs in the sea and land economic corridors) = 16.8 percent. Assuming that BRI does not affect the payments flows of other currencies, the BRI would increase the RMB's global payment share to about 1.62 percent × (1 + 16.8 percent) = 1.9 percent in 2016.[5] However, this share is still lower than the 7th ranked AUD's payment share of 2.11 percent. Consequently, the RMB would still rank 8th in payment share in 2016. Thus, our conclusion is that the BRI would not substantially improve the payment share of the RMB in global payments. The result is summarized in Table 8.4.

8.2.2 The Increase in RMB-Denominated International Debt Securities

According to the official document issued by the Chinese government in March 2015, "Vision and Actions on Jointly Building Silk Road Economic Belt," cited above, the Chinese government:

262 8 THE POTENTIAL OF THE RMB AS A PAYMENT CURRENCY

will support the efforts of governments of the countries along the Belt and Road and their companies and financial institutions with good credit-rating to issue renminbi bonds in China. Qualified Chinese financial institutions and companies are encouraged to issue bonds in both renminbi and foreign currencies outside China, and use the funds thus collected in countries along the Belt and Road.

Thus, it is expected that the BRI would lead to RMB-denominated financing of projects in the B&R countries, notably through the issuance of RMB-denominated bonds in the onshore and offshore markets. This would enhance RMB internationalization. We offer a rough estimate of the impact below.

What is the current status of the RMB in denominating international debt securities? As of 2020 Q1, out of a total outstanding stock of international debt securities of USD 24.91 trillion, the amount (share) denominated in USD was USD 11.8 trillion (47.4%); in euro, USD 9.45 trillion (37.9%); in pounds sterling, USD 1.97 trillion (7.9%); in yen, USD 448 billion (1.8%); and in RMB, USD 101 billion (0.41%). Thus, the share of the RMB is tiny indeed (see columns (1)–(3) of Table 8.5). To what extent can the BRI boost this share?

First, we estimate how much RMB-denominated bonds will be issued as a result of the BRI. The total amount of investment in the BRI is uncertain. But according to different sources, the total amount of investment in the BRI has been estimated to be about USD 4 trillion to USD 8 trillion. Some of the investments (an amount equal to about USD 1 trillion) have been sunk as of the time of writing (July 2020).[6] In addition to uncertainty concerning the total amount of investment, the exact length of time for the total investment to be fully spent is also uncertain. However, one should expect the time it takes to be at least several decades. After examining the estimates from various sources, we think it is not unreasonable to assume that there is an additional amount of USD 6 trillion to be invested in the next 35 years.[7]

Table 8.5 Currency shares of outstanding stock of international debt securities in 2020 Q1 (out of a total of USD 24.91 trillion) and rough projection of the shares in 2030 Q1 (out of an estimated total of USD 31.88 trillion) with and without BRI

Current status of the RMB (2020 Q1)			Projection for 2030 Q1 – without BRI			Projection for 2030 Q1 – with BRI		
(1)	(2)	(3)	(4)	(5)	(6)	(7)	(8)	(9)
Rank	Currency	Share (percentage)	Rank	Currency	Share (percentage)	Rank	Currency	Share (percentage)
1	USD	47.4	1	USD	47.4	1	USD	47.4
2	EUR	37.9	2	EUR	37.9	2	EUR	37.9
3	GBP	7.9	3	GBP	7.9	3	GBP	7.9
4	JPY	1.8	4	RMB	2.7	4	RMB	5.4
					(optimistic)			(very optimistic)
?	RMB	0.41	?	JPY	1.8	?	JPY	1.8

For a liberal estimate, suppose half of the USD 6 trillion (i.e., USD 3 trillion) worth of BRI investment is to be financed by RMB-denominated international debt securities over a period of 35 years, starting from 2020. This is equivalent to USD 86 billion per year, or USD 0.86 trillion per decade. That is, there is a cumulative amount of USD 0.86 trillion worth of RMB-denominated international bonds issued from 2020 (the time of writing) to 2030. Let us compare this with the estimated total global stock of international debt securities in 2030. The data from BIS shows that the total global amount of outstanding stock of international debt securities increased from USD 19.44 trillion in 2010 Q2 to USD 24.91 trillion in 2020 Q1 (i.e., a period of ten years). This is an increase of 28 percent in ten years.[8] If we extrapolate by assuming that there is a 28 percent increase in the next ten years, then there will be a total stock of outstanding international debt securities of about USD 31.88 trillion by 2030 Q1. Thus, BRI will boost the share of outstanding RMB-denominated international debt securities by 0.86/31.88 = 2.7 percent by 2030 Q1.

It is reasonable to assume that the share of the RMB will increase in the next decade even without BRI, as China is an ascending country. The outstanding stock (share) of international debt securities denominated in RMB was USD 11.98 billion (0.062 percent) in 2010 Q2. The rate of increase during the ten years from 2010 Q2 to 2020 Q1 was 8.4 fold. Suppose this growth has nothing to do with BRI. If we extrapolate by assuming the same rate of increase in the next ten years starting from 2020 Q1, then by 2030 Q1, even without BRI, the share of the RMB in international debt securities will become USD 101 billion × 8.4 = USD 848 billion, which is equivalent to a share of 0.848/31.88 = 2.66% ≈ 2.70%. Together with the estimated increase in share due to the BRI, the total share of RMB-denominated international debt securities will be 2.70% + 2.70% = 5.40% in 2030 Q1. Assuming that the shares of those denominated in other currencies remain the same, then RMB will become the fourth currency (behind the USD, euro, and GBP, but ahead of JPY) used to denominate international debt securities by 2030 Q1. This can put the RMB ahead of the JPY to become the fourth-ranked currency by 2030 if the share of JPY remains unchanged. However, the impact of the BRI alone is still too small to catapult the RMB ahead of the USD, euro, and GBP. Note, however, that this is a liberal estimate. A less liberal, but still plausible, estimate can easily cut the amount by half or even three-quarters, reducing the share of RMB to 2.7 percent or even 1.4 percent. Refer to columns (7)–(9) of Table 8.5.

In sum, the BRI can probably increase the international use of the RMB as a funding currency by increasing the share of RMB-denominated international debt securities, but it will very likely still leave the RMB far behind the top three currencies in this regard. The result of the projection is summarized in Table 8.5. Columns (1)–(3) show the current status of the currency shares as of 2020 Q1. Columns (4)–(6) show the projection for 2030 Q1 without BRI, while columns (7)–(9) show the projection for 2030 Q1 with BRI.

Our conclusion is, therefore, that to the extent that the BRI increases the uses of the RMB for international payments and denominating international debt securities, the effects are too small to have any substantial impact on the internationalization of the RMB. Financial development and capital account openness are still the two most important factors that can have first-order impact on the internationalization of the RMB.

However, there can be intangible benefits from the BRI for China regarding RMB internationalization. As Aliber (2011) pointed out, one important attribute of an international currency is its brand name. The BRI can in fact help China to build trust with the B&R countries, which can improve China's brand name. This can increase the appeal of the RMB to foreigners and make them more willing to hold it for store of value and use it for payments and even use it as a reserve currency.

8.3   CONCLUSION

Our thought experiments based on the gravity model reveal that capital account liberalization and financial market development have a distinctly stronger impact on the payment share of the RMB than the increase in China's GDP. This is because China's financial development and capital account openness are both low even by developing-country standards, and so there is a lot of room for China to improve along these two dimensions. On the other hand, China is already the second largest economy in the world, and its growth rate is diminishing over time. So, there is not much room for the increase in its GDP to have a large impact on the payment share of its currency even if it catches up with the largest economy, namely the United States.

Our conclusion, therefore, is that China must greatly speed up its financial development and open its capital account if it wants the RMB to become a significant international payment currency. Economic size alone will not catapult the RMB into the league of major payment currencies.

Concerning the BRI, our quantitative estimates indicate that, to the extent that the BRI increases the uses of the RMB for international payments and denominating international debt securities, the effects are too small to have any substantial impact on the internationalization of the RMB. Nonetheless, the BRI can deliver an intangible benefit of building up the brand name of China, which can facilitate RMB internationalization.

NOTES TO CHAPTER 8

1 Among the East Asian countries, the major emerging economies with higher share ratios than that of China in 2016 were South Korea 0.43, Taiwan 0.43, and Thailand 0.33. The financial development and openness of these economies are not considered particularly high even by developing-country standards.

2 See, for example, Li, Gao, Oxenford, et al. 2017.

3 See "Vision and Actions on Jointly Building Silk Road Economic Belt and 21st-Century Maritime Silk Road," issued by the National Development and Reform Commission, Ministry of Foreign Affairs, and Ministry of Commerce of the People's Republic of China, with State Council authorization, March 2015 (www.chinese-embassy.org.uk/eng/zywl/t1251719.htm).

4 From de Soyres, Mulabdic, Murray, et al. 2018: "the Belt and Road Initiative includes efforts to improve the efficiency of customs, reduce border delays or to improve management of economic corridors. As an extension of our main database, we present two scenarios where those elements are explicitly taken into account. We find that the implementation of complementary policy reforms magnifies the impact on shipment times and trade costs, especially along the corridors. For instance, if border delays were reduced by half, the reduction of shipment times along corridors would range between 7.7 percent for the China-Indochina Peninsula Economic Corridor (CICPEC) and 25.5 percent of the China-Central Asia-West Asia Economic Corridor (CCWAEC). Similarly, trade costs would fall by 5.6 percent for the China-Indochina Peninsula Economic Corridor (CICPEC) and by 21.6 percent for the China-Central Asia-West Asia Economic Corridor (CCWAEC). These large effects are not surprising given the importance of trade facilitation bottlenecks in BRI economies [M. Bartley Johns, C. Kerswell, J. L. Clarke, and G. McLinden 'Trade Facilitation Challenges and Reform Priorities for Maximizing the Impact of the Belt and Road Initiative', MTI discussion paper No. 4, World Bank, 2018]."

5 This is not exact, as the shares of the other currencies would fall. However, it is a good enough approximation given the small initial share of the RMB.

6 See *South China Morning Post*, 27 September 2017 and 21 February 2019: www.scmp.com/special-reports/business/topics/special-report-belt-and-road/article/2112978/cost-funding-belt-and; www.scmp.com/print/week-asia/explained/article/2187162/explained-belt-and-road-initiative; and OECD 2018.

7 A report published in 2016 by PWC estimates that as large as USD 5 trillion was going to be spent in 30 to 40 years, with most of the

expenditure expected to have been incurred by 2049, the 100th anniversary of the People's Republic of China: www.pwc.com/gx/en/growth-markets-center/assets/pdf/china-new-silk-route.pdf.

8 See BIS website: www.bis.org/statistics/about_securities_stats.htm?m=6%7C33.

9 The Prospects of RMB Internationalization

As we have seen, RMB internationalization requires not only a large economic size, capital account opening, and financial market reforms, but also state-owned enterprise (SOE) reforms and institutional reforms such as establishing a credible legal system and a system of checks and balances in the government.

China's strategy of launching the internationalization of RMB is underpinned by the creation of the offshore RMB market, or what I call "one currency, two markets," which in turn is inspired by the "one country, two systems" concept. The reason "one currency, two markets" is so attractive to the leaders of China is that, at its current stage of development, China does not want to be fully integrated with the West (at least it is not yet prepared to do so), but it wants to open up to the West in a controlled manner so as to stimulate domestic economic development. China is wary of the risks of free capital mobility, and it is not prepared to relinquish capital controls any time soon. Although the creation of the offshore market alone cannot be the main driver of RMB internationalization, it greatly amplifies the impacts of capital account opening and financial development, which are the ultimate drivers of RMB internationalization.

How likely is it that RMB internationalization will succeed? There are plenty of reasons to be pessimistic. First, the growth rate has declined almost continuously from 10.6 percent in 2010 to 6.1 percent in 2019.[1] In addition to the decline in the growth rate of total factor productivity, the population is ageing, and the working-age population (16–59 years old) has already begun to shrink in 2012.[2] The shrinking labor force can have a pivotal impact on economic growth. Without a sufficiently large economic size, it is hard for China's currency to attain the market thickness in the foreign exchange market and the broad and deep financial markets necessary for internationalization of the RMB.

Second, China is too wary of the risks of free capital mobility to relinquish capital controls in the onshore market any time soon. The offshore market is a place where China experiments with full convertibility of the RMB and free capital mobility in a controlled manner. There is a firewall that separates the onshore from the offshore markets, providing safety to the former. Thus, the offshore market is an important component of the RMB internationalization strategy. If necessary, the authority can strengthen capital controls between the offshore and onshore markets through administrative measures. Unfortunately, it is this option of imposing capital controls in a discretionary manner that becomes the enemy of RMB internationalization. Every time discretionary capital controls are imposed, it would damage the credibility of the Chinese government, and hurt the offshore market. One reason for the aversion to free capital mobility is China's desire to maintain the stability of its financial markets, which are still underdeveloped. Another reason is its desire to prevent excessive volatility of its exchange rate. According to the open-economy trilemma, maintaining a stable exchange rate implies that it has to impose capital controls from time to time so as to preserve autonomy in monetary policy. This hurts RMB internationalization.

Third, a key obstacle to RMB internationalization is that the development of a deep, broad, and liquid financial market in the onshore market will probably take a long time. It requires the rule of law, freedom of capital mobility, an independent judiciary, the effective enforcement of contracts, well-enforced bankruptcy laws, and the credibility of the government. A sophisticated and fair legal system that guarantees the proper functioning of the financial system at all times is crucial. China is a long way from that goal. Furthermore, the liberalization of the financial sector is met with strong resistance from vested interests, such as the large state-owned commercial banks and state-owned enterprises that rely on easy access to credit from the banking system to keep them afloat. As long as SOEs continue to serve not just economic but also social and political functions, they will continue to receive special treatment in the financial market, and they will continue to be an obstacle to financial sector reforms. For better or for worse, a sizable SOE sector may be here to stay for a long time. The reason is that SOEs are regarded as the foundation of the political power of the Communist Party of China (CPC). Not only do SOEs serve political and social functions, they are also a tool for the planning of the economy. For many in the party, SOEs and central planning are the foundation for the CPC to stay in power. As long as the CPC continues to claim to be adhering to the ideology of Marx, Lenin, and Mao, it is hard for it to rationalize a substantial downsizing of the SOE sector and central planning. Adhering to such an ideology is important for the legitimacy of the party.[3] The public announcement concerning the outcome of the fourth plenum of the 19th session of the CPC released in October 2019 went so far as to state that "public ownership is the main body" of the economic system. It goes on to state that the party should "fully develop the decisive role of the market in the allocation of resources" but also "fully develop the function of the government." These seemingly contradictory statements signify the continuation of the pragmatic approach of "crossing the river by feeling for the stones" that ignores the contradiction between practice and theory as long as it serves the purpose of the day. Yet the sacrosanct nature of the SOE sector and central planning is unmistakable.[4]

Last but not least, in order for the RMB to be a "safe-haven currency," China must gain foreigners' trust in China's institutions, such as having an independent judiciary, an independent and transparent central bank, checks and balances in the government, and freedom in general (see, for example, Prasad 2017b).[5] It seems unlikely that a one-party state, without a contestable democracy and citizens' freedom to challenge government policies, can sustain sufficient trust from the rest of the world. Aliber (2011) suggests that whether a currency is widely accepted as international money depends to a large extent on its "brand name." He argues that the brand name of the

USD is supported by the size of the US economy, the stability of its financial markets, a long history of a low rate of inflation, and its military and political security. However, he forgets to mention that trust also plays a very important role in the brand name of the USD. It is in the area of trust that it is hard for the RMB to compete with the USD (or the euro for that matter) in the developed world. This is because of history, culture, and politics. Most countries in the developed world share their history and culture with the United States. Western European countries and Japan have been the allies of the United States since the end of World War II. They have similar political and economic systems. They have enjoyed the military protection of the United States and close economic ties with the United States. Thus, they feel comfortable with the United States, and by extension the USD, being the leader. China, on the other hand, is an outsider. It does not share its history, culture, or ideology with most countries in the developed world. Thus, it will take time and effort for China to win the trust of the developed world.

Recent events have made it even harder for China to build trust with Western countries. At the time of writing (the end of 2020), the US government, under President Donald Trump, had been engaging in a vigorous campaign to discredit China. The Belt and Road Initiative of China was harshly attacked and characterized as debt traps by the Secretary of State, Mike Pompeo. China's territorial claims in the South China Sea was criticized as completely illegitimate. The treatment of the Uighur ethnic group in Xinjiang was attacked as an appalling human rights violation and the officials responsible were subject to sanctions by the United States. In fact, Mike Pompeo used a highly controversial term "genocide" to describe China's policy in Xinjiang just before he left office on 20 January 2021. The enactment of the national security law in the Hong Kong SAR was denounced as a gross violation by China of the agreement to allow it to have a high degree of autonomy under "one country, two systems," and so the Hong Kong and Mainland Chinese officials responsible were subject to sanctions. The telecommunications giant Huawei was accused of being a security threat and banned from doing business in the United States. At the time of writing, the highly successful social media app TikTok was forced to be sold to US companies for national security reasons. China was accused by Donald Trump of withholding the facts about COVID-19 and of failing to warn the rest of the world in time about its seriousness. China was accused of hacking into US computers to steal information about COVID-19 vaccines. The CPC and even its highest leader were vilified: On 23 July 2020, in a speech titled "Communist China and the Free World's Future" delivered in the Richard Nixon Presidential Library and Museum, in California, Secretary of State Mike Pompeo called Xi Jinping a "true believer in a bankrupt, totalitarian ideology," – a scathing attack. There were too many such attacks to be fully documented here for lack of space. The United States even mobilized its allies, such as the UK, Canada, Australia, and New Zealand, to join in the discrediting campaign. Although there is a lack of evidence regarding many of the accusations by the United States, China's image was greatly hurt, and so was its brand name. At the time of writing, the international political environment was very unfavorable to building up trust for RMB internationalization.

However, there are reasons for cautious optimism as well. First, despite a possible slowdown in the growth rate, China's economy is likely to continue to grow faster than the United States in the next one or two decades, and it is likely going to become the largest economy by market exchange rate before 2040, giving it size advantage. For the same reason, China will probably continue to be the largest trading economy. In 2016, China's GDP was USD 11.23 trillion, while that of the United States was USD 18.71 trillion, which was 1.67 times that of China. In 2019, the gap narrowed: China's GDP was USD 14.34 trillion while that of the United States was USD 21.43 trillion, being 1.49 times that of China.[6] So, as long as China's nominal growth rate in USD terms is more than 2 percent higher than that of the United States in each of the following 20 years from 2019, China's nominal GDP in USD terms will be as large as that of the

United States by 2039. Given the track records of China and the United States, this is likely to happen. The total factor productivity (TFP) of China is still very low compared with, say, South Korea, Taiwan, and Japan. There is a lot of room for TFP growth through technological progress, further human capital accumulation, and better resource allocation through capital market reforms.[7]

Second, China has more incentives than other countries, such as Japan, to internationalize its currency. The first incentive is that, because of its ideological differences with the United States, China has a strong desire to be more independent from the United States and the USD than countries like Japan, which is an ally of the United States. The second incentive, unique to China, is the possibility of using the capital account opening that comes with RMB internationalization to *daobi* domestic financial sector reform. This is similar to using the market opening that came with accession to the WTO to stimulate domestic industrial sector reform back in 2001. Today, the domestic financial sector is so fraught with special interests that it is hard to reform it without opening the market to foreign competition and opening its financial assets to foreign investment. So, one way to move the reform forward is to liberalize the capital account and the financial market in tandem, but in a gradual and interactive fashion. Capital account opening can prompt financial market liberalization, which in turn can justify further capital account opening. This provides the rationale for using RMB internationalization as an external commitment to force the reform of the domestic financial market.

The favorable news is that the pace of opening of China has not slowed down in recent years. In the last few years, there have been a large number of entries of foreign financial institutions with majority ownership, fast development of the bond market, the introduction of the Bond Connect and Stock Connects with Hong Kong, interest rate reform (e.g., introduction of the market-based loan prime rate), and stock market reform.

As for SOE reform, an alternative model to maintain the existence of unprofitable SOEs that perform social and political functions without interfering with the efficient operation of the financial markets is to support them through fiscal subsidies instead of credit subsidies. That way, the state-owned banks can focus on their economic functions and compete on a level playing field with other competitors in the financial markets, such as the private domestic and foreign financial institutions. More generally, under this alternative model, other than providing fiscal subsidies to SOEs, the government need not interfere in the markets so that the markets can work efficiently. Then, the interest rate can be truly market-determined and the financial markets can become more efficient in the allocation of resources. It should be noted that one condition for this alternative model to work is that the share of tax revenue in GDP has to be sufficiently high. Another issue with this alternative model is that, while it can correct the distortion in the financial market, it does not fundamentally solve the problem that real resources are used to prop up unprofitable enterprises. Thus, in the long run, most of the SOEs need to be phased out from the economic efficiency point of view.

Third, a counterpoint to the view that the RMB cannot be a "safe-haven currency" because China does not have enough political freedom is that what matters for whether a currency can be a "safe-haven currency" is the economic freedom, not political freedom, of the issuing country. China can possibly commit to allowing a lot of economic freedom but restrict political freedom to a level compatible with its history and stage of development. China has made a lot of progress in reducing corruption, strengthening the rule of law and the enforcement of contracts, and establishing an independent judiciary, especially in economic affairs. In this regard, Singapore may be an example that China wants to follow. Singapore is an economic powerhouse. It was ranked "the most competitive economy" in the world in the Institute for Management Development (IMD) World Competitiveness Ranking 2019 and ranked highest in the world in the Heritage Foundation 2020 Index of Economic Freedom. However, it is not highly ranked in terms of political freedom and human rights. In Singapore, the incumbent People's Action Party (PAP) is the

276 THE PROSPECTS OF RMB INTERNATIONALIZATION

dominant party by a large margin. The opposition is very weak. According to Wikipedia, "Singapore has consistently been rated as the least-corrupt country in Asia and amongst the top ten cleanest in the world by Transparency International. The World Bank's governance indicators have also rated Singapore highly on rule of law, control of corruption and government effectiveness. However, it is widely perceived that some aspects of the political process, civil liberties, and political and human rights are lacking. The Economist Intelligence Unit rated Singapore a 'flawed democracy' in 2019. Freedom House deemed the press 'not free' in 2015."[8] In another entry of Wikipedia, it is pointed out that, "[in] 2018, Singapore was ranked 151st by Reporters Without Borders in the Worldwide Press Freedom Index. US-based Freedom in the World scored Singapore 3 out of 7 for 'political freedom', and 3 out of 7 for 'civil liberties' (where 1 is the 'most free'), with an overall ranking of 'partly free' for the year 2015."[9] In other words, it is possible for a country with a lot of economic freedom but limited political freedom to win the trust of foreigners concerning its handling of economic affairs.

Checks and balances in the government are in general good, but central bank independence is not necessarily always a virtue. First, it may not be necessary if the government does not have the incentive to run an excessive fiscal deficit or prefers growth over stable price levels in the short term so as to increase its chance of getting re-elected. Second, the ability of the central bank to coordinate with other government departments can in fact be a virtue. Former PBC governor Zhou Xiaochuan once pointed out that by being part of the government, the PBC could more effectively participate in the broader policy debate and decision-making, thus playing a more influential role than an independent central bank could. In fact, even the most important central banks, such as the US Federal Reserve, the European Central Bank, and Bank of Japan, are not always independent, as their governments sometimes find it necessary for the central bank to coordinate with other branches of the government. For example, former Fed Chairman Ben Bernanke once told his successor Janet Yellen during his handover that she needed to heed the US Congress. The point is that the central bank (and maybe some other branches of the government for that matter) should be given the freedom to carry out independent professional analysis and make independent judgements in its professional area, but the final action to be taken may have to be a compromise with the central government. This compromise is sometimes necessary to achieve the best outcome for the country as a whole. One can argue that what is most important for a central bank is the track record in maintaining price stability, exchange rate stability, and financial stability. In these regards, the PBC has performed very well. In addition, it has played a pivotal role in spearheading financial sector reforms, capital account liberalization, and internationalization of the RMB. This record proves that the central bank need not be fully independent to be effective and influential.

While China has to make an effort to build its brand name, that of the United States is not as illustrious as it used to be. There are multiple reasons. First, the United States continues to run a current account deficit year after year since the early 1980s. It is now the largest debtor country. This creates pressure for the USD to depreciate. A number of economists have warned against a possible sudden loss of confidence in the dollar. For example, Obstfeld and Rogoff have argued (2001; 2007) that the likely future reversal of the US current account would lead to a 30 percent depreciation of the dollar.

Another reason the brand name of the United States was damaged recently is that its credibility in international affairs plummeted as it pursued an "America First" agenda under President Donald Trump. The United States blatantly violated WTO rules by unilaterally erecting trade barriers on goods such as steel and aluminum and specifically targeting China. In September 2020, the WTO expert panel ruled that the US unilateral imposition of tariffs on Chinese goods in 2018 had violated WTO rules. However, the United States ignored the ruling. At the same time, the United States refused to confirm any judge to fill the vacancies in the Appellate Body of the WTO, making it short of the minimum number of judges required, thus rendering the dispute settlement procedure of the organization non-functional. Therefore, the United States, under Donald Trump, effectively tore apart the WTO (whose predecessor was GATT), the institution that has championed free trade for all countries based on the principle of multilateralism since the end of World War II under the leadership of the United States.[10] It withdrew from the Trans-Pacific Partnership trade agreement initiated by Barack Obama and a group of Pacific countries including Japan, puzzling its allies. In addition, it withdrew from the 2015 Paris Agreement on climate change mitigation signed by Barack Obama, the nuclear deal with Iran signed by Barack Obama and US allies, and the WHO during the COVID-19 pandemic. President Trump frequently contradicted himself, saying one thing at one point and then the opposite thing later on. Some may say that all these are just temporary phenomena, and that the policies can be reversed after Donald Trump leaves office. Others, however, argue that the fact that Donald Trump was elected and that he continues to be influential in the Republican Party after he left office signals a fundamental change in the United States in that a large percentage of Americans desire to have a nationalistic government that focuses only on its national interests and ignores those of foreigners, and this situation will not go away any time soon. At the end of the day, it is not at all clear whether the United States will feel any moral obligation to honor its implicit promises toward foreigners when its national interest is on the line, according to this view. For example, will it expropriate the properties of foreigners in the United States based on economic and ideological rivalry (and not on justice), thus violating the property rights of the owners? More importantly, will the US government intentionally cause or allow the USD to depreciate so as to reduce its net external liabilities? This leads us to the next point.

The fourth, but not least, argument in support of cautious optimism about the RMB becoming a major international currency in the long run is related to the limitation of the United States itself. The USD is the dominant reserve currency by a large margin (with a reserve currency share of about 60 percent to 65 percent), with the euro being a distant second (with a reserve currency share of about 20 percent). The euro is more a regional currency than the USD, as most of the countries that hold large amounts of euro as foreign reserves are located near the eurozone or have close ties to it. The eurozone sovereign debt crisis of 2009 exposed the weakness in the governance of the monetary union. Moreover, the GDP share of the eurozone is shrinking. Thus, the euro has limited capacity to expand its reserve-currency share. Given that the USD is the only truly global reserve currency, the Triffin dilemma described in Chapter 3 may be triggered as the relative economic size of the United States falls over time, and this can cause people to lose confidence in the exchange value of the USD. To the central banks of many countries (especially those that do not have close ties to the eurozone), if there is an alternative to the USD, they would probably diversify away from the USD. However, currently, there is no real alternative to the USD as a global reserve currency. In Chapter 3, I mentioned that there is potentially a long-run problem with the current IMS, under which there is only one truly global reserve currency, the USD. This is because, as the rest of the world grows more quickly than does the United States, their demand for foreign reserves will grow faster than the fiscal capacity of the United States to repay the dollar-denominated US government debt that it issued to meet this demand. This will cause the United States to either depreciate its currency over time so as to inflate away the debt, or to default. The anticipation of such an event can trigger a confidence problem that can cause the IMS to collapse. This was what happened to the Bretton Woods system in 1973. Can this happen again under the current IMS?

Farhi and Maggiori (2018) argue that the Triffin dilemma is present under both a fixed and a floating exchange rate regime, and that the high demand for reserves in the post-Asian Financial Crisis era with large global imbalances may activate the Triffin margin. They point out that the American role as a "world banker" is per-formed today on a much larger scale than when originally debated in the 1960s. In other words, the "bank of the world," which the United

States is supposed to be, has gotten bigger, and so the scale of the potential problem has gotten larger. The US external debt, which in 2015 stood at 158 percent of GDP, of which 85 percent was denominated in USD, heightens the possibility of a Triffin-like event.[11] They go on to point out that, "[i]f the history of the IMS is any guidance, then this possibility should not be discarded since the system tends to undergo long spells of tranquility that breed complacency before investors suddenly wake up to the reality that even anchors of stability such as world providers of reserve currencies do end up sharply devaluing under bad enough circumstances."

In other words, in the long run, outside the euro-bloc countries, the world demands an alternative choice of reserve currency other than the USD. Another reserve currency is needed to fill the gap. The RMB is an obvious candidate because China is likely going to be the largest economy in the world in the not too distant future and it is rapidly opening up to the rest of the world. So, it may not be too far-fetched to imagine that, at some point in the future, the IMS would become a truly multi reserve currency one, with the USD, euro, and RMB being the three main reserve currencies. Perhaps there will be a RMB bloc, which includes China, East and Southeast Asia (except Japan), most developing countries along the Belt and Road, and some other developing countries, a euro bloc, which includes Europe and some historically related countries, and a USD bloc, which includes most of the rest of the world.

However, even in a multi reserve currency IMS, it is likely that the USD will continue to be the dominant reserve currency of the world in the foreseeable future. First, the expansion of the share of the euro as a reserve currency is probably quite limited, as it is more like a regional currency than a global currency. Second, as pointed out earlier in this chapter, the growth rate of China is likely going to slow down markedly in the coming decades due to the shrinkage of its labor force and other reasons. Although this effect can in principle be offset by further capital accumulation and the growth of its total factor productivity, perhaps through technological progress, human capital accumulation, and better allocation of resources, it is not clear how much progress can be made on these fronts. Much hinges on further reforms and the opening and stability of the regime. By contrast, the labor force of the United States is forecast to increase in the coming decades, favoring the sustenance of its past growth rate. In the end, even if China becomes a larger economy than that of the United States, it probably will not be much larger. This, together with the fact that the US financial system is much more mature and open (which makes the US Treasury bond by far the most liquid safe asset of the world), will probably sustain the status of the USD as the dominant reserve currency for many more decades to come. In addition, in the foreseeable future, the USD will probably continue to be the single/ dominant vehicle currency of the world for invoicing homogeneous primary goods such as energy and commodities like oil, minerals, and agricultural products. This is because, as we pointed out in Chapter 5, the network effect (thick market externalities) is particularly strong in the invoicing of homogeneous goods, leading to the existence of one single/dominant vehicle currency for invoicing. This explains the persistence of the use of a currency as a vehicle currency even long after the issuing country ceases to be the largest economy in the world. This will likely apply to the USD.

So, what is in store for the future? We carried out some quantitative analyses in Chapter 8 to predict the extent of RMB internationalization in the future. Although we focused only on the potential of the RMB as a payment currency, the result can be interpreted as a prediction about the extent of RMB internationalization as a whole, as the roles of unit of account, medium of exchange, and store of value mutually reinforce each other. One important message we hope to convey from this book is that, in addition to economic stability and economic size, financial development and capital account openness of China are two most important pillars in making the RMB an important international payment currency. At the current stage of China's development, these two factors are more important than the economic size of China in determining the share of the RMB in international payments. Our quantitative analysis reveals that, although China has employed a plethora of policies to facilitate the internationalization of the RMB, the RMB can at best only rank a distant third in the global ranking of payment currencies by 2030. The main reason for this somewhat modest pace of internationalization of the RMB is that becoming a major payment currency might require China to reach a higher level of financial development and to open its capital account more than it is capable of doing. There has been speculation that the Belt and Road Initiative would greatly enhance RMB internationalization by promoting RMB trade invoicing, RMB-denominated outward direct investment, and the development of RMB financing of offshore projects, including the bond market. However, we think that the effect is very limited as long as the BRI does not contribute significantly to the financial development and capital account openness of China. Nonetheless, the BRI can carry an intangible benefit of building the trust for China, which can enhance RMB internationalization.

Our quantitative analysis indicates that it is possible that the RMB can become the third most used payment currency in the world by around 2030, after the USD and the euro, due to China's increasing relative economic size, capital account opening, and financial sector liberalization. However, the payment share of the RMB depends on the pace of capital account opening and financial market reforms in China. Even if the pace of these reforms is fast (when its financial development and openness in 2030 is about the same as that of Thailand in 2016), the RMB can only be a distant third in the ranking of payment currencies in 2030, behind that of USD and EUR, with a payment share of about 6.6 percent. This is not an implausible scenario, but it requires China to reform its financial sector and to open its capital account fast in the next decade.

Recent events, especially the enactment and implementation of the national security law for the Hong Kong Special Administrative Region, have thrown doubts on "one country, two systems" and the future of Hong Kong. Some people say that "one country, two systems" has failed because of the direct intervention of the Mainland into Hong Kong. Some even think that Hong Kong's status as an international financial center will come to an end. A few questions need to be answered. Will the intervention of the Mainland into Hong Kong jeopardize the credibility of its legal system so much that it undermines Hong Kong's status as an international financial center? Will Western companies leave Hong Kong because of the sanctions and decoupling of the United States and its allies? Will the competitiveness of Hong Kong suffer because of such sanctions and decoupling? My view is that "one country, two systems" is going to be alive and well when all the dusts have settled. My view is based on two arguments. First, it is in China's interest to make "one country, two systems" work, as it needs Hong Kong to be China's window and gateway to the rest of the world. Specifically, it wants Hong Kong to be the facilitator for China's reforms and opening by serving as China's international financial center, among other roles. The purpose of the introduction of the national security law in Hong Kong was to sustain the social, economic, and political stability of Hong Kong so that it can serve its roles better. Therefore, China will try its best to keep its intervention into Hong Kong at a minimum, focusing only on a small minority of cases that truly jeopardize national security. In particular, it will make sure it does not undermine the credibility of Hong Kong's legal system. Second, because China is still growing and opening at a fast pace, it is still a very attractive place for Western companies to do business with and to invest in. If Western companies, including American ones, flock to Mainland China, where the market institutions and business environment are less well-developed and freedom is more limited, there is really no reason for them to leave Hong Kong, where the market institutions and the business environment are world-class and there is still a lot more freedom than the Mainland (and many other parts of the world for that matter). So, I believe Hong Kong's competitiveness will not be compromised at the end of the day, despite sanctions and decoupling by the US government and its allies. Western companies will continue to go to China and Hong Kong as long as these places are good for doing business.

It is very likely that China will continue to open itself, but in a gradual and controlled manner. It is still very wary of fully integrating with a world dominated by a financial system it considers to be controlled by the United States, not totally reliable, and prone to crises. For this reason, it is quite likely that, for a long time, China will continue to rely greatly on the offshore markets, particularly Hong Kong, as it still wants to have a firewall between the onshore and offshore markets. The offshore centers help to separate the currency risks from the country risks for overseas investors. All the offshore centers are places with free capital mobility and robust legal frameworks for contractual enforcement. When overseas investors invest in Chinese assets through an offshore RMB center such as Hong Kong, the contracts are signed and enforced under the jurisdiction of Hong Kong, which is governed by British common law. This facilitates capital flows and helps capital account liberalization by increasing the confidence of the foreign investors that their investment is legally protected by a common law regime. Viewed in this light, Hong Kong will probably continue to prosper as an international financial center, thanks to its role as an important offshore RMB center and a window for China to the rest of the world.

In sum, one has to bear in mind that China is still a developing country. It started reforming and opening only 42 years ago, in 1978. At that time, the country had only one formal financial institution, the PBC. This served as both the central bank and the commercial bank and accounted for 93 per cent of the country's total financial assets. The legal system was very rudimentary.[12] The patent laws were first enacted only 36 years ago, in 1984. The Shanghai Stock Exchange and Shenzhen Stock Exchange started operation only as recently as 1990. Only in 2003 did the central bank, the PBC, acquire its current legal status and mandates. Today, many of the institutions are still underdeveloped. Today, the country still retains many characteristics of financial repression. In order to internationalize its currency, China must improve its institutional quality to international standards. The most important institution is the legal system. The second is a system of transparency and checks and balances. The third is a well-functioning financial market. Regarding all these, China still has a lot of work to do. In addition, the country is governed by a one-party state that has a different ideology from essentially all of the Western developed countries. This makes it hard for China to win the trust of the West. After the discrediting campaign of Donald Trump's administration, China has to fight an even harder uphill battle to build the trust of foreign countries in China and its currency. In any case, it takes a long time to build a brand name for a currency to be trusted as an international safe asset. Although China has made a lot of progress in the last 42 years, it still does not have a long enough history of credibility. Thus, RMB internationalization is going to be a long process.

Nonetheless, regardless of how long it takes for the RMB to become a significant international currency, one should not lose sight of the fact that RMB internationalization, in addition to being a long-term goal, is also a tool to stimulate financial market reforms and opening at the current stage of China's development. The ultimate goal of the initiative is to facilitate economic development. Even if the RMB does not become a significant international currency in the near future, if the process of seeking RMB internationalization serves as a catalyst for financial development and opening, the initiative should still be considered a success. RMB internationalization needs not be an end in itself.

NOTES TO CHAPTER 9

1 Refer to the World Bank.
2 Refer to *Caixin* magazine and National Bureau of Statistics www
.caixinglobal.com/2019-01-29/chart-of-the-day-chinas-shrinking-
workforce-101375782.html.
3 See "Ideology of the Chinese Communist Party": Wikipedia 2021b.
4 中共十九届四中全會全民公告 (二零一九年十月) (in Chinese) "Public
Announcement about the Fourth Plenary Session of the 19th CPC Central
Committee (October 2019)."

5 According to Prasad's definition, the role of a safe-haven currency is not just for investors seeking temporary refuge in times of international turmoil but also for people seeking a safe harbor for long-term store of value.

6 Refer to the World Bank (https://data.worldbank.org/indicator/NY.GDP .MKTP.CD?locations=EU-US-CN&most_recent_value_desc=true).

7 See Zhu 2012 and Zhang 2017 for some in-depth discussion about TFP growth in China.

8 See "Politics of Singapore": Wikipedia 2021d.

9 See "Human Rights in Singapore": Wikipedia 2021a.

10 For some in-depth discussion of the political economy of the China–United States trade war, see Lai 2019.

11 According to Farhi and Maggiori 2018, in 2015, US external liabilities (excluding financial derivatives) were USD 28.28 trillion against a GDP of USD 17.94 trillion (source: Bureau of Economic Analysis). US external liabilities are mostly denominated in USD, 85 percent on average, while US external assets are mostly denominated in foreign currency, 61 percent on average. (Source: Bénétrix, Lane, and Shambaugh 2015, average for the period 1990–2012.)

12 See, for example, Huang and Wang 2018.

References

Aliber, Robert. 2011. *The International Money Game*. Basingstoke: Palgrave Macmillan.

Anderson, James E., and Eric van Wincoop. 2003. "Gravity with Gravitas: A Solution to the Border Puzzle." *American Economic Review* 93(1): 170–192. http://doi.org/10.1257/000282803321455214.

Bacchetta, Philippe, and Eric van Wincoop. 2005. "A Theory of the Currency Denomination of International Trade." *Journal of International Economics* 67(2): 295–319. http://doi.org/10.1016/j.jinteco.2004.01.006.

Bacchetta, Philippe, Eric van Wincoop, and Toni Beutler. 2010. "Can Parameter Instability Explain the Meese–Rogoff Puzzle?" In Lucrezia Reichlin and Kenneth D. West (eds.). *NBER International Seminar on Macroeconomics 2009*. Chicago: University of Chicago Press, pp. 125–173.

Balding, Christopher. 2017. "Can China Afford Its Belt and Road?" *Bloomberg Opinion*. May 17. www.bloomberg.com/opinion/articles/2017-05-17/can-china-afford-its-belt-and-road.

Bank for International Settlements. 2003. "A Glossary of Terms Used in Payment and Settlement Systems." Committee on Payment and Settlement Systems. March. Basel, Switzerland.

Bénétrix, Agustín S., Philip R. Lane, and Jay Shambaugh. 2015. "International Currency Exposures, Valuation Effects, and the Global Financial Crisis." NBER Working Paper w20820.

Bhagwati, Jagdish. 1998. "The Capital Myth: The Difference between Trade in Widgets and Dollars." *Foreign Affairs* 77(3): 7–12. http://doi.org/10.2307/20048871.

Bosworth, Barry. 2012. "Conflicts in the U.S.–China Economic Relationship: Opposite Sides of the Same Coin?" Paper presented at Nomura Foundation's Macro-economic Conference in Tokyo. https://www.brookings.edu/wp-content/uploads/2016/06/20-china-us-economic-relationship-bosworth.pdf.

Boughton, James M. 1998. "Harry Dexter White and the International Monetary Fund." *Finance and Development* 35(3): 39–41. www.imf.org/external/pubs/ft/fandd/1998/09/boughton.htm.

Boyreau-Debray, Genevieve, and Shang-Jin Wei. 2005. "Pitfalls of a State-Dominated Financial System: The Case of China." NBER Working Paper 11214.

"Buttonwood." 2014. "What Was Decided at the Bretton Woods Summit." *The Economist*. 1 July. www.economist.com/the-economist-explains/2014/06/30/what-was-decided-at-the-bretton-woods-summit.

Calvo, Guillermo A., and Carmen M. Reinhart. 2002. "Fear of Floating." *Quarterly Journal of Economics* 117 (2): 379–408. http://doi.org/10.1162/003355302753650274.

Chen, Hongyi, and Wensheng Peng. 2010. "The Potential of the Renminbi as an International Currency." In Wensheng Peng and Chang Shu (eds.). *Currency Internationalization: Global Experiences and Implications for the Renminbi*. London: Palgrave Macmillan, pp. 115–138. https://link.springer.com/chapter/10.1057/9780230245785_5.

Cheung, Yin-Wong. 2015. "The Role of Offshore Financial Centers in the Process of Renminbi Internationalization." In Barry Eichengreen and Masahiro Kawai (eds.). *Renminbi Internationalization: Achievements, Prospects, and Challenges*. Washington, DC: Brookings Institution Press, pp. 207–235.

Cheung, Yin-Wong, Kenneth K. Chow, and Fengming Qin. 2017. *The RMB Exchange Rate: Past, Current and Future*. Singapore: World Scientific Press.

Cheung, Yin-Wong, Menzie Chinn, and Xin Nong. 2017. "Estimating Currency Misalignment Using the Penn Effect: It's Not as Simple as it Looks." *International Finance* 20: 222–242. https://doi.org/10.1111/infi.12113.

Chinn, Menzie D., and Hiro Ito. 2006. "What Matters for Financial Development? Capital Controls, Institutions, and Interactions." *Journal of Development Economics* 81(1): 163–192.

Chinn, Menzie D., and Hiro Ito. 2008. "A New Measure of Financial Openness." *Journal of Comparative Policy Analysis: Research and Practice* 10(3): 309–322. http://doi.org/10.1080/13876980802231123.

Chinn, Menzie D., and Jeffrey A. Frankel. 2007. "Will the Euro Eventually Surpass the Dollar as Leading International Reserve Currency?" In Richard Clarida (ed.). *G-7 Current Account Imbalances: Sustainability and Adjustment*. Chicago: University of Chicago Press, pp. 283–338.

Chinn, Menzie D., and Richard A. Meese. 1995. "Banking on Currency Forecasts: How Predictable is Change in Money?" *Journal of International Economics* 38: 161–178.

Chorzempa, Martin. (PIIE). 2018. "China's Restructuring of Financial Regulation Is Good News for Reform." March 19. www.piie.com/blogs/china-economic-watch/chinas-restructuring-financial-regulation-good-news-reform.

Čihák, Martin, Aslı Demirgüç-Kunt, Erik Feyen, and Ross Levine. 2012. "Benchmarking Financial Development Around the World." World Bank Policy Research Working Paper 6175, Washington, DC: The World Bank.

Coeurdacier, Nicolas, and Philippe Martin. 2009. "The Geography of Asset Trade and the Euro: Insiders and Outsiders." *Journal of the Japanese and International Economies* 23(2): 90–113. http://doi.org/10.1016/j.jjie.2008 .11.001.

Corden, W. Max. 2009. "China's Exchange Rate Policy, its Current Account Surplus, and the Global Imbalances." *Economic Journal* 119(541): F430–F441. doi:10.1111/j.1468–0297.2009.02319.x.

Corte, Pasquale Della, and Ilias Tsiakas. 2012. "Statistical and Economic Methods for Evaluating Exchange Rate Predictability." In Jessica James, Ian W. Marsh, and Lucio Sarno (eds.). *Handbook of Exchange Rates*. Hoboken, NJ: John Wiley & Sons, pp. 221–263.

Davis, Scott, Giorgio Valente, and Eric van Wincoop. 2019. "Global Drivers of Gross and Net Capital Flows." Hong Kong Institute of Monetary Research Working Paper No. 07/2019.

de Soyres, Francois, Alen Mulabdic, Siobhan Murray, Nadia Rocha, and Michele Ruta. 2018. "How Much Will the Belt and Road Initiative Reduce Trade Costs?" Policy Research Working Paper No. 8614. Washington, DC: The World Bank. https://openknowledge.worldbank.org/handle/10986/30582.

Dollar, David, and Shang-Jin Wei. 2007. "Das (Wasted) Kapital: Firm Ownership and Investment Efficiency in China." NBER Working Paper 13103. www.nber .org/papers/w13103.

Du, Julan, and Yifei Zhang. 2018. "Does One Belt One Road Initiative Promote Chinese Overseas Direct Investment?" *China Economic Review* 47: 189–205. https://doi.org/10.1016/j.chieco.2017.05.010.

Du, Wenxin, Alexander Tepper, and Adrien Verdelhan. 2018. "Deviations from Covered Interest Rate Parity." *Journal of Finance* 73(3): 915–957. http://doi .org/10.1111/jofi.12620.

The Economist. 2019. "Uncle Sam's Game America's Legal Forays against Foreign Firms Vex Other Countries." 19 January. www.economist.com/ business/2019/01/19/americas-legal-forays-against-foreign-firms-vex-other-countries.

Eichengreen, Barry. 2011a. "The Renminbi as an International Currency." *Journal of Policy Modeling* 33(5): 723–730.

Eichengreen, Barry. 2011b. *Exorbitant Privilege*. Oxford: Oxford University Press.

Eichengreen, Barry. 2013. "Renminbi Internationalization: Tempest in a Teapot?" *Asian Development Review* 30(1): 148–164.

Eichengreen, Barry, and Masahiro Kawai (eds.). 2015. *Renminbi Internationalization: Achievements, Prospects, and Challenges*. Washington, DC: Brookings Institution Press.

Eichengreen, Barry, and Ricardo Hausmann. 1999. "Exchange Rates and Financial Fragility." In *New Challenges for Monetary Policy*. Kansas City, MO: Federal Reserve Bank of Kansas City, pp. 329–368.

Eichengreen, Barry, Arnaud Mehl, and Livia Chiṭu. 2018. *How Global Currencies Work: Past, Present and Future*. Princeton, NJ: Princeton University Press.

Einzig, Paul, and Brian Scott-Quinn. 1977. *The Euro–Dollar System, Practice and Theory of International Interest Rate*, 6th edn. London: Macmillan.

Farhi, Emmanuel, and Matteo Maggiori. 2018. "A Model of the International Monetary System." *Quarterly Journal of Economics* 133(1): 295–355.

Feige, Edgar L. 2012. "New Estimates of U.S. Currency Abroad, the Domestic Money Supply and the Unreported Economy." *Crime, Law and Social Change* 57(3): 1–35. https://ssrn.com/abstract=2735044.

Fratzscher, Marcel. 2012. "Capital Flows Push versus Pull Factors and the Global Financial Crisis." *Journal of International Economics* 88(2): 341–356. http://doi.org/10.1016/j.jinteco.2012.05.003.

Frankel, J. A. 2011. "Historical Precedents for Internationalization of the RMB." CGS/IIGG Working Paper, New York: Council on Foreign Relations. www.cfr.org/china/historicalprecedents-internationalization-rmb/p26293.

Gelos, R. Gaston, and Shang-Jin Wei. 2005. "Transparency and International Portfolio Holdings." *Journal of Finance* 60 (6): 2987–3020. http://doi.org/10.1111/j.1540-6261.2005.00823.x.

Gilmore, S., and F. Hayashi. 2011. "Emerging Market Currency Excess Returns." *American Economic Journal: Macroeconomics* 3(4):85–111.

Goldberg, Linda S., and Cédric Tille. 2008. "Vehicle Currency Use in International Trade." *Journal of International Economics* 76(2): 177–192. http://doi.org/10.1016/j.jinteco.2008.07.001.

Gopinath, Gita, and Jeremy C. Stein. 2018. "Banking, Trade, and the Making of a Dominant Currency." NBER Working Paper 24485.

Habib, Maurizio Michael. 2010. "Excess Returns on Net Foreign Assets: The Exorbitant Privilege from a Global Perspective." European Central Bank Working Paper Series No. 1158. www.ecb.europa.eu/pub/pdf/scpwps/ecbwp1158.pdf.

Han, Xuehui, and Shang-Jin Wei. 2018. "International Transmissions of Monetary Shocks: Between a Trilemma and a Dilemma." *Journal of International Economics* 110: 205–219. http://doi.org/10.1016/j.jinteco.2017.11.005.

Hasbrouck, Joel, and Richard M. Levich. 2018. "FX Market Metrics: New Findings Based on CLS Bank Settlement Data." NBER Working Paper 23206.

Hassan, T. A. 2013. "Country Size, Currency Unions, and International Asset Returns." *Journal of Finance* 68(6): 2269–2308.

He, Dong, and Paul Luk. 2017. "A Model of Chinese Capital Account Liberalization." *Macroeconomic Dynamics* 21(8): 1902–1934.

He, Dong, and Robert N. McCauley. 2012. "Eurodollar Banking and Currency Internationalization." In M. C. S. Wong and W. F. C. Chan (eds.). *Investing in Asian Offshore Currency Markets*. London: Palgrave Macmillan. https://doi .org/10.1057/9781137034649_13.

Hong Kong Exchanges and Clearing Limited. 2018. "The RMB Reference Currency Basket and the Implications of a Market-Based RMB Currency Index." Hong Kong Exchange Research Report, July. www.hkex.com.hk/-/media/HKEX-Market/News/Research-Reports/HKEx-Research-Papers/2018/CCEO_RXY_201807_e.pdf?la=en.

Huang, Yiping, and Xun Wang. 2011. "Does Financial Repression Inhibit or Facilitate Economic Growth? A Case Study of Chinese Reform Experience." *Oxford Bulletin of Economics and Statistics* 73(6): 833–855. https://doi.org/10 .1111/j.1468-0084.2011.00677.x.

Huang, Yiping, and Xun Wang. 2018. "Strong on Quantity, Weak on Quality: China's Financial Reform between 1978 and 2018." In Ross Garnaut, Ligang Song, and Cai Fang (eds.). *China's 40 Years of Reform and Development: 1978–2018*. Canberra: ANU Press. https://press-files.anu.edu.au/downloads/ press/n4267/html/ch16.xhtml?referer=&page=25#.

Hurley, John, Scott Morris, and Gailyn Portelance. 2018. "Examining the Debt Implications of the Belt and Road Initiative from a Policy Perspective." CGD Policy Paper 121, March 2018, Washington, DC: Center for Global Development. www.cgdev.org/sites/default/files/examining-debt-implications-belt-and-road-initiative-policy-perspective.pdf.

International Monetary Fund. (IMF) 2011. "People's Republic of China: Financial System Stability Assessment." IMF Country Report No. 11/321. November 2. Washington, DC. www.imf.org/external/pubs/ft/scr/2011/cr11321.pdf.

International Monetary Institute of Renmin University of China. *Annual Report on the Internationalization of the Renmin*. 2015, 2016, 2017. In Chinese. [中国人民大学国际货币研究所《人民币国际化报告》（2015, 2016, 2017）].

Ito, Takatoshi. 2011. "The Internationalization of the RMB: Opportunities and Pitfalls." A CGS–IIGG Working Paper. New York Council on Foreign Relations.

Ito, Takatoshi, Satoshi Koibuchi, Kiyotaka Sato, and Junko Shimizu. 2010. "Why Has the Yen Failed to Become a Dominant Invoicing Currency in Asia? A Firm-Level Analysis of Japanese Exporters' Invoicing Behavior." NBER Working Paper 16231. July. http://doi.org/10.3386/w16231.

Johansson, Anders C. 2012. "Financial Repression and China's Economic Imbalances." In Huw McKay Huw and Ligang Song (eds.). *Rebalancing and Sustaining Growth in China*. Canberra: ANU Press, pp. 45–64. www.jstor.org/stable/j.ctt24hd16.10.

Judson, Ruth. 2012. "Crisis and Calm: Demand for U.S. Currency at Home and Abroad from the Fall of the Berlin Wall to 2011." Board of Governors of the Federal Reserve System, International Finance Discussion Papers, IFDP 1058. November. www.federalreserve.gov/pubs/ifdp/2012/1058/ifdp1058.pdf.

Kenen, Peter B. 1983. "The Role of the Dollar as an International Currency." Group of Thirty Occasional Papers 13, Washington, DC.

Kindleberger, Charles P. 1981. *International Money*. London: George Allen & Unwin.

King, Robert G., and Ross Levine. 1993. "Finance, Entrepreneurship, and Growth: Theory and Evidence." *Journal of Monetary Economics* 32(3): 513–542.

King & Wood Mallesons. 2014. "What Does a Sydney RMB Clearing Bank Mean?" 19 November. www.lexology.com/library/detail.aspx?g=83df73cd-772f-4133-8ecb-983727f917ef.

Kongmin, Li, Gao Haihong, Matthew Oxenford, Xu Qiyuan, Li Yuanfang, Paola Subacchi, and Song Shuang. 2017. "The 'Belt and Road' Initiative and the London Market – The Next Steps in Renminbi Internationalization, Part 3. Framework for Policy Discussion." Research Paper, International Economics Department, Chatham House. January. www.chathamhouse.org/publication/belt-and-road-initiative-and-london-market-next-steps-renminbi-internationalization.

Kongmin, Li, Gao Haihong, Xu Qiyuan, Li Yuanfang, and Song Shuang. 2017. "The 'Belt and Road' Initiative and the London Market – The Next Steps in Renminbi Internationalization, Part 1. The View from Beijing." Research Paper, International Economics Department, Chatham House. January. www .chathamhouse.org/publication/belt-and-road-initiative-and-london-market-next-steps-renminbi-internationalization.

Kose, M. Ayhan, Eswar S. Prasad, Kenneth Rogoff, and Shang-Jin Wei. 2009. "Financial Globalization: A Reappraisal." *IMF Staff Papers* 56(1): 8–62.

Krugman, Paul R. 1984. "The International Role of the Dollar: Theory and Prospect." In John F. O. Bilson and Richard C. Marston (eds.). *Exchange Rate Theory and Practice*. Chicago: University of Chicago Press, pp. 261–278.

Krugman, Paul R., Maurice Obstfeld, and Marc Melitz. 2018. *International Economics: Theory and Policy*. 11th edn. Cambridge, MA: Pearson Publishing.

Lai, Edwin L.-C. 2015. "Renminbi Internationalization: The Prospects of China's Yuan as the Next Global Currency." Thought Leadership Brief, 2015–09, Institute for Emerging Market Studies, Hong Kong University of Science and Technology. https://iems.ust.hk/publications/thought-leadership-briefs/renminbi-internation alization-the-prospects-of-chinas-yuan-as-the-next-global-currency.

Lai, Edwin L.-C. 2019. "The US–China Trade War, the American Public Opinions and Its Effects on China" *Economic and Political Studies* 7(2): 169–184. A Special Issue on the Sino–US Trade War. https://doi.org/10.1080/20954816 .2019.1595330.

Lai, Edwin L.-C., and Isabel K.-M. Yan. 2020. "International Payment Flows and the Potential of the RMB as a Significant Payment Currency." Hong Kong University of Science and Technology Working Paper. July. https://edwin-lc-lai.weebly.com/.

Lai, Edwin L.-C., and Xiangrong Yu. 2015. "Invoicing Currency in International Trade: An Empirical Investigation and Some Implications for the Renminbi." *World Economy* 38(1): 193–229. https://doi.org/10.1111/twec.12211.

Lane, Philip R., and Gian Maria Milesi-Ferretti. 2004. "International Investment Patterns." *Review of Economics and Statistics* 90(3): 538–549. http://doi.org/10.1162/rest.90.3.538.

Lardy, Nicholas R. 1998. *China's Unfinished Economic Revolution*. Washington, DC: Brookings Institution.

Lardy, Nicholas R., and Tianlei Huang. 2020. "Despite the Rhetoric, US–China Financial Decoupling Is Not Happening." Peterson Institute for International Economics (PIIE), China Economic Watch. July 2. www.piie.com/blogs/china-economic-watch/despite-rhetoric-us-china-financial-decoupling-not-happening.

Lee, S. S., and P. Luk. 2018. "The Asian Financial Crisis and International Reserve Accumulation: A Robust Control Approach." *Journal of Economic Dynamics and Control* 90:284–309.

Levich, Richard M., and Frank Packer. 2017. "Development and Functioning of FX Markets in Asia and the Pacific." *Financial Markets, Institutions & Instruments* 26(1): 3–58. http://doi.org/10.1111/fmii.12079.

Li, Kongmin, Haihong Gao, Matthew Oxenford, Qiyuan Xu, Yuanfang Li, Paola Subacch and Shuang Song. 2017. "The 'Belt and Road' Initiative and the London Market – the Next Steps in Renminbi Internationalization, Part 3: Framework for Policy Discussion." Research Paper, International Economics Department, Chatham House, January 2017. https://www.chathamhouse.org/publication/belt-and-road-initiative-and-london-market-next-steps-renminbi-internationalization.

Li, Bo. 2013. "The Prospect of Renminbi Pricing in Cross-Border Trade." *China Finance* 23:47–48. In Chinese. [李波 "跨境人民币计价的前景", 《中国金融》].

Li, Kongmin, Haihong Gao, Qiyuan Xu, Yuanfang Li and Shuang Song. 2017. "The 'Belt and Road' Initiative and the London Market – the Next Steps in Renminbi Internationalization, Part 1: The View from Beijing." Research Paper, International Economics Department, Chatham House, January 2017. https://www.chathamhouse.org/publication/belt-and-road-initiative-and-london-market-next-steps-renminbi-internationalization.

Li, Jingya, and Ming-Hua Liu. 2019. "Interest Rate Liberalization and Pass-Through of Monetary Policy Rate to Bank Lending Rates in China." *Frontiers of Business Research in China* 13(8). https://doi.org/10.1186/s11782-019-0056-z.

Lin, Justin Yifu, Fang Cai, and Zhou Li. 2003. *The China Miracle: Development Strategy and Economic Reform*. Hong Kong: Chinese University Press.

Lu, Susan Feng, and Yang Yao. 2009. "The Effectiveness of Law, Financial Development, and Economic Growth in an Economy of Financial Repression: Evidence from China." *World Development* 37(4): 763–777. https://doi.org/10.1016/j.worlddev.2008.07.018.

McKinnon, Ronald I. 1973. *Money and Capital in Economic Development.* Washington, DC: Brookings Institution.

McKinnon, Ronald I., and Gunther Schnabl. 2004. "The East Asian Dollar Standard, Fear of Floating, and Original Sin." *Review of Development Economics* 8(3): 331–360. http://doi.org/10.1111/j.1467-9361.2004.00237.x.

Mark, Nelson C. 1995. "Exchange Rates and Fundamentals: Evidence on LongHorizon Predictability." *American Economic Review* 85: 201–218.

Martin, Philippe, and Hélène Rey. 2004. "Financial Super-Markets: Size Matters for Asset Trade." *Journal of International Economics* 64(2): 335–361. http://doi.org/10.1016/j.jinteco.2003.12.001.

Matsuyama, Kiminori, Nobuhiro Kiyotaki, and Akihiko Matsui. 1993. "Toward a Theory of International Currency." *Review of Economic Studies* 60(2): 283–307. http://doi.org/10.2307/2298058.

Meese, Richard A., and Kenneth Rogoff. 1983a. "Empirical Exchange Rate Models of the Seventies: Do They Fit Out of Sample?" *Journal of International Economics* 14(1/2): 3–24. http://doi.org/10.1016/0022-1996(83)90017-x.

Meese, Richard A., and Kenneth Rogoff. 1983b. "The Out-of-Sample Failure of Empirical Exchange Rate Models: Sampling Error or Misspecification?" In Jacob A. Frenkel (ed.). *Exchange Rates and International Macroeconomics.* Chicago: University of Chicago Press, pp. 67–112.

Mitsuhiro Fukao. 2003. "Capital Account Liberalisation: The Japanese Experience and Implications for China." BIS Papers, *China's Capital Account Liberalisation: International Perspective* 15: 35–57.

Moser, Joel. 2017. "China's Bridge to Nowhere." *Forbes.* September 7. www.forbes.com/sites/joelmoser/2017/09/07/chinas-bridge-to-nowhere/.

National Bureau of Statistics of China. 2007. *Chinese Statistical Yearbook.* www.stats.gov.cn/tjsj/ndsj/2007/indexeh.htm.

Naughton, Barry. 1995. *Growing Out of the Plan: Chinese Economic Reform, 1978–1993,* Cambridge: Cambridge University Press. doi.org/10.1017/CBO9780511664335.

Nixon, William, Eden Hatzvi, and Michelle Wright. 2015. "The Offshore Renminbi Market and Renminbi Internationalisation." In Ligang Song, Ross Garnaut, Fang Cai, and Lauren Johnston (eds.). *China's Domestic Transformation In a Global Context.* Canberra: ANU Press.

Obstfeld, Maurice, and Kenneth Rogoff. 2001. "Perspectives on OECD Capital Market Integration: Implications for the US Current Account Adjustment." In *Global Economic Integration: Opportunities and Challenges*. Kansas City, MO: Federal Reserve Bank of Kansas City, pp. 169–208.

Obstfeld, Maurice, and Kenneth Rogoff. 2007. "The Unsustainable US Current Account Position Revisited." In R. H. Clarke (ed.). *G7 Current Account Imbalances: Sustainability and Adjustment*. Chicago: University of Chicago Press, pp. 339–376.

Obstfeld, Maurice, Jay C. Shambaugh, and Alan M. Taylor. 2005. "The Trilemma In History: Tradeoffs among Exchange Rates, Monetary Policies, and Capital Mobility." *Review of Economics and Statistics* 87(3): 423–438.

OECD. 2018. "China's Belt and Road Initiative In the Global Trade, Investment and Finance Landscape." *OECD Business and Financial Outlook*. chap. 2. www.oecd.org/finance/Chinas-Belt-and-Road-Initiative-In-the-global-trade-investment-and-finance-landscape.pdf.

Okawa, Yohei, and Eric van Wincoop. 2012. "Gravity In International Finance." *Journal of International Economics* 87(2): 205–215. http://doi.org/10.1016/j.jinteco.2012.01.006.

Overholt, William, Guonan Ma, and Cheung-Kwok Law. 2016. *Renminbi Rising*. London: John Wiley & Sons.

Pei, Changhong, Chunxue Yang, and Xinming Yang. 2015. *The Basic Economic System of China: A Perspective Based on Quantitative Analysis*. Beijing: Chinese Academy of Social Science Press. In Chinese. [裴长洪、杨春学、杨新铭：《中国基本经济制度 – 基于量化分析的视角》, 北京：中国社会科学出版社2015年版。].

People's Bank of China. 2017. *RMB Internationalization Report*. Beijing: PBC.

Portes, Richard, and Hélène Rey. 2005. "The Determinants of Cross-Border Equity Flows." *Journal of International Economics* 65(2): 269–296. http://doi.org.10.1016/j.jinteco.2004.05.002.

Prasad, Eswar S. 2017a. "China Needs to Come Clean on its Exchange Rate Policy: the Central Bank Must Let the Renminbi's Value Go Where Market Forces Take It." *Financial Times*. September 14 . www.ft.com/content/725cd994-9931-11e7-8c5c-c8d8fa6961bb.

Prasad, Eswar S. 2017b. *Gaining Currency*, New York: Oxford University Press.

Prasad, Eswar S., and Raghuram G Rajan. 2006. "Modernizing China's Growth Paradigm." *American Economic Review* 96(2): 331–336. http://doi.org/10.1257/000282806777212170.

Prasad, Eswar S., and Raghuram G Rajan. 2008. "A Pragmatic Approach to Capital Account Liberalization." *Journal of Economic Perspectives* 22(3): 149–172. http://doi.org/10.1257/jep.22.3.149.

PwC. 2016. "China's New Silk Route: the Long and Winding Road." PWC's Growth Markets Center. February. www.pwc.com/gx/en/growth-markets-center/assets/pdf/china-new-silk-route.pdf.

Rey, Hélène. 2001. "International Trade and Currency Exchange." *Review of Economic Studies* 68(2): 443–464. http://doi.org/10.1111/1467–937x.00176.

Rey, Hélène. 2015. "Dilemma not Trilemma: The Global Financial Cycle and Monetary Policy Independence." NBER Working Paper 21162.

Rodrik, Dani. 1998. "Who Needs Capital-Account Convertibility?" In Stanley Fischer, et al. *Should the IMF Pursue Capital-Account Convertibility?* Princeton, NJ: Princeton Book Company.

Rogoff, Kenneth S. 1996. "The Purchasing Power Parity Puzzle." *Journal of Economic Literature* 34(2): 647–668.

Rossi, Barbara. 2013. "Exchange Rate Predictability." *Journal of Economic Literature* 51(4): 1063–1119.

Santos Silva, J. M. C., and Silvana Tenreyro. 2006. "The Log of Gravity." *Review of Economics and Statistics* 88(4): 641–658. http://doi.org/10.1162/rest .88.4.641.

Sarno, Lucio, Giorgio Valente, and Hyginus Leon. 2006. "Nonlinearity in Deviations from Uncovered Interest Parity: An Explanation of the Forward Bias Puzzle." *Review of Finance* 10(3): 443–482.

Sarno, Lucio, Ilias Tsiakas, and Barbara Ulloa. 2016. "What Drives International Portfolio Flows?" *Journal of International Money and Finance* 60: 53–72. http://doi.org/10.1016/j.jimonfin.2015.03.006.

Shioji, Etsuro. 2013. "The Bubble Burst and Stagnation of Japan." In Randall E. Parker and Robert Whaples (eds.). *Routledge Handbook of Major Events in Economic History.* London: Routledge, Taylor and Francis Group.

Shu, Chang, He Dong, and Xiaoqiang Cheng. 2015. "One Currency, Two Markets: The Renminbi's Growing Influence in Asia-Pacific." *China Economic Review* 33: 163–178. http://doi.org/10.1016/j.chieco.2015.01.013.

Song, Zheng, Kjetil Storesletten, and Fabrizio Zilibotti. 2011. "Growing Like China." *American Economic Review* 101(1): 196–233. https://doi.org/10.1257/ aer.101.1.196.

State Council of the People's Republic of China. 2017. "*China Establishes Financial Stability and Development Committee.*" November 9. http://english.www.gov .cn/news/top_news/2017/11/08/content_281475936107760.htm.

Steil, Benn. 2013. *The Battle of Bretton Woods: John Maynard Keynes, Harry Dexter White, and the Making of a New World Order.* Princeton, NJ: Princeton University Press.

Steil, Benn. 2019. "Central Bank Currency Swaps Tracker." Council on Foreign Relations, 5 November. www.cfr.org/article/central-bank-currency-swaps-tracker#!/?cid=otr-marketing_use-currency_swaps.

Stiglitz, Joseph E. 1994. "The Role of the State In Financial Markets." In M. Bruno and B. Pleskovic (eds.). *Proceedings of the World Bank Annual Conference on Development Economics, 1993: Supplement to the World Bank Economic Review and the World Bank Research Observer.* Washington, DC: The World Bank.

Stiglitz, Joseph E. 2000. "Capital Market Liberalization, Economic Growth, and Instability." *World Development* 28(6): 1075–1086. https://doi.org/10.1016/S0305–750X(00)00006-1.

Stiglitz, Joseph E. 2002. *Globalization and Its Discontents.* New York: W. W. Norton.

Stiglitz, Joseph E., and Andrew Weiss. 1981. "Credit Rationing In Markets with Imperfect Information." *American Economic Review* 71(3): 393–410.

Subacchi, Paola. 2017. *People's Money.* New York: Columbia University Press.

Subacchi, Paola, and Matthew Oxenford. 2017. "The 'Belt and Road' Initiative and the London Market – The Next Steps In Renminbi Internationalization, Part 2. The View from London." Research Paper, International Economics Department, Chatham House, January. www.chathamhouse.org/publication/belt-and-road-initiative-and-london-market-next-steps-renminbi-internationalization.

Svirydzenka, Katsiaryna. 2016. "Introducing a New Broad-based Index of Financial Development." International Monetary Fund Working Paper WP/16/5, Strategy, Policy, and Review Department. www.imf.org/external/pubs/ft/wp/2016/wp1605.pdf.

Swoboda, Alexander. 1968. "The Euro–Dollar Market: An Interpretation." In Peter B. Kenan (ed.). *Essays in International Finance.* Princeton, NJ: Princeton University Press.

Swoboda, Alexander. 1969. "Vehicle Currencies and the Foreign Exchange Market: The Case of the Dollar." In Robert Z. Aliber (ed.). *The International Market for Foreign Exchange, Praeger Special Studies In International Economics and Development.* New York: Frederick A. Praeger.

Tobin, James. 1982. "A Proposal for International Monetary Reform." In *Essays In Economics,* Cambridge, MA: MIT Press.

Triffin, Robert. 1960. *Gold and the Dollar Crisis: The Future of Convertibility.* New Haven, CT: Yale University Press.

Walter, Carl, and Fraser Howie. 2011. *Red Capitalism.* Singapore: John Wiley & Sons.

Wang, Ming, Jerome Yen, and Kin-Keung Lai. 2014. *China's Financial Markets: Issues and Opportunities.* London: Routledge.

Wang, Xuanwen (ed.). 2016. *China's State-Owned Assets Supervision and Administration Yearbook 2016*. In Chinese. ISBN 978-7-5136-4505-8. [王选文主编《中国国有资产监督管理年鉴 2016》《中国国有资产监督管理年鉴》编委会, 中国经济出版社出版, 2016。].

Wikipedia. 2021a. "Human Rights In Singapore." https://en.wikipedia.org/wiki/Human_rights_In_Singapore.

Wikipedia. 2021b. "Ideology of the Chinese Communist Party." https://en.wikipedia.org/wiki/Ideology_of_the_Chinese_Communist_Party.

Wikipedia. 2021c. "Internationalization of the Renminbi." https://en.wikipedia.org/wiki/Internationalization_of_the_renminbi.

Wikipedia. 2021d. "Politics of Singapore." https://en.wikipedia.org/wiki/Politics_of_Singapore.

Wikipedia. 2021e. "Society for Worldwide Interbank Financial Telecommunication." https://en.wikipedia.org/wiki/Society_for_Worldwide_Interbank_Financial_Telecommunication.

Wu, Ying. 2015. "The Open-Economy Trilemma In China: Monetary and Exchange Rate Policy Interaction under Financial Repression." *International Finance* 18(1): 1–23.

Yang, Charlotte, and Baili Ke. 2019. "Caixin Explains: Why It's So Hard To Kill Zombies In China." *Caixin*. January 24. www.caixinglobal.com/2019-01-24/caixin-explains-why-its-so-hard-to-kill-zombies-In-china-101374079.html.

Yu, Yongding, 2012. "Revisiting the Internationalization of the Yuan." Asian Development Bank Institute Working Paper 366.

Zhang, Liqing, and Kunyu Tao. 2015. "The Benefits and Costs of Renminbi Internationalization." In Barry Eichengreen and Masahiro Kawai (eds.). *Renminbi Internationalization: Achievements, Prospects, and Challenges*. Washington, DC: Brookings Institution Press, pp. 348–376.

Zhang, Yanqun. 2017. "Productivity In China: Past Success and Future Challenges." *Asia-Pacific Development Journal* 24(1). www.un-ilibrary.org/content/journals/24119873/24/1/1.

Zhang, Yuan, Ting Shao, and Qi Dong. 2018. "Reassessing the Lewis Turning Point In China: Evidence From 70,000 Rural Households." *China & World Economy* 26(1): 4–17. http://doi.org/10.1111/cwe.12226.

Zhu, Xiaodong. 2012. "Understanding China's Growth," *Journal of Economic Perspectives* 26(4): 103–124. https://pubs.aeaweb.org/doi/pdfplus/10.1257/jep.26.4.103.

Further Reading

Aliber, Robert Z. 1980. "The Integration of the Offshore and Domestic Banking System." *Journal of Monetary Economics* 6(4): 509–526.

Ba, Qing. 2019. *The Pivotal Force In RMB Internationalization: The Construction of the Offshore RMB Market Mechanism.* Kowloon: City University of Hong Kong Press. In traditional Chinese [巴晴 《人民幣國際化的關鍵》香港城市大學出版社 , 2019年 。].

Bank for International Settlements. 2014. "Triennial Central Bank Survey of Foreign Exchange and Derivatives Market Activity In 2013." Basel, Switzerland.

Chang, Chun, Liu Zheng, and Mark M. Spiegel. 2015. "Capital Controls and Optimal Chinese Monetary Policy." *Journal of Monetary Economics* 74(C): 1–15.

Cheng, Siwei. 2015. *RMB Towards Internationalization.* Singapore: World Scientific Press.

Cheung, Yin-Wong, Guonan Ma, and Robert McCauley. 2011. "Why Does China Attempt to Internationalise the RMB?" In Jane Golley and Ligang Song (eds.). *Rising China: Global Challenges and Opportunities*, Canberra: ANU Press.

Cohen, Benjamin J. 2011. "The Benefits and Costs of an International Currency: Getting the Calculus Right." *Open Economies Review* 23(1): 13–31. http://doi.org/10.1007/s11079–011-9216-2.

Dobbs, Richard, David Skilling, Wayne Hu, Susan Lund, James Manyika, and Charles Roxburgh. 2009. "An Exorbitant Privilege? Implications of Reserve Currencies for Competitiveness." McKinsey & Company. www.mckinsey.com/global-themes/employment-and-growth/an-exorbitant-privilege.

Dufey, Gunter, and Ian H. Giddy. 1994. *The International Money Market.* Englewood Cliffs, NJ: Prentice Hall International.

He, Dong, and Robert N. McCauley. 2013. "Offshore Markets for the Domestic Currency: Monetary and Financial Stability Issues." In Yin-Wong Cheung and Jakob de Haan (eds.). *The Evolving Role of China In the Global Economy.* Cambridge, MA: MIT Press, pp. 301–337.

He, Dong, L. Cheung, W. Zhang, and T. Wu. 2012. "How Would Capital Account Liberalisation Affect China's Capital Flows and the Renminbi Real Exchange Rates?" *China & World Economy* 20(6): 29–54.

Kawai, Masahiro, and Victor Pontines. 2015. "The Renminbi and Exchange Rate Regimes In East Asia." In Barry Eichengreen and Masahiro Kawai (eds.). *Renminbi Internationalization: Achievements, Prospects, and Challenges.* Washington, DC: Brookings Institution Press.

Kindleberger, Charles P. 1984. *A Financial History of Western Europe.* London: George Allen & Unwin.

Minikin, Robert, and Kelvin Lau. 2013. *The Offshore Renminbi.* Singapore: Wiley.

Osugi, K. 1990. "Japan's Experience of Financial Deregulation Since 1984 In an International Perspective." Bank for International Settlements (BIS) Economic Papers 26.

Subramanian, Arvind. 2012. "The Renminbi Bloc is Here: Asia Down, Rest of the World to Go?" Peterson Institute of International Economics (PIIE) Working Paper 12-19.

Takagi, Shinji. 2011. "Internationalizing the Yen, 1984–2003: Unfinished Agenda or Mission Impossible?" In Yin-Wong Cheung and Gounan Ma (eds.). *Asia and China In the Global Economy.* Singapore: The World Scientific Publishing, pp. 219–244.

Wong, Michael C. S. and Wilson F. C. Chan (eds.). 2013. *Investing In Asian Offshore Currency Markets, the Shift from Dollars to Renminbi.* Basingstoke: Palgrave Macmillan.

Index